AMERICA APART

AMERICA APART

The Inconvenient Truth
About Multiculturalism
&
Racism Today

James Long

BANNOCKBURN
PRESS

America Apart

Bannockburn Press Logo Design: Richard Dix
Layout & Design: Denise Rutledge
Index: Denise Rutledge
Typeset: Electra

ISBN-13: 978-0-9963351-0-2

Names of current and former inmates have been altered to protect privacy.

attn.pc@bannockburnpress.org

To order books, visit BannockburnPress.org

DEDICATION

To my daughter and the rest of the future.

10% of the proceeds from the sale of this book will be donated to Forgiven Ministries (ForgivenMinistries.com), a not-for-profit organization that enables inmates to enjoy day-long visits with their children through its *One Day With God Camp*.

CONTENTS

INTRODUCTION

Several years ago, Pulitzer Prize winner Leonard Pitts Jr. wrote in his syndicated column that there was a public uproar over Marvel Comics making Spiderman bi-racial. He asserted this was proof of white people feeling "angst" and discomfort over America becoming "a country where no group" will command a numerical majority, where "whites will be just another minority group." He went on to say, whites can "gnash" their teeth and attempt to "seal the borders," but that "a smart nation" would prepare for "the coming demographic shifts," and it will "be interesting to see what this nation does."

Indeed, Pitts seems to be suggesting, as he often does, that the changing racial composition of America will be more of a problem for whites than for other racial or ethnic groups. He started another column in a similar "the white folks can't handle it" fashion, saying that his column for that day would be "about race—but not racist." However, someone would tell him it was—and that person would be white.

This of course suggests that non-white people have some ability, some sensory acuity, which allows them to distinguish when something is, or is not, racist. Something that apparently white people must lack. These condescending notions (of white people being more cowardly and less informed on issues of race than non-whites) are very popular on the political left, and are not limited to Pitts. However, he is at least right about the changing racial makeup of America's population. Most estimates have white Americans ceasing to be the majority by 2040. What, if anything, this portends is more than worthy of discussion.

Pitts, along with most people on the left—henceforth referred to collectively as the clique*—see the changing demographics as a chance for the oppressed, that is any non-white person, to finally transcend that

---

* I believe this is an apt description considering how they operate.

Introduction

historical yoke which their persecutors have held around their necks for centuries. When Pitts says, "A smart nation prepares" for something like this, I hear: "There should be dialogue on the matter, so that those asleep at the wheel (teeth-gnashing white people) can learn to deal with the loss of their 'privilege.' Meanwhile Pitts and his cohorts hope dialogue will stem further uproars from said confused white people.

One of the reasons some whites are reluctant to engage in discussions of race is because they see an undulating playing field rife with double standards. In the spring of 2014, 'a friend' released the now infamous private conversation of Donald Sterling, the owner of the National Basketball Association's Los Angeles Clippers and his then girlfriend V. Stiviano. The recording caught Sterling saying he did not want Stiviano bringing black people to Clipper games. This became the number one story on every ESPN program and all the major networks and cable news channel flagship world news programs.

America was outraged. Even the majority owner of the NBA's Charlotte Bobcats, Michael Jordan, who has notoriously avoided discussing anything remotely controversial, immediately took to social media to express his anger over Sterling's private comments. TNT analyst and former NBA player Charles Barkley said Sterling's comments were especially troublesome because the NBA is a "black league."

But just a couple of weeks before this story broke, the rapper Jay-Z, who owned part of the Brooklyn Nets and a sports agency that represents professional athletes in all sports, was seen at a Nets game on national television wearing a Five Percent Nation Medallion the size of a hub cap.

The Five Percent Nation is a black supremacist group that believes black men alone (not black women) have God inside of them, and that all white people are wicked and weak. ESPN and their self-perceived race experts like Jamelle Hill and Stephan A. Smith had nothing to say about Jay-Z.

Nor has Michael Jordan said anything about one of his co-owners of the Bobcats, the rapper Nelly who has had ties to the Five Percenters for quite some time. His Airness, Lebron James and all the others who rightfully castigated Sterling have never publicly said anything about Nelly, who like Jay-Z is a serial objectifier of women. (i.e. Don Imus has nothing on these guys.)

No one so much as batted an eye at Charles Barkley's comment that the NBA was a "black league." Nevertheless, can you imagine what would have happened to Berry Melrose, the white ESPN hockey analyst had he labeled the National Hockey League a white league? ESPN would have fired him quicker than you can say Rush Limbaugh.

This 'Black Privilege' of not being called a racist, when similar actions or comments would undoubtedly get a white person labeled as the second coming of Hitler, discourages whites from engaging others in conversations about race. Like everyone else, whites do not want to play a game in which different sets of rules apply to each player, especially based upon something they cannot control, such as the color of their skin.

The consequences of biased reporting of racial incidents by mainstream media have recently proven much more severe than merely discouraging whites from talking about race. Just ask the business owners of Ferguson, Missouri. Clique journalists convinced scores of people that Darren Wilson, a white police officer, killed Michael Brown, an unarmed black teenager, in cold blood. Their 'news' programs and papers made little mention of the publicly known facts corroborating Wilson's story. In the rage that followed, whose establishments did an angry non-white population loot and burn in response? Mostly black-owned businesses.

NPR coverage was especially shameful. I listened to it every day from the time of the incident to when the Grand Jury decided not to indict. "Brown was unarmed and on his way to college" was repeated frequently. I heard nothing about the photographs showing Wilson's swollen jaw, corroborating his claim Brown had hit him and reached for his service weapon. Forensics expert's conclusions that Brown was not likely to have been standing still with his hands raised weren't presented. Nor were the descriptions of the 12 witnesses, six of whom were black, which matched Wilson's story, shared. Even Eric Holder's Justice Department had to admit, after a six-month investigation, it had found no evidence to indict Wilson.

The clique often portrays discussions concerning race as only taking place in their own echo chambers like President Clinton's advisory board in the 1990s or some PBS talk show. This is simply not the case. Conversations about race occur on practically every right-wing radio talk or TV show I have ever heard or seen. None of these are acknowledged by the clique because they challenge their beliefs on the subject and most clique members have learned to reflexively scream racism anytime someone even suggests that racial group X's problems may not be the result of the one-size-fits-all cause—white supremacy. Because of this, the discussion on race has been anything but.

Pitts and the rest of the clique like to believe that white people just do not 'get it.' In one of his column's he even recommended a list of books that he thought white people needed to read. From that list, I selected three titles: *Mirror to America*, which turned out to be the autobiography of historian Dr. John Hope Franklin, *Been in the Storm So Long*, and *The New Jim Crow*, which Pitts seems especially smitten with, as he has mentioned it in numerous subsequent columns.

After reading these books and many others, and culling information from other sources dealing with racial issues, I came away with three beliefs about the subject matter:

1) Human nature does not vary between the so-called races while attitudes and customs are another animal entirely;

2) Because our brains are products of evolution by natural selection, we are not as rational as we like to believe, and at times exhibit self-defeating behavior because it is emotionally satisfying, and, most importantly;

3) If the racial narrative promoted by the clique continues to dominate issues and discussions on race—with identity politics, racially selective indignation, and victimology forming the core theme—America will certainly come to resemble the environment in which I reside. It is a place where no one lacks racial esteem or pride—things whites are often told America's minorities need in order to compete. It is a place where, because of the clique's dominance in America's education and entertainment industries, everyone believes their grievances, historical or contemporary, are the only legitimate ones. It is one of the most violent, culturally chauvinistic police states you will find on earth.

Being a natural pessimist, I fear it is perhaps already too late for a warning such as this to do any good. There is a mountain of scientific data showing that our brains lead us to do what feels right instead of what is right. Just as discouraging is the fact that the clique's loudest voices live mostly within gated communities where they will never encounter the dissonance and furor their notions and vendettas have wrought, unless they fail to pay their security guards their non-living wages.

I often hear, "Decline is a choice." I hope this is true, and people realize as much.

Unfortunately, the clique has been so successful at propagating their vision a large segment of America has come to believe it is the right choice. Cut her down to size. She is merely the product of white supremacist enslavement of Africans and genocide of her natives. You can't let the "original terrorist state" continue to lead the world, can you?

Be careful what you wish for. America could very well become that nation of squabbling nationalities our forefathers warned us about. A nation in which polarized racial and ethnic groups compete for the title of Utmost Victim and lay the blame for their ancestors misfortunes at the feet of people who bear no responsibility whatsoever for them. That's how it is where I live, and none of you wants to live here.

James Long
Texas Department of Criminal Justice
October 2015

CHAPTER 1

YOUR MOTHER LIED —
THAT BOWL OF SALAD IS NOT HEALTHY

Notwithstanding the members of a few racial supremacy groups, (The Nation of Islam, La Raza, Aryan Nation, etc.), I believe most Americans consider it imperative to the furthering of our society that our country's many varied ethnicities 'get along.' A friend of mine in the free world told me before the election in 2008 that she thought the American people were looking for a president who could "bring everyone together" as she put it. Many people in polls, water cooler conversations, and everywhere in between expressed this sentiment. This being the case, a good question to ask would be whether or not a racially heterogeneous society like America should have a model, or at least some sort of philosophy to follow, in order to "bring everyone together."

In America, two such templates claim to unite groups of differing people even though their respective means to accomplishing this goal could not be more different. Figuratively, you may know them as the 'salad bowl' and 'melting pot.'

Those in the salad bowl camp believe people in a given society should retain as much of their culture as possible, and assimilation should not be promoted. Hence, the salad bowl into which you throw many ingredients. Yet each continues to look as it did beforehand. In this vision, stark contrasts between groups are celebrated. Its proponents also tend to believe no culture is better than another. Outsiders should not criticize another culture's customs. Often called 'Multiculturalists,' most adherents to this philosophy lean to the left politically. They believe in bi-lingual education, mass-immigration, and fill-in-the-blank 'heritage months' for non-white groups.

The fact there are few if any examples of successful societies based upon this salad bowl model has never deterred its advocates. In reality, there are quite a few examples of failed societies based upon it. Sri Lanka is one. Germany, France, and Great Britain—supposedly so much more advanced and refined then the United States with their social democracies and universal health care—have recently seen each of their elected leaders denounce their state-sponsored multi-cultural/salad bowl experiments as abject failures. In all three of these countries, the problems mostly stem from Muslim immigrants refusing to assimilate.

There is no incentive to do so. In fact, the welfare laws are so generous some immigrants have been in these countries for over a decade and have never had to get a job, which would have at least encouraged them to learn the language.[1]

How this makes for a better society, I do not know. Moreover, if you think language does not matter, you may want to ask the friends and family members of the UK man who died from an overdose of pain killers because his doctor could not speak English clearly.[2]

Americans should take note of the fact these failures occurred in countries that are not nearly as despised as the U.S. is by these immigrants. Perhaps the problem is not the tenets of multiculturalism but that white privilege and racism in the West are so pervasive that an otherwise very plausible model has never been given a fair shake. The notions of white supremacy, a clique member might say, are so entrenched and ubiquitous that the salad bowl model or anything not Euro-centric is unable to get a toehold; and that if not for "whiteness," the aforementioned European countries would be reaping the benefits of "diversity."

However, for better or worse, evolution by natural selection (or the tower of Babel if you must) is a process that has made human beings noticeably different in physical appearance and culture. It has also programmed our brains to notice and record these differences. Having this ability would allow one to discriminate between a type of fruit that you saw your friend eat and caused him to die from poisoning, and the type you ate that tasted good and did not harm you. In fact, nine tenths of human existence has been spent in small tribes hunting and gathering food. It was this environment— not multicultural metropolises—that our brains adapted to.[3]

Steven Pinker, a renowned Harvard psychiatrist, explains why being able to discriminate and classify has nothing to do with white supremacy and everything to do with the costs conferred upon our ancestors:

> An intelligent being cannot treat every object it sees as a unique entity unlike anything else in the universe. It has to put objects in categories

so that it may apply its hard-won knowledge about similar objects encountered in the past to the object at hand.[4]

In other words, evolution favors efficiency, and because of this, we are all primed for stereotyping. Dr. Pinker further:

> Experiments in cognitive psychology have shown that people are bigots about birds, other animals, vegetables, and tools. People share a stereotype, project it to all members of a category, recognize the stereotype more quickly than the nonconformists, and even claim to have seen the stereotypes when all they saw were examples similar to it.[5]

Selection of our genes began long before a single white person considered their race, their tribe, or even themselves superior. After seeing one eat a buddy, humans of every color learned to avoid predators. While it is possible not all alligators would eat every human they possibly could, it is impossible to investigate the chances of this being the case because to do so would most likely remove your genes from the gene pool by satisfying the reptile's appetite. These verifiable facts are not 'constructs' of the white man. Nor are they proof America should return to its days of racial segregation. They simply point out that when racially heterogeneous societies are attempting to live in unison, the human brain is not doing them any favors, and most likely hinders their progress. Since our brains are programmed to identify differences in appearance, it would seem illogical to encourage people to forsake assimilation into the mainstream if the goal is for everyone to 'get along.'

In prison, identity politics are the default setting for the average inmate's beliefs. Everybody is quick to assert what they believe, and even quicker to tell you they believe it because of their skin color. Forget the fact that we know with certainty that the skin does not tell the brain what to do. In here, as is the case with the clique, everything is color-coded; inmates walk, talk, or act color X, Y, or Z. There is no room for variation. Your skin is who and what you are. Period.

When it comes to the mind and how it operates amongst the different races, there are few if any differences[6] despite what the Reverend Jeremiah Wright told the national press club, and Al Jazeera's Soledad O'Brien fawning over his remarks. The truth is, "Peoples of the world share an astonishingly detailed universal psychology."[7] So initially, biology forces us to make more out of our differences than necessary, but since our most pressing needs are identical, regardless of race or ethnicity, we should be able, with the right framework, to 'get along.'

Dr. Pinker again:

> Cultures surely differ in how often their members express, talk about, and act on various emotions. But that says nothing about what their people feel. The evidence suggests that the emotions of all normal members of our species are played on the same keyboard.[8]

The clique would do well to search for common ground as vigorously as they do for reasons to claim, "Diversity is our strength." I have seen inmates of different colors who get along fine on football Sundays get into a riot with one another for the slightest of infractions. This happens because every time there is a disagreement between two or more individuals of different races, it quickly turns into a referendum on the entire history—as taught by the clique with no perspective whatsoever—of the groups these two people come from. Their dispute becomes retroactive and all of the injustices of the past, that these two individuals have nothing to do with, are somehow available for adjudication. This happens in the free world as well when the reverends Jesse Jackson and Al Sharpton, or some other self-anointed 'community activist,' attempts to put the entire western world on trial when something like the Duke Lacrosse case or Trayvon Martin tragedy happens. Members of the clique seem to have no concept of the resentment and strife their writings, movies, and teachings have caused. When you consider the constraints and incentives under which they operate, and where they live cocooned away with security guards monitoring their neighborhoods how could they?

In 2011, several dozen black teenagers descended upon an outdoor fair in Milwaukee, Wisconsin. They bull-dozed over white children and ransacked the Midway games, stealing all they could. They yanked whites out of their cars, beat them down and stomped on them. When the mayhem was over, at least 18 people, including some police officers, had been assaulted and/or robbed. The Associated Press reported that at least one of the black assailants/robbers admitted that the group specifically targeted whites.[9]

In August of 2010, at the Iowa state fair, a large group of black teenagers assaulted whites on what they called 'beat whitey night.' At least one kid had his skull fractured, and they hit one police officer so hard from behind both his eye sockets were 'busted.'[10] During the summer of 2011 in Philadelphia, Pennsylvania, 'flash mobs' of Blacks pummeled and robbed numerous whites, putting at least one victim in the hospital with a fractured skull. In Kansas City, Missouri, on March 4, 2012, a thirteen year-old boy had two older black teens douse him with gasoline and set him on fire before exclaiming, "You get what you deserve, white boy."[11] In Chicago during the summer of 2011, Mayor Rahm Emanuel had to order the city's beaches to close because groups of Blacks were "terrorizing white families."[12]

However, Pitts and the rest of the clique will continue telling us Blacks cannot be racist, or their racism does not harm anyone because they have no power. The people of Milwaukee, Iowa, Philadelphia, and Kansas City respectfully disagree. In short, the problems I am illustrating are not exclusive to penal institutions.

So no, it is not white supremacy that keeps ideas like multiculturalism or identity politics from working in a given society. Those super computers between our ears are mostly responsible for this, regardless of origin:

> My fifteen assistants in New Guinea's Fak Fak mountains all looked pretty similar to me, but eventually they began explaining to me which of them were Muslims and who were Christians, and why the former (or the latter) were irredeemably lower humans. There is an almost universal hierarchy of scorn, according to which literate peoples with advanced metallurgy (e.g. white colonists in Africa) look down upon herders, (e.g. Tutsi, Hottentots), who look down on farmers (e.g. Hutu) who look down on nomads or hunter-gatherers (e.g. Pygmies, Bushmen).[13]

Jared Diamond, an evolutionary biologist from Berkley and Pulitzer prize-winning author of the seminal book *Guns, Germs, and Steel*, made this observation. As a very educated, politically correct observer, he is not stereotyping the many different ethnic groups he has worked with. He is merely relating his observations of a universal, human characteristic. This means that when First Lady Michelle Obama says it's easier for people to keep their stereotypes about each other instead of doing otherwise because, "That's America," she could not be more wrong.

This type of behavior happens everywhere, because it is human in nature, not American. The clique needs to be reminded, "Jingoism is alarmingly easy to evoke."[14] There have been numerous experiments conducted by social psychologists that prove this.

In one such experiment, subjects were grouped by the results of tests in which they counted the number of dots on a computer screen, a very trivial matter. Once in their respective groups, they immediately judged the people in the other groups to be less desirable and attempted to keep them from receiving rewards even though doing so penalized their own group.[15] "This instant ethnocentrism can be evoked even if the experiment drops the charade with the dots and divides the people into groups by flipping a coin before their eyes."[16]

As Arthur Schlesinger Jr. said, "The hostility of one tribe for another is among the most instinctive human reactions."[17] Another stalwart of the clique, progressive president Woodrow Wilson, said in an address, "You cannot become Americans if you think of yourselves in groups. America does not consist of groups. A man who thinks of himself as belonging to a particular national group in America has not yet become an American."[18]

The point thus far: It is difficult enough for the people of a culturally heterogeneous society to live and work in peace, and despite their stated intentions, identity politics and multiculturalism make this task more arduous and more difficult by stiffening the walls that enclose each group. Telling individuals they are members of the Chinese-American or African-American communities, and therefore are required to walk, talk, act, and vote a certain way or else they are selling-out their race has not produced income, housing, or educational equality with whites as promised. (In fact, Americans of Chinese descent have surpassed whites in these categories while Blacks still lag behind them.) Nor has teaching school children lies about the advancements of some cultures with the hope that it will boost their self-esteem. More often than not, this actually makes them worse off because you are robbing them of vicarious feedback that would have helped them learn to think critically.

Imagine a history class in which the teacher told the students that the culture of the Irish immigrants to America in the 1800s—particularly their penchant for alcohol and fighting—was no better or worse than that of West-Indian Blacks in the early 1900s who were, "frugal, hard-working, and entrepreneurial."[19] By 1901, West Indians owned 20 percent of all the black owned businesses in Manhattan, even though they made up only 10 percent of the black population.[20] If the teacher proceeded to teach this faux-equality of these two cultures, how would they explain the help-wanted ads in white-owned businesses which read "A cook, washer, and ironer who perfectly understands her business; any nationality except Irish?"[21]

"Coachman wanted, a man who understands horses...a colored man preferred. No Irish need apply?"[22]

What will the teacher say? That the white man's Eurocentric exploitative, capitalist mindset made him biased against the Irish because they were white?

The culture of the Irish produced a worker with habits that were not as effective at performing most jobs as that of the West Indians. While a teacher might be able to get away with this example because the non-preferred group is white, in all likelihood that same teacher would be fired for using an equally factual example if the skin color and roles were reversed. This is form over function, in the name of sensitivity, and it does not help its intended beneficiaries.

The melting pot is the model America followed for over a hundred years. This is why large waves of immigrants were assimilated so successfully in the past. It promotes speaking a single language and adoption of America's unique culture, which of course came to be over generations of cultures intermingling. This philosophy says you are not an African-American or a Mexican-American unless you were born on the continent of Africa, or in the country of Mexico, and then moved to the United States afterward.

The melting pot concept looks to promote the common ground individuals have instead of their differences. It rejects identity politics and the notion that an individual must think or act in a certain way, according to their skin color. Above all, the melting pot template seeks to keep society from balkanizing into a nation of nations.

THE FASTEST GROWING MINORITY GROUP

Your tax dollars subsidize the career of Jose Angel Gutiérrez, a professor of political science at the University of Texas. This professor once told a crowd of college students, "We have an aging white America. They are not making babies. They are dying. The explosion is in our population. They are shitting in their pants in fear. I love it."[23] Very professorial indeed, no? Gutiérrez is also the director of the Mexican-American Study Center at the university. Would you expect this man to encourage students to respect America's traditions?

Ricky Sierra shares this belief with Pitts and Gutiérrez that whites are afraid of non-whites. A member of the 'Chicano National Guard,' he claims, "We're recolonizing America, so they're afraid of us. It's time to take back what is ours."[24] Clique members like Pitts will say, "So what if these guys have taken a few digs at white guy's manhood. That does not compare to years of institutional oppression!"

Of course, it does not. However, if we are all going to live together and get along, it is disturbing when leaders of the fastest growing minority group voice such polarizing ideas. You cannot ask white people to have this conversation on race while someone like professor Gutiérrez can say such incendiary, self-gratifying things without the mainstream Latino population condemning it.

Yes, I know. There are plenty of whites who have avoided minorities because they thought they were criminals, and therefore were scared. Unfortunately, Hispanics commit crimes at three times the rate of whites and are 19 times more likely to join a gang.[25] Maybe you think that what Gutiérrez and Sierra said is inappropriate, but harmless because everyday people do not listen to speeches from professors or members of the Chicano National Guard. This seems plausible. However, large numbers of people have adopted beliefs that would be right at home in one of Gutiérrez's lectures, even though they have never set foot inside one of his classrooms.

A 2006 joint poll conducted by Zogby International and a Mexican polling company surveyed 1,000 Mexicans and Americans to discover their attitudes about each other. The results were stark and disheartening to say the least. While 78 percent of Americans considered Mexicans to be hard workers, only 25 percent of Mexicans thought the same about their American neighbors.[26] While 44 percent of Americans thought Mexicans were tolerant, a whopping 73 percent of Mexicans said Americans were racist. When it comes to the nation's wealth, 62 percent of Mexicans said America's wealth is greater because they exploit other people's money. Only a mere 10 percent of Mexicans thought Americans were honest.[27]

However, this is a poll of Mexicans you say, not Americans of Mexican descent, so therefore it is an apples and oranges comparison. Not exactly. Of the 40 million or so foreign-born people in America today, about 30 percent of them are Mexicans, and over half of them are here illegally.[28] The census bureau showed that "almost half of the Hispanic adults counted in the 1990 census had been born outside the U.S."[29] This means that today, in 2015, of the roughly 45 million Hispanics (most of Mexican descent) at least 13 million of them were born in Mexico where Zogby conducted the poll.

Mexican immigrants outnumber all others by a ratio of a least 6:1. In other words, it is not that much of a stretch to impute the Zogby poll results to the millions of people classifying themselves as Mexican-Americans in the U.S.

In July of 2002, the Mexican government's website declared that Juan Hernandez, a native of Fort Worth, Texas, with a Mexican father and American mother, was "to bring a strong and clear message to Mexicans abroad. Mexico is one nation of 123 million–100 million who live in Mexico and 23 million who live in the Unites States. Most importantly, he was to say that although far, they are not alone."[30] While heading the office for Mexicans abroad from 2000–2002, Hernandez told the Denver Post that immigrants from Mexico "are going to keep one foot in Mexico," and "are not going to assimilate in the sense of dissolving into not being Mexicans."[31]

In an interview with Ted Koppel of ABC News, Hernandez said he wanted all Mexican-Americans in the United States to think "Mexico first," and that he wanted the "third generation" and "seventh generation" to "all think Mexico first."[32]

Hernandez is by no means an anomaly amongst influential people in the ever-growing world of racial lobbyists with multiculturalist, anti-assimilationist views. Mario Obeldo, who is the co-founder of the Mexican American Legal Defense Fund (MALDEF), once said, "California is going to be a Hispanic state and anyone who doesn't like it should leave. They should go back to Europe." MALDEF is a zealous supporter of bi-lingual education.[33] As we have seen in Quebec, and other places, this actually proves an impediment to the students' development and functioning of society. However, not to worry, you can trust the lobbyists and their politicians as they issue their dictums from their gated estates. In fact, Obeldo even received the Medal of Freedom from President Clinton in 1998.

I have no idea how telling whites they can go back to Europe (especially considering most whites have never been there), and Mexican immigrants they need to think 'Mexico first,' will benefit either group or American society as a whole. And while I do understand that poor people, taking it one day at a time in the barrio are much more concerned with getting ahead economically than they are 'getting along' with the gringos, I would still like to think a more unified coexistence is on their list of desirable things in life. In addition, if a group is truly concerned with economic advancement, why not look to the successful examples of other immigrants, which usually included assimilation, or at least learning English?

However, because of the changing demographics, the Hispanic community's leaders may believe the most effective strategy for accomplishing their goals is to lobby the Equal Employment Opportunity

Commission, and the Department of Justice, to obtain for Hispanics what other immigrants got through assimilation and self-improvement. It appears MALDEF, LULAC and La Raza (The Race) may also believe they can indoctrinate enough young people into thinking 'Mexico first' to guarantee they accomplish their goals.

In 2005, the Mexican government, headed by Vicente Fox, had approximately 50 consulates in the United States with the number growing virtually every year. According to Heather MacDonald, every one of the consulates "has a mandate to introduce Mexican textbooks into schools with significant Hispanic populations."[34] In the textbooks, students are taught about the Mexican War in a way that is very sympathetic to Santa Ana, portraying him and Mexico as the 'good guys.'[35]

The Los Angeles consulate heaped almost 100,000 such textbooks into 1500 schools in Los Angeles in just one year and "Hundreds of thousands have gone to school districts across the country." These textbooks end by "celebrating Mexican patriotic symbols, the flag, the currency, and the National anthem," declaring, "We love our country because it is ours."[36] Hispanics promoting themselves as a separate nation within a nation, whether through lobbyists or textbooks may not be that serious of a problem. Then again, the last time a large faction of Americans thought of themselves as a separate nation, America was plunged into a ruinous war that left the South in a shambles, and the country as a whole, on life support.

In prison, we have an abundance of ethnocentrism. Senor's Hernandez and Obeldo would surely be proud. Tattoos of Pancho Villa, the Mexican flag, and Aztec pyramids are all the rage for discriminating Hispanic convicts system-wide. Along with the obligatory 'Brown Pride' tattoo, you also see the names of cities converted: Houston becomes Houstone; San Antonio becomes San Anto. Many of these inmates are here illegally and have no intention of assimilating or reforming whatsoever. Like the 'Chicano student movement of Aztlán' whose motto is "Por La Raza todo, Fuera da La Raza" (for the race, everything, outside the race nothing), these unabashedly ethnocentric inmates believe they are in a righteous battle against their gringo oppressors who stole the land of their ancestors. Therefore, they are doing nothing wrong by committing crimes against white Americans. I wonder how many of them have even heard of Professor Gutiérrez or Hernandez. As I said before, these views are very prevalent.

I will never forget the time I saw a very dubious expression of this 'Brown Pride.' After transfer to a prison unit that had college available, I signed up for American History 101. The teacher of the class was a Vietnam veteran and county judge who happened to be of Mexican descent. The man really knew his stuff and turned out to be the best teacher the college had. He would often mix in a personal anecdote about his family while giving the day's lecture, which suggested he did not view us as monsters.

One particular day, he told us his daughters were giving him a hard time about speaking Spanish, the language he spoke growing up even though he grew up in America. Several of the Hispanic students in my class commented on this, some in English, and some in Spanish because that was all they knew.

They exchanged opinions about their families and Mexican culture, most saying something along the lines of, "My grandmother always tried to get me to speak Spanish." One Hispanic student, who looked much more Caucasian than native, got up abruptly and marched to the teacher's desk. He stopped just as suddenly as he got up, yanking his shirt off over his head like we do in here when we are about to fight someone. I was almost certain he wasn't going to call the teacher 'to a square' as we say, but stranger things have happened.

I began going through a list of scenarios in my head. *He's going to hit the teacher, because he disrespected the bronze people by fighting for America, or because he got a bad grade. What will the other prideful bronze people in the classroom do when I jump up to stop this guy?*

The inmate jerked forward and planted his hands on the teacher's desk, bracing himself. Still shirtless, he said sternly, "This is our culture." I had no idea what he was talking about but was relieved none of the above scenarios were being played out. My relief quickly changed to bewilderment when I figured out what he meant. Aztec pyramids and warriors covered the inmate's torso. These tattoos were the 'our culture' he was referring to.

In spite of his shock, the teacher played it off really well. He reared back in his chair and ostensibly admired the 'work,' as we call tattoos in here, as if nothing out of the ordinary was transpiring.

Why do I bring this up? Because the young Aztec invoker had colored eyes, light brown hair, and attended an 'all-white school' before coming to prison. How he came up with this idea that those Aztec pyramids and warriors were his culture is beyond me. He looked much more like the conquistadors than the indigenous Aztecs to me. This sort of selective gene acceptance, like Elizabeth Warren and President Obama engage in, enables its practitioners to see themselves as underdogs and rebels.

John McWhorter and others have often pointed out the problems inherent in seeing oneself as a perpetual underdog/victim who everyone (i.e. white men) wants to 'keep down.' McWhorter says it is an 'ironic joy' they are caught up in. I imagine an evolutionary psychologist could find an adaptive advantage to this mindset. It is not difficult to conceptualize how convincing people to feel sorry for you could increase your access to shelter and food. And when it comes to attracting mates, men casting themselves as David taking on Goliath are telling everyone, "My genes must be superior for I am taking on a giant most of my competition cannot." Women could also find rebels attractive because in the same sense their behavior may be saying, "My genes are so fit I can rock the boat and risk ostracism." These would be fairly low-risk strategies for increasing your attractiveness to potential mates.

Think about the number of Hollywood movies that are about underdogs. *Rocky, Hoosiers, Rudy, Invincible*—they are too numerous to name. They are what we like because we wish we could get that fame and notoriety and show a large group of people how fit our genes are. There are practically no movies that tell stories about something like, say, the early 1990s UNLV men's basketball team that won every game one year because it's starting-five had at least 4 if not 5 future professional basketball players on it. This is because they elicit no sympathy. They were supposed to win.

None of this is to say non-whites have some sort of personality disorder that causes them to see themselves as victims, rebels, or underdogs more often than whites. We all have these tendencies. However, in America, non-whites have more reasons—legitimate and illegitimate—to see themselves as such.

The inmate who saw the Aztecs as his culture came from the west Texas town of Odessa. He did not grow up in a barrio, nor did he speak any Spanish before he came to prison. Judging from our conversations and things I had overheard him saying to other inmates, he encountered little if any racism growing up. He seemed to enjoy mentioning that he had plenty of 'snow-bunnies' (the term non-white inmates use to refer to white women) throw themselves at him. However, if he ever writes a memoir, I would be willing to bet a chance at parole it will be in the mold of President Obama's *Dreams From My Father*, playing up or completely fabricating incidents of racism.

The Problem With Preferences

Since we may have evolved a predisposition to see ourselves as victims and underdogs, and doing so can bring preferential treatment, many people have learned to don the hat of victimhood. However, like everything else in life, it comes with a cost: When you derive your power from a strategy that requires you to remain a casualty, you must remain infirm or else lose your preferential treatment. As Shelby Steele has said, "victimization, like implied inferiority, is what justifies preference, so that to receive the benefits of preferential treatment one must to some extent become invested in the view of one's self as a victim."[37] This mindset causes numerous problems in a society in which people see themselves as members of groups — either privileged (whites) or oppressed (non-whites) — exactly what the clique's salad bowl/multiculturalism model produces, instead of individuals. One such problem is that it creates a counter-productive competition amongst assumed victims for the right to be the 'Greatest Victim of All Time.' Preferences also lower the standards of those who are supposed to be benefiting in more ways than most can imagine.

During my 17 years of incarceration, I have done my time on two units in south Texas. Both of these units are staffed with a majority of Hispanic guards.* I mention their ethnicity because when it comes to the lowering of standards for non-whites, white liberals are usually the only ones indicted, and while they are no doubt serial offenders of this should-be crime, they are by no means its only perpetrators. I have honestly lost count of the number of times I have seen corrections officers (of all colors) hold white inmates to a higher standard than they do non-white inmates. This is especially the case when it comes to remedying a problem like, say, the confiscation of an inmate's property.

Black inmates seem to get away with the most histrionics when putting up their beef, but Hispanic inmates are not far behind them. This causes even the most objective white inmates to assume the correctional officers (COs) are racist. This is problematic for at least two reasons:

1) It incentivizes non-whites to act in a way that will obviously make it harder for them to function in society.
2) It helps drive white inmates into various gangs, which engage in organized criminal activity and promote racial separation.

The CO in prison reasons much like the white liberal in the admissions department at Diversity-At-All-Costs University. They are from the ghetto/barrio; it is not their fault; the white man's oppression has held them back,

---

* Several Mestizo Hispanic guards and inmates have told me they prefer to be called Mexican because a Hispanic is 'black,' and they look down on them.

etc. etc. However, even W.E.B. Dubois has called preferential treatment "indiscriminate charity,"[38] and rightfully condemned it for the harm he saw it cause black people. Nevertheless, the COs and Bill Ayers of the world mean well we are all assured. Unfortunately for non-whites who need honest feedback, these do-gooders rarely consider the results of their virtuous goals. They would do well to consider where the road leads that is paved with such intentions.

When it comes to preferential policies, most people assume that the pros outweigh the cons. For instance, with affirmative action, it is obviously an injustice to put one student ahead of another for admission to college based on their skin color. However, most left-leaning Americans think giving non-white students preferential treatment over whites is a reasonable trade off in order to counteract past discrimination. They will argue fervently that if not for affirmative action Blacks would be relegated to the lower rungs of society because of racist whites and their discrimination.

Professor Cornel West, one of President Obama's favorite intellectuals said, "It is a virtual certainty that racial...discrimination would return with a vengeance" if affirmative action were done away with.[39] Although I am quite certain Professor West is firmly ensconced in the camp that believes racism is just as rampant today, in 2015, as it was 60 years ago, am I wrong in saying Blacks, as well as whites, are better off in most regards? He calls America a "racist patriarchal" country that refuses to accept "the humanity of Blacks."[40] If he were to agree with me, I imagine he would say affirmative action policies are the only reason Blacks are better off. This belief is a basic consensus amongst not only those on the left but people in general. Mention to the average black inmate that most black business districts like Bronzeville thrived before the Great Depression, and therefore obviously before affirmative action, and you will get a befuddled glance followed by a very dismissive reply of, "Hell no."

Here are the facts: In 1940, 87 percent of black Americans had incomes that put them below the poverty line. By 1970, that number had plunged 57 percentage points to 30 percent. In 1995, it was down to 26 percent.[41] The latest census bureau figures I could find put the African-American poverty rate at 27.4 percent.[42] Read those numbers again if you need to.

Since affirmative action policies became an integral part of American society, sometime around the late 1960s, the poverty rate for black folks in America has remained largely unchanged. Incomes for black families show the same surprising trajectory. In 1940, only 1 percent of black families had incomes that were at least double the poverty line.[43] By 1970, that number had soared to 39 percent. However, from 1970–1995, there was only a 10-point increase to 49 percent.[44] Keep this in mind when considering these statistics. A much larger proportion of Blacks lived in the south (77 percent) in 1940 than whites (27 percent). Wages were lower for all.

The point of course is that Blacks made their greatest gains in income before the era of affirmative action began in earnest. However, Professor West works in academia, and he may have very well been referring to black's gains in those institutions of higher learning where he is employed.

In 1965, 15.2 percent of Blacks and 26.2 percent of whites ages 25–29 had attended college.[45] Of those college students, 6–8 percent of the Blacks, and 13 percent of the whites had completed 4 years or more of schooling. Blacks were attending and graduating college at a little over half the rate of whites. By 1995, the percentage of Blacks attending college had increased to 44.9 from 15.2, an increase of 195 percent. Amongst whites, the same numbers increased from 26.2 to 55.4 percent.[46] Therefore, over a period of 30 years in which affirmative action policies figured predominately, Blacks went from attending college at 58 percent of the rate of whites to 81 percent.

This looks good for proponents of affirmative action.

Unfortunately, the increasing rates of attendance have never been transferred to rates of completion. In 1995, 26 percent of whites completed 4 years of college versus 13 percent in 1965. For Blacks, the numbers were 15.3 percent in 1995 and 6.8 percent in 1965.[47] The rate of completion essentially doubled. The problem with this doubling of the completion rates for both Blacks and whites is that it equates to a drastically different dropout rate between the two groups. Only about 1 in 7 Blacks between the ages of 25–29 have earned a bachelor's degree even though almost half of the demographic has attended college.[48] One study showed that within a six year period 57 percent of whites earned a degree while only 34 percent of Blacks did.[49] That means that while affirmative action may have increased the rate of enrollment, it also may have decreased the graduation rate.

Many will reflexively argue that the reason Blacks are less likely to complete college is because they lack financial resources to do so. However, in the 1990s about 40 percent of Blacks were receiving federal grants to help cover the cost of tuition, a number double that of white students.[50] A much better explanation for the black dropout rate is that affirmative action policies mismatch black students with colleges. Since there are thousands of colleges with clique-approved diversity policies and only so many qualified minority students, colleges often take a minority student who is not academically prepared for their institution's curriculum. Take the Massachusetts Institute of Technology for example. MIT accepts the top 1 percent of America's engineering students every year.[51] The black students enrolled at MIT have very impressive SAT scores that place them in the top 10 percent of all students nationwide. However, these same promising SAT scores place them in the bottom 10 percent at MIT. In fact, if MIT admitted Blacks based on the same criteria as whites their numbers would decrease 400 percent.[52]

This ends up putting a non-white student in a tier 1 school when he or she is only qualified for admission to a tier 2 school. The same is true for a minority student that should be at a tier 3 school, but because tier 2 students are going to tier 1 colleges, the tier 3 qualifier ends up at a tier 2 school. In addition to sending minority students to schools they are not academically prepared for, once there, they often have to major in subjects that are less academically challenging and which lead to careers that are less rewarding from an income standpoint.

The book *The Shape of the River* by William Bowen and Dereck Bok, who were both college presidents, was supposed to have disproven the mismatching proposition. In reality, the evidence they offer to disprove the claim actually bolsters it. Bowen and Bok pointed to higher rates of graduation among black students at colleges like Harvard where the admission requirements were more stringent than they were at schools like Duke and Rice. What they missed, however, was that the gaps between white and black student's SAT scores at Harvard was 95 points while at Duke it was 184 points and at Rice 271. This means that Harvard was admitting black students who on average scored much more similarly on the SAT to the school's white students while Duke and Rice were admitting Blacks whose scores were not nearly as competitive. It should be no surprise that black students whose test scores were comparable to the students who got in on merit alone did better than those whose test scores were not. It is rumored that Bok and Bowen refuse to release the data from which they drew their conclusions.[53]

President Johnson once said, in an attempt to justify affirmative action:

> "You do not take a person who, for years, has been hobbled by chains and liberate him, bring him up to the starting line of a race and then say, 'You're free to compete with others,' and justly believe that you have been fair."

Your Mother Lied

Unfortunately, he did not take into consideration that it might not be a good idea to take someone who can run a 5K race (state college) and put them in a marathon (Ivy League).

The main reason preferential policies should be done away with is this: They do not help non-whites as advertised. Secondly, they widen that already vast gulf that exists between the races by making the competition unfair for the sake of payback. Were it possible to bring back the whites of the past that excluded non-whites, and pay them back, you would be on to something. Attempting to get that revenge however by punishing their descendants is a lose-lose proposition if ever there was one.

THE EFFECTS OF PREFERENCE

Sri Lanka is an island located off the coast of southern India. Its population of around 20 million is made up of two ethnic groups: the majority Sinhalese (74 percent) and minority Tamil (18 percent). Under British colonial rule, the Tamil minority took advantage of schooling offered by the Brits and various Christian missionaries for well over 100 years. The Sinhalese majority did not. Discrimination was not to blame. Because of this, by 1948, the Tamil minority had become over represented in every high-paying profession. They were 32 percent of the countries doctors, 40 percent of its engineers, and 46 percent of its accountants.[54] The Sinhalese majority occupied most of the less rewarding, manual labor jobs. However, these differences in occupations and incomes, combined with differences in ethnicity and religion, had never caused any animosity or violence between the two groups.

Then in 1956, S.W.R.D. Bandaranaike appeared. A demagogic Sinhalese politician, Bandaranaike managed to get elected Prime Minister by creating ethnic unrest between the two groups. Once in office, he instituted a very polarizing set of policies to please his ethnic supporters.[55] Sinhalese became the official language of Sri Lanka, and affirmative action-type preferences were soon to follow. First, the nation's college for teachers began accepting only Sinhalese students. Before long, all the nation's colleges had lowered their standards for the Sinhalese and introduced strict quotas to keep the Tamils out. After just a few years, these policies had reduced the percentage of Tamil medical students to 17 percent, even though in 1948 Tamils were 32 percent of practicing doctors. The number of Tamil engineering students was purposefully reduced as well. In 1975, only 14 of Sri Lanka's engineering students were Tamils even though 40 percent of the countries engineers were.[56]

Initially, Tamil leaders tried appeals to reason when voicing their displeasure to the Sinhalese government officials. When this did not work, the Tamils produced their own ethnocentric, demagogic, politicians. Before long, these equally polarizing pols were calling for their fellow Tamils to secede from the Sinhalese majority. Inter-group violence was soon to follow. During the 1970s, Tamil resistance groups engaged in numerous crimes including arson, robbery, and hundreds of murders.[57]

The Sinhalese military was dispatched to Tamil areas to quell the violence. In addition, as you probably guessed, they had revenge on their minds. Innocent Tamil civilians were slaughtered in droves.

Once the divisive preferential policies were combined with the equally alienating politics of identity, it took less than 25 years for an all-out civil war to tear the country apart and claim the lives of 51,000 people.[58] These once congenial compatriots acquired all the trappings of the racialist groups where I reside.

Here in prison, every inmate thinks his race is the chosen one, or at least it is superior to all others. The whites think they are superior because of European conquests and economic power. The Blacks think they are the Asiatic-Africanic—prominent, dominant, original Hebrews from the lost tribe of Shabazz—and because Jesus was black, they are therefore superior. The Hispanics think they are superior because they were in the new world before the 'Ladinos' and had a calendar that is better that everyone else's. They all have their own incendiary, fanciful histories. So do the Tamils and Sinhalese.

The Tamils claim that they discovered America hundreds of years before Columbus. And, like all good racialists, they believe they are God's chosen ones. In case you did not know, one of the three wise men who travelled to Bethlehem was a Tamil.[59] The Sinhalese are known for asserting their 'Aryan' superiority, as Hitler's *Mein Kampf* nonsense was very popular amongst them for generations.

Considering these Sri Lankan events, the distinguished economist Dr. Thomas Sowell pointed out, "Intergroup relations in the United States… have never been as good as they once were in Sri Lanka nor, fortunately, are they as bad as they later became in Sri Lanka."[60] Of course, this doesn't mean they couldn't become worse in the future.

One of the reasons telling everyone to hold on to their ethnic 'identity' (salad bowl) is a bad idea is because if you look back far enough, almost every ethnicity can claim victim status. When this is the case, the power hungry like Sri Lanka's S.W.R.D. Bandaranaike will always take advantage of it by pitting groups against one another even when, as was the case in Sri Lanka, they have no history of one group oppressing the other. Countries with histories like America would seem to be even more susceptible to such demagoguery.

Like Sri Lanka, the country of Nigeria also had different groups supposedly 'under-represented' and 'overrepresented' in various parts of its workforce. As was the case in Sri Lanka, this was not due to anything sinister. In northern Nigeria, the citizenry is mostly made up of the Havsa and Fulani ethnic groups, who together account for 30 percent of the country's population.[61] In southern Nigeria, the Yorubas and Ibos, like the Tamils in Sri Lanka, took advantage of educational opportunities offered to them by Christian missionaries during the colonial era.[62] Unfortunately, the missionaries could only do so much, and their work remained in the south, never reaching the Havsa and Fulani in northern Nigeria. Predictably, this led to the Yorubas and Ibos from the south becoming 'overrepresented' amongst doctors, artisans, clerks, mechanics, and college students.

There were disparities between Nigerian schoolchildren. As late as 1957, children from the North (which has a larger population than the south) only made up 10 percent of the entire country's school enrollment. In 1960, after gaining independence from colonial rule, northern Nigerian politicians started instituting preferential policies that were purposefully biased against southerners in employment and employment training programs. Job openings were filled by practically anyone other than southerners, including expatriates. As the extent of biased policies grew, southern Nigerians found themselves prohibited from owning land, engaging in retail trade, attending college, and of course, holding government jobs.[63] As you can imagine, it did not take long for violence to erupt.

The Ibos, in 1966, carried out a bloody military coup. The North struck back with their own coup. Before long, marauding groups of Northerners wielding knives, clubs, poison arrows, and shotguns were maiming and killing Ibos on a regular basis. Tens of thousands of Ibos were methodically slaughtered before they decided to flee from their own nation. In 1967, Biafra was established as being completely independent from the rest of Nigeria. A civil war began, and over the next two years, more than a million human beings lost their lives.[64]

Those in the clique blame these types of disasters on colonialism and imperialism. Doing so allows them to ignore the results of their own policies while engaging in their favorite tradition: blaming white men.

Although India is better known for Mahatma Gandhi, and ironically peace (Gandhi was killed by his own countryman because of his pacifist views), examples of ethnic violence abound in its history. This is understandable when you consider there are approximately 180 different languages spoken across the country which is demarcated across ethnic and religious lines, making it difficult to get to know people not from your own group; and therefore almost impossible for society to function coherently.

Before it became fashionable to never criticize Islam, India was home to barbaric carnage between its Hindu and Muslim populations. Typically, most people are therefore aware of the bloodshed these religions caused millions of people. What they are not usually aware of is the murder and mayhem preferential policies have been causing there since the 1960s.

In the state of Assam, located in northwestern India, Bengali immigrants had come to be overrepresented amongst the physicians, attorneys, educators, journalists, and government bureaucrats. (See the pattern here?) At the same time, the Marwaris, also immigrants to Assam, had become renowned in finance and industry. Envious of these immigrants' successes, the indigenous Assamese, who were mostly poor farmers, decided they could improve their lot with the enactment of preferential policies and began to lobby the government accordingly. In the 1980s, they demanded that the official language taught in schools be changed from Bengali to Asamalese. Even though the immigrants were obviously a net benefit to the economy, the native Assamese lobbied the government to begin curbing their immigration.[65]

Insistence upon quotas in government hiring came next in the form of threats, demonstrations, and riots. Already tense intergroup relations became even more problematic when the Assamese nationalists demanded that all business be conducted solely in their native language. After years of increasing tension, Marwari businesses were ransacked and burned by rioters who believed the Marwaris were not hiring enough Assamese. The Assamese then intensified their demands for their native language to be used and violence with Bengali militants ensued. The Assamese massacred 1,000 Bengali Muslims in mob violence.[66]

Preferential policies also caused polarization that led to intergroup violence and chaos in the Indian state of Maharashtra. After forming a group called Shir Sera and protesting 'immigrant dominance,' Maharashtrians decided to intensify their efforts. They began engaging in mob violence that killed over 200 people and left 10,000 homeless in a single year.[67]

When the Indian government decided in 1950 that the 'untouchables' should have more essential human rights, they quickly became the victims of violent protests against their newly-granted preference regarding college admission. Murders were in the hundreds and 300 villages and 2,000 homes were leveled.[68]

IT COULD HAPPEN HERE

Keep in mind, while assuring yourself that "this could never happen here," that none of these groups' ancestors had been owned as slaves by their counterparts ancestors. Nor did any of them claim that their ancestors had a large portion of their country taken from them in 1848. Nor did they have a Hollywood machine to exaggerate those very real injustices. In some cases, majority groups were attacked by minorities; in others, the attackers were majorities.

In short, America has all the ingredients (and then some) necessary to produce atrocities every bit as horrifying as those in Sri Lanka, Nigeria, and India. You have racially polarizing leaders such as the Reverends Al Sharpton, and Jesse Jackson. You have politicians like President Obama and government officials like Eric Holder taking sides on racial issues based on color—before they know all the facts. You have academicians like Bill Ayers and Jose Angel Gutiérrez misrepresenting the story of western civilization by teaching that conquest and slavery were never known by Africans or Native Americans until white men built boats, even though there is nothing further from the truth.

They all tell us that any disparities in achievement, whether in education, employment, or income, are due to past discrimination—white supremacy. Add to this mix the changing demography of America, and it becomes all too easy to envision a society polarized and on the brink, and much sooner than 2040.

In his exemplary book *Race and Culture*, Dr. Thomas Sowell, who literally traveled the world to research the book's content, lays out the necessary elements for turning ethnic polarization into a viable political strategy.[69] First, a party must derive the majority of their votes from an electorate defined mostly by ethnicity/race. Second, the politicians in that party have to have little to no chance of getting the votes of anyone apart from that ethnically characterized electorate. Lastly, blatant animosity toward other groups cannot cause them to lose support amongst their ethnically defined base or in society at large.[70]

This is how the Democratic Party operated in the American South for almost 100 years. Dr. Sowell writes on how this phenomenon can burgeon:

> The transition from the initial condition of mutual tolerance in Sri Lanka to the threshold of group level antagonism necessary to create ethnic-issue parties was produced in a few years by the skilled political demagoguery of Sinhalese political leader S.W.R.D. Bandaranaike, as part of his campaign to become prime minister in 1956. Once ethnic issues became preemptive for parties of all ideological leaning, ever more extreme demands from both the Sinhalese and the Tamils followed. Moreover, this political polarization has in turn increased cultural polarization, even among the cosmopolitan elements of both groups. Whereas highly educated Sinhalese or Tamils once spoke English in their homes, and spoke their respective group languages only to servants or other lower class people, that changed after political polarization. In short, the highly educated, cosmopolitan, elements of both Sri Lankan groups—once looked to hopefully as a bridge between the two communities, in part because they literally spoke the same language—have themselves joined in the general polarization, now cultural as well as political.[71]

In America right now, you have ethnic lobbies like MALDEF who conspicuously solicit support along ethnic/racial lines without any meaningful consequences from the larger society. The Ford Foundation and many other non-ethnically defined organizations donate money to groups like MALDEF all the time. Apparently, they are not bothered by these groups' overt appeals to ethnocentrism, as MALDEF has "raked in $30 million from Ford and tens of millions more from other corporations,"[72]— despite having their co-founder say anyone who does not like California being a Hispanic state should go back to Europe. No, MALDEF is not a political party. However, they and other similar groups are already deeply entrenched in the Democratic Party, which could therefore begin making polarizing appeals to their constituencies well before 2040. By openly campaigning on racial grievances, real or imagined, a well-defined constituency of non-whites could be created with demographic changes alleviating the current need to appeal to all Americans. You could very well have someone as polarizing as S.W.R.D. Bandaranaike running for office as a Democrat.

Today, at least in national elections, no Democrat can come out and say, "Black/brown people vote for me because I will seek racial justice against the white man." The question is, "Could that ever be the case?"

Currently, politicians still operate under a set of constraints and incentives that keep them from running for office on a platform of redressing racial grievances by punishing whites. However, if a coalition of non-whites and whites who think like Bill Ayers could organize, much like the Democratic Party already is, it might be possible for a politician to run a racially polarizing campaign and win in the near future.

Instead of turning America into a nation of 'squabbling nationalities' as President Theodore Roosevelt warned against, a shrewd politician might be able to succeed in creating an us-against-them environment, where the 'us' becomes all non-whites, and the 'them' is of course all whites.

In Leesburg, Virginia, during the spring of 2002, members of the Black, Hispanic, and Asian Pacific Caucuses of the House of Representatives held a collaborative retreat.[73] Their objective? To "create an atmosphere of understanding among groups that have often felt pitted against one another for resources and recognition." The attendees found common ground on the issue of expanding the food stamp program in general and for immigrants in particular.[74] No whites were invited, nor were any members of the press. Since there were no reporters there, we are left to speculate just who it is these groups believe are pitting them against one another. Judging from the poem read by Beau Sea, it is obvious whom these groups identified as the cause of their troubles:

> We are everywhere
> We are programming your websites
> Making your executives look smart
> And getting into your schools for free
> And you know what?
> It's only gonna get bigger.[75]

The name of the poem is *The Asians Are Coming*. It was part of the entertainment in Leesburg. Ever since I first read this, I have wondered how someone who comes from an ethnic group that does better in regards to earning educational achievements than the 'privileged' white majority could feel compelled to write something like this. Someone should tell Mr. Sea, someone of Chinese descent, the Asians came a long time ago; were discriminated against, and now do better than everyone else! My only guess as to why Mr. Sea feels as he does is that if he imagines himself as an underdog and/or victim, then whenever he does accomplish something, it is all the more praiseworthy and gratifying.

Of course, the flipped side to that coin is this. When he fails, it is not his fault, for he was not supposed to succeed anyway, the forces of white supremacy stacked against him as they were. Victimhood: the opiate for the clique's masses.

WHY YOU WILL NOT HAVE TO WAIT FOR 2040

You do not need a majority of non-whites in America in order to have large-scale violence between the races, or to at least change the country so dramatically no one alive today would recognize it. You may not even need the Democratic Party to become anymore racially and ethnically polarized than it is today. There are already plenty of whites in the clique who desire nothing more than the opportunity to prostrate themselves before non-whites and commence with their self-flagellation. Andrew Hacker, Father Pflager, John Rawls, et.al. would gladly vote for a politician who campaigned along racial lines. These are the whites who live in the gated community with Pitts. They are the types of white people who sat approvingly in Jeremiah Wright's church while he called white America the "U.S. of KKK," as his majority black congregation, 7,000 strong, applauded his racist tirade. T.S. Elliot gave an apt description of these whites:

> Half the harm that is done in this world is due to people who want to feel important. They don't mean to do harm—but the harm does not interest them. Or they do not see it, or they justify it because they are absorbed in the endless struggle to think well of themselves.[76]

In addition to ethnomasochist whites like Michael Moore and Bill Clinton, there are over a million immigrants entering America each year. Since 1965, 85 percent of these immigrants have come from the third world where the rulers and people lean much further to the left politically than the average native-born American does. Even if America manages to avoid the violent fates of Sri Lanka, Nigeria, India, and many others, she could still very well cease to exist as we know her today via majority vote.

A recent Harris poll reported that 81 percent of native-born citizens believe our public schools should teach children to be proud of their country. When America's naturalized citizens were polled that number dropped to 50 percent. On the question of whether or not the United States Constitution should supersede international law, 67 percent of native-born answered, "Yes," while only 37 percent of naturalized citizens agree with them.

Your Mother Lied

When it comes to affirmative action policies, only 35 percent of native-born Americans are in favor of preference. America's immigrants, however, support these same policies that helped beget the bloodshed in the aforementioned countries at a 58 percent clip; including 64 percent of Asians even though those of Chinese, Japanese, and Korean descent out perform their 'privileged' white oppressors in myriad categories of outcomes.

A poll from the Pew Research Center found that 55 percent of Latinos, native and foreign born, viewed capitalism unfavorably. Also only 27 percent supported gun rights, compared to 57 percent of non-Hispanic whites.

Fifty-five percent of Asian immigrants and a whopping 75 percent of Latino immigrants support bigger government. This does not change much after even three generations in the U.S. The grandchildren of Latino immigrants favor bigger government 55 percent to 36 percent even though the average American opposes bigger government 48 to 41 percent.

In other words, the things that make America 'America' are overwhelmingly opposed by most of our immigrants and our largest minority group. No wonder the clique keeps screaming for 'comprehensive immigration reform' and amnesty for illegal aliens. They are guaranteed tens of millions of votes for the Democratic Party.

Long before 2040, at the intersection of identity politics and the clique's false narrative, America will choose its future. Regardless of the choice, America will still be at least a geographic location. The question is whether she will be one nation, indivisible, or a barely functioning, balkanized police state divided along racial or ethnic lines—like it is where I live.

Will Americans heed the examples of Sri Lanka, Nigeria, India, and the many others, which Dr. Sowell and others have been proffering? Or will the clique continue to keep the faith in what can only be described as the left-wing version of American exceptionalism: believing the salad bowl/multicultural model, combined with identity politics, can work in America even though its track record everywhere else is on par with that of communism. Only time will tell. There are reasons for pessimism when groups like the League of United Latin American Citizens (LULAC) with mottoes such as "We cannot assimilate! We will not assimilate!" become more and more accepted.†

---

† In 2014, President Obama's appointee to head the Consumer Financial Protection Bureau, Richard Cordray, gave a speech to LULAC in which he bragged about new federal laws that would benefit immigrants and illegal aliens. Having a government representative speak to a group with such a motto, thereby demonstrating official approval, should give everyone pause.

America Apart

I happen to believe that much of what divides the races in America is not so much an inherent inability to get along, but a false narrative that propagates an erroneous vision. Unfortunately, this vision so greatly benefits its proponents they go to great lengths to preserve it. And preserve it they must. Their egos, incomes, and entire lives all rest upon it.

CHAPTER 2

THE NARRATIVE

The facts are these: Blacks in the United States suffer disproportionately from the lack of substantive healthcare, access to employment opportunities and to educational equality. In addition, Blacks make up a disproportionate portion of the prison population.[1]

~ Michelle Alexandre, Teacher of Critical Race Theory
University of Mississippi

Long before we came to this country, we were kings and queens, never porch monkeys.[2]

~ NAS, *I Know I Can*

In 2010, Barry Bujol Jr., a black American living in Hempstead, Texas, was arrested and charged with attempting to aid Al Qaeda terrorists. Why would an American citizen want to help Islamo-fascists inflict harm upon his country? After Bujol's arrest, a neighbor had this to say about Bujol and his wife: "They'd talk about white people always wanting to overpower everything."[3]

Think back to October of 2002. A seventeen-year-old illegal alien named John Lee Malvo and his surrogate father, John Allen Muhammad were on a murderous tour of the Washington, DC area in which they shot 13 people, killing 10 of them.[4] Most people remember the beltway sniper. What they do not remember—probably because they never heard them—are the beliefs that drove the pair to shoot over a dozen people in cold blood. Drawings made by Malvo depicting Blacks being tortured by whites with phrases of revenge scrawled about them were found in his cell.[5] Apparently, the demand for money was not the only thing motivating the pair. Teenagers are easily influenced, and Malvo was no doubt under the spell of the older Muhammad. However, what convinced Muhammad, a grown man, that it was a good idea to indoctrinate a teenager from Jamaica with such beliefs?

In December of 1997, Colin Ferguson boarded a train in Long Island, New York. Out of respect for New York Mayor David Dinkins being black, he waited until the train was outside Dinkins jurisdiction before he opened fire on the train's white passengers. When some heroic passengers finally tackled him, Ferguson had shot twenty-three whites and Asians, killing six of them.[6] Not long after his arrest, it came out that Ferguson's rampage was racially motivated. He had sought revenge against whites for their supposed racism. Strangely enough Ferguson was an immigrant to the U.S. from Jamaica, and could have returned anytime the racism became too much to bear. A lawyer for the NAACP; an organization Pitts claims is "distrusting of the bold" and the "most conservative" of the civil rights groups; said on a radio show that she "grieved" for Ferguson. She wanted to know, "How could we permit a man to walk around with such bottled up rage?"[7] The host of this talk radio show, Clayton Riley, went even further down this road of rationalization by saying Ferguson was, "no more enraged about a whole lot of things than I am and a whole lot of other people are."[8] A caller to the show however took the cake with a very telling claim: "These people who enslaved our fathers, enslaved our mothers, they earned it."[9] As if Ferguson's victims had been the actual slave traders from over a hundred years ago.

However, a lawyer, talk-show host, and the show's callers cannot speak for an entire race of people. I agree, and I hope the survey done by the National Law Review that found 68 percent of Blacks believe white racism could have caused Ferguson to do what he did, does not either. However, I doubt it. The gulf between the races is awfully wide.

The above incidents are admittedly extreme manifestations of what the narrative can cause people, especially black Americans, to do. What I see and hear on a day-to-day basis, which should especially concern the Pitts of the world who believe there are too many non-whites in prison, are men coaxing themselves into believing they cannot make it in society because of racism from whites. "The brain is a belief engine... once beliefs are formed, the brain begins to look for and find confirmatory evidence in support of those beliefs, which adds an emotional boost of further confidence in the beliefs and thereby accelerates the process of reinforcing them, and round and round the process goes in a positive feedback loop of belief confirmation."[10] The narrative also widens the gulf between the races by convincing non-whites their ancestors were subjected to a unique form of evil simply because they were not white.

The passage by Ms. Alexandre I began this chapter with covers most of the narrative's bases. It is what Pitts in particular, and the vast majority of the political left—the clique—believes concisely. John Hope Franklin, a historian recommended by Pitts, states it this way. "...white Americans are a bigoted people and have always been."[11] This is seen in the nation's healthcare system where "poor black patients [are] slighted" as reported by the New York Times. It appears in the denial of educational opportunities because of funding and because tests like the SAT are, according to Richard Seymour of the Lawyers' Committee for Civil Rights, "an engine for the exclusion"[12] of Blacks. Lastly, discrimination appears in prison populations where Blacks make up a disproportionate share of America's inmates because they are, according to Pitts, 'funneled' into the criminal justice system by racist whites. This justice system, claims civil rights litigator and Ohio State law professor Michelle Alexander, is therefore "the new Jim Crow," meaning whites still to this day want to see Blacks remain second class citizens.

These strongly held beliefs, and the "solutions" their holders are hell-bent on imposing, are the main cause of what separates the races—not white supremacy. While the above quotes are all in reference to black Americans, you could easily replace "Blacks" with "Latinos" and none of the believers would bat an eye. As long as you are talking about non-whites, the claims for the most part are interchangeable. This is why there is affirmative action for Asians and Hispanics even though they or their ancestors came here under their own power. This has not stopped them from clamoring for separate Asian and Hispanic study halls, dorms, yearbooks, graduation ceremonies, and copious amounts of racially based "studies programs." The point most take away from all this is that all non-whites are victims and all whites are privileged because of their victimizing of those non-whites.

The song lyrics from NAS represent a supplementary part of the narrative and one of the ways it is spread to everyday people who never took fill-in-the-blank "victim studies" classes or read Cornel West, Ms. Alexandre, or even Pitts. The notion that things were better for Blacks in Africa before the white men came upon the scene is a common falsehood taught by Afrocentric professors at colleges all across America.* Musicians

---

* Africans and Arabs were conquering and enslaving Blacks for centuries before whites ever set foot on the African continent.

and filmmakers get these notions from books like *Racist America* by former head of the American Sociological Association, Joe Feagin. These of course intellectually rigorous tomes are teeming with incontrovertible facts such as, "every part of the life cycle... [is] shaped by the racism that is integral to the foundation of the United States."[13] America has "a centuries old system intentionally designed to exclude Americans of color from full participation in the economy, polity, and society." Books like this, or the more popular *A Peoples History of The United States* by Howard Zinn, inspire movies and documentaries that the average Joe will see or be influenced by.

In prison, we can get books. On lockdown (time when we are locked in our cells 24 hours a day, except for three five-minute showers a week), we have plenty of time to read. Books like *Message to the White Man, The New Jim Crow* or *Makes Me Wanna Holler* are all allowed in and very popular amongst black inmates. We also are allowed radios on which you can hear song lyrics like those from NAS or "and the white man gets paid off all of that" by Kanye West. There are TVs on which to watch movies like "American Beauty" and shows like "Law and Order" where the criminals are mostly white people — even though Blacks commit, according to their percentage of the population, an outsized proportion of criminal activities no matter what form of crime statistics you choose, whether drawn from police reports or victim surveys.

HEALTH DISPARITIES BETWEEN WHITES AND NON WHITES

An article in the New York Times claimed Blacks received "worse care than any other equally sick Medicare patient in every type of hospital in America."[14] The Pitts' of the world see something like this and accept it as the gospel truth without any further investigation because they know, as Joe Feagin says, America is a "total[ly] racist society."[15] Yet further into the article, we find out that the total long-range survival rate for white and black patients is precisely the same. In addition to that, we also learn that black heart-attack patients have an 18 percent higher survival rate than whites over the short term.

Will any of the clique's many columnists, Maureen Dowd, Pitts, Eugene Robinson, et.al. write a column about how the health care system discriminates against white-heart-attack victims? Of course not. So why is it assumed that when the roles are reversed and Blacks are shown to be doing worse than whites by any given measuring stick, that racism is to blame?

The Narrative

The National Center for Health Statistics released a study that claimed black women were receiving less prenatal care than white women were, and that black babies were three times as likely to die as white babies were.[16] This of course got the clique in an uproar as a famous author asked the question, "Do black newborns die at three times the rate of white babies because of some factor intrinsic to blackness, or because being black means they're treated by society as only one-third as valuable as white newborns?"[17] Fortunately this study did not just involve white and black women. It also had Americans of Chinese, Mexican, Japanese, and Filipino descent participating. If the reason black infant mortality rates are three times as high as those of whites is because of the amount of prenatal care, we should see this same correlation amongst all the other women in the study.

Yet we do not. In fact, American women of Mexican descent got less prenatal care than black women, yet they had the same infant mortality rates as white women. Even more damning to the 'one-third-as valuable as whites' notion was that American women of Chinese, Japanese, and Filipino descent received less prenatal care than white women, yet these groups had significantly lower infant mortality rates than whites. In other words, according to the disparities equal racism school of thought, there must be a conspiracy amongst Asians to oppress whites by killing their babies. However, this would be difficult to pull off considering most doctors are white. I guess those Asians really are sneaky! Maybe Beau Sea took time off from writing thought provoking poems and is leading this conspiracy. He did warn us they were coming.

Prenatal care, at least in the era of Medicaid, is available to most women who want it. However, infant mortality rates are influenced by a number of things, quite possibly the least of which is prenatal care. According to the U.S. census bureau, in 2010 18.1 percent of Asians lacked health insurance while 11.7 percent of whites did. That means that even though the percentage of Asians without health insurance is almost twice as high as that of whites, their infant mortality rates are lower, their incomes are higher, and they are more likely to have a college degree than whites. In other words, amongst relatively healthy people, there will be no correlation between health insurance and success in life, just as the amount of prenatal care received does not correlate to mortality rates.

So just why are black infant mortality rates higher than those of whites? One explanation could be the attitude of the mothers. If a woman smokes, drinks, or uses drugs while she is pregnant there is a good chance any of these behaviors will harm the child. One study compared black women with only other black women and found that those that did not get prenatal care were twice as likely to smoke, and six times likely to drink, as black women who did get prenatal care. This shows that some women are more concerned about their babies than others. Another reason for the infant mortality rates being different could be that black children, when born to unmarried mothers, are twice as likely to be addicted to drugs at birth as Hispanic or Asian babies.[18]

Another problem affecting infant mortality rates is the weight of the child at birth. The Family Research Council says, "Teenage single-parent mothering is the single greatest contributor to low-birth-weight babies." The studies they reviewed also showed "that the high [rate of] out of wedlock births to young mothers is the primary explanation for America's low international standing on measures of infant mortality."[19] This is especially troubling when you consider that 70 percent of black newborns enter the world with unmarried parents.

In short, there are many more logical explanations for black infant mortality rates than the clique wishes to consider. Everyday facts do not bring as much notoriety as calling an entire country racist. Pitts will never win another Pulitzer for operating "at room temperature"[20] when he writes. These people know that the best way to be noticed is to cast themselves as "defender[s] of the downtrodden."[21] Therefore, instead of seeing these women as having done something they should not have done, they see a failure of 'society' because anyone can defeat a pregnant teenager, but no one can defeat an entire society. They are David taking on Goliath, and therefore very worthy of your praises.

These types of problems in which "disparities" are blamed on racism will be examined throughout this book.

Like every prong of the narrative, the "medical system is racist" claim does not stand up to verifiable evidence. Although banal, mundane explanations are of no use to clique members, they could provide invaluable feedback to non-whites who, because of the narrative, may be close to giving up and doing something that could cause them to become my next cellmate inside this razor-wire-wrapped salad bowl I live in.

CHAPTER 3

EMPLOYMENT DISPARITIES

Blacks suffer from a lack of employment opportunities. This is the second strand of Alexandre's abbreviated version of the narrative. Likewise, Pitts laments the fact that the "black unemployment rate stands at twice the national average."[1] Michelle Alexander, author of *The New Jim Crow* says it should come as no surprise that a large number of black men are unemployed "given the high level of discrimination suffered by black men in the job market and the structural barriers to employment in the new economy."[2]

Alexander claims that globalization and deindustrialization took factory jobs out of American cities and sent them overseas—causing skyrocketing unemployment[3] amongst Blacks. When new factory jobs did come into existence, they were located in the suburbs where Blacks were unable to travel because they lacked transportation. This is called a spatial mismatch, when job seekers are located in areas where there are not enough jobs to satisfy their demand, while the areas with plenty of jobs do not have enough job seekers. Alexander freely admits that in 1954 unemployment amongst black and white youths was equivalent. Yet this gives her no pause whatsoever when leveling her discrimination argument.

It seems logical to conclude that white employers were more discriminatory in the 1950s than they are today. However, she says that the blue-collar jobs that employed 70 percent of black males in the 1950s and 1960s had 'suddenly disappeared' and that by 1987 only 28 percent of black men held such jobs.[4] In short, the problem is black unemployment, the cause, according to the clique, is globalization and discrimination.

THE PROBLEM WITH MINIMUM WAGE

In 1910, 71 percent of Blacks over the age of nine were employed.[106] That number will surprise most considering the racial climate during that era. What is even more surprising is that amongst whites age nine and older, the percentage of those employed was 51 percent—a full 20 percentage points lower than the black employment rate. Also in 1910, 89 percent of Blacks still lived in the south where there were few if any blue-collar manufacturing jobs.[6]

In 1930, 60.2 percent of Blacks were employed compared to 44.7 percent of whites.[7] Around this same time, a man from Alabama managed to underbid the competition for a government contract to build a veteran's hospital in New York. The main reason he was successful in this endeavor was that he employed black workers from the south at wages white workers in New York would not accept. Upset that the locals lost out to a southerner, and no doubt seeing an opportunity to garner votes in the future, Representative Robert Bacon from New York, brought forth H.R. 17069. This bill would, "Require Contractors and Subcontractors... to comply with state laws relating to hours of labor and wages of employees on state public works." This would make it impossible for a contractor to win a bid by paying a lower wage to his workers than the competition paid theirs. In March of 1931, after numerous other bills regulating wages had been submitted, the Davis-Bacon act was passed and federally decreed super-minimum wages became the law for the construction industry.[8]

When the Davis-Bacon act was passed, Blacks made up over 80 percent of the unskilled laborers in six southern states as well as 17 percent of carpenters.[9] At this same time they were also moving north in greater numbers and gaining a toehold in the Yankee construction industry. This did not bode well for union bosses. If black workers were willing to work for less, how would they guarantee Jobs to the white workers? More importantly, as far as the union bosses were concerned, from whom would they collect dues? In other words, the government and labor unions—who the clique says have always been great friends to underdogs—made it much more difficult for Blacks to get and maintain jobs.

How would mandating a minimum wage put Blacks out of work you ask? Because if you have to pay $7.25 an hour—no matter who you hire—for whatever job, you are going to hire the most skilled worker you can get, not the most cost effective worker available. Think about it like this: You own a small retail store and you need to hire someone to watch the place from time to time when you cannot be there. Two people apply for the opening. Both are high school graduates but one is computer literate while the other is not. You really only need someone to run the cash register and answer the phone. If there were no minimum wage, you would ask the two applicants what was the least amount they would be willing to do the job for and hire accordingly. However, since you have to pay $7.25 an hour regardless of which one you hire, you might as well hire the one with the computer skills in case your business develops a use for them.

Again if there were no minimum wage, and the lesser skilled applicant were willing to work for less than their competition, they would get the job every time. Indeed. The executive director of the National Association of Minority Contractors, Ralph C. Thomas, says Davis-Bacon leaves "no choice but to hire skilled tradesmen" and that the majority of them are white. The act "closes the door in such activity in an industry most capable of employing the largest number of minorities."[10]

In 1948, the unemployment rate for Blacks aged 16—17 was 9.4 percent. For the same aged group of whites it was 10.2 percent. That is, more white 16—17 year-olds were unable to find a job than were their black counterparts in 1948. In 1957, after two increases in the federal minimum wage, black unemployment for 16–17 year-olds had risen to 16.3 percent while only rising to 11.9 percent (from 10.2 percent) for whites of the same age. The disparity was even more pronounced amongst 18–19 year-olds with the percentage of unemployed Blacks jumping to over 20 percent (from 9.4 in 1948) versus only 11.2 percent for whites. In 1967, after two more increases in the minimum wage, black 16–17 year-olds had an unemployment rate of 28.9 percent compared to 12.7 percent for whites. By 1973, two more increases in the minimum wage had come to pass and the rate of unemployment for black 16–17 year-olds was a previously unconscionable 45.2 percent. The white rate had risen to 19.7 percent. In 2009 after 13 more increases, the unemployment rate amongst black 16–19-year-olds was 52 percent compared to 27 percent for same-aged whites.[11]

And remember, Alexander's contention is that black unemployment was not a problem until the 1970s when the unquenchable thirst for profits took all the great factory jobs overseas. But as we have just seen the black unemployment rate was already rising precipitously and tracking very closely with the increases in the minimum wage, before the 1970s when the factory jobs began to 'suddenly' disappear. Also problematic for Alexander's hypothesis is that since free trade has flourished, at least up until the great recession, the black unemployment rate has fluctuated without rhyme or reason when it should have increased dramatically if her assumptions are correct.

In 1995, the book *Myth and Measurement: The New Economics of the Minimum Wage* was published and the clique rejoiced. The authors, two Princeton University economists, argued that they had proven through research on fast food restaurants in New Jersey that raising the minimum wage did not reduce employment. However, in 1996 the Employment Policies Institute released a paper called "New Evidence on the Minimum Wage: The Crippling Flaws in the New Jersey Fast Food Study." This paper showed that wage raises did decrease employment opportunities as the vast majority of economic studies have shown over the years.[12] Researchers who took a closer look at the data determined that the Princeton Professors had collected the information for their thesis incorrectly. Another study done by a presidential commission that came out in 1980 showed that unemployment rose one to three percent for every 10 percent increase in the minimum wage.

Skeptical of arguments like this, economics professor Bernard Anderson says: "The minimum wage argument does not explain why black youths are so disproportionately affected; then why doesn't it reduce as much for white youths as it does for black youths."[13] Unfortunately, black youths on average have lower levels of educational accomplishment than white youths. Even when you are comparing two high school graduates, one white and one black, there are normally marked differences in their scholastic abilities. For instance, the average black twelfth grader's reading ability tests as being equal to that of the average white eighth grader.[14] This may be blamed on poverty or a Eurocentric curriculum by the Pitts of the world, but even Blacks who came from families making over $70,000 a year score lower on the SAT than whites whose families make less than $10,000 a year.[15] As for the SAT in particular or the curriculum in general being Eurocentric, Asian students happen to do better than whites on all standardized tests even though they do not have a single 'Asian Heritage Day' much less an entire month devoted to their culture as Blacks and Hispanics do.

What this boils down to is that having a minimum wage forces younger, less skilled workers out of the labor market. And that this affects Blacks more than whites because a larger portion of the black population is less skilled than their white peers. This will be a problem for the near future because the clique's members derive tremendous emotional satisfaction from waxing righteously indignant on a presumed injustice, which in reality is that—while there is still a minimum wage—whites and Asians are more employable than Blacks and Hispanics. If they really wanted the unemployment rate for Blacks to go down, they would call their Democratic comrades in Congress and demand they introduce legislation to abolish the minimum wage. The Republicans would check their calendars to make sure it was not April 1, and then we would see a rare demonstration of bipartisanship as the bill passed unanimously.

Another problem with Alexander's globalization/discrimination hypothesis as the cause of high black unemployment is that many Asians and Hispanics live in the exact same cities, in neighborhoods just as afflicted as Blacks do. Yet they have neither as high an unemployment rate, nor as low a labor force participation rate, as do Blacks. For example, in California, males of Mexican ancestry have higher labor force participation rates, and lower unemployment rates than black males. Also, in Chicago, Puerto Rican and Mexican descendants are significantly more likely to be employed than Blacks are. For various reasons—mainly high taxes and regulatory costs—businesses have fled California in droves, taking the jobs they provide with them. Yet this has not affected non-black minorities. And remember, in 2010, the rates of poverty were nearly identical among Blacks and Hispanics. Alexander never offers an explanation as to why minorities living in the same cities and states as Blacks do not have as much difficulty working jobs. Lucky for us, the book she actually got the information from for her argument, does.

The book *When Work Disappears* by William Julius Wilson is where Alexander gets most of her information. In it, Wilson claims that unemployment and poverty, along with a host of other problems those in the clique believe are consequences thereof, have increased exponentially since globalization began. He says the infrastructure of the economy changed, (factories moved), and that this hurt Blacks living in cities disproportionately.[16] But to his credit, Mr. Wilson made note of the problem with his argument as it relates to Hispanics and Asians. In fact, I have to assume Alexander completely skipped over this portion of the book. Wilson himself says that Blacks are less likely to have good attitudes about working and are less likely to put together car pools than Hispanics.[17] Alexander fails to mention this. This is very common amongst those in the clique for to do otherwise would be a case of "blaming the victim." To the Alexanders of the world, nothing is ever the fault of Blacks, because they have been discriminated against.

Joel Kotkin, writing in the Washington Post, echoed the sentiments of Mr. Wilson, which Alexander is loath to admit. He claimed that even though black males in south central Los Angeles had unemployment rates of 50 percent, most of them would not take the jobs that were available from small businesses in the city. Meanwhile the Asians and Hispanics in the city wasted no time taking those jobs. A black community organizer named George Givens told Kotkin, "Young Blacks today don't want to start at the bottom." And, that "after the civil rights movement, there was a false message that you didn't have to work your way up. If a job didn't pay $15.00 an hour, you didn't want to do it."[18]

A Newsweek piece by Joe Klien, titled, *There Are Jobs in Chicago* also claimed that a lack of opportunities were not to blame for the high rates of unemployment amongst black males. "The problem isn't jobs," said Harriet Dawson, who was in charge of Project Match, a program being run in the notorious Cabrini Green housing project that sought to help its tenants find work. According to Ms. Dawson, "There are jobs in Chicago. We don't have trouble placing our people. Whether they'll be motivated to do those jobs is another matter." Along with motivation, the young have to be able to get up on time, improvise on the job, and at a minimum speak correct English.[19] Fixing the language problem is more daunting than it seems. It is not merely a matter of education. There are black figures held in high regard that believe and preach that speaking English correctly makes someone less black. Malcolm X, for example, equated good diction with being a house slave—that is, the lowest of the low; the sell-out who sided with the white slave master against Blacks—the last thing on earth anyone black wants to be.

In *Still The Promised City? African-Americans and new immigrants in postindustrial New York*, Roger Waldinger writes that Blacks from the Caribbean do not have the same problems with unemployment American Blacks do because their attitudes towards the available jobs are different.[20] This is a better, more apples to apples comparison than those mentioned above involving Asians and Hispanics. It eliminates the possibility employers are only racists towards Blacks and no other minorities because Blacks from the Caribbean look identical to American Blacks. Also, Blacks from the Caribbean are the descendants of slaves, and therefore were also cut off from their cultural heritage from Africa just as American Blacks were.

The immigration of Blacks from the British West Indies (Barbados, Jamaica, Trinidad, etc.) began in earnest in the early 1900s in Harlem, New York.[21] Initially, West Indians faced discrimination identical to that of American Blacks. As they searched for employment, even those who were educated or skilled had trouble finding an employer that would look past their skin color. Eventually, these black immigrants from the Caribbean managed to save up enough money as a group to invest in rental properties or to bank roll their own small businesses. West Indians developed reputations as "frugal, hardworking, and entrepreneurial." And because of these traits, as early as 1901, they owned 20 percent of all black businesses in Manhattan even though they were only 10 percent of the population there.[22] By the new millennium, their descendants, along with recent black immigrants from the West Indies, had come to own over 50 percent of all black businesses in New York. Indeed. Their success has been so pronounced some black Americans have taken to calling them "black Jews."[23] In light of the success Blacks from the West Indies have had, it seems almost absurd to claim that black Americans lack employment opportunities.

THE PROBLEM WITH LABOR FORCE PARTICIPATION

The labor force participation rate (LFP) is the percentage of a population, 16 years or older, either already working or diligently looking for work. It differs from the unemployment rate by measuring individuals' intentions toward working instead of the percentage of people who looked for work in the last month but could not find any. LFP is important when examining Alexander's claim about globalization and discrimination because these two forces cannot directly affect it. She and the rest of the clique will disagree. They will say globalization and racism caused non-whites, especially Blacks, to give up looking for jobs that were not there, that the government should have done something, and that Blacks did not change their attitudes towards work.

In her book *The New Jim Crow*, Alexander informs us of the following:

> In 1954, black and white youth unemployment rates in America were equal, with Blacks actually having a slightly higher rate of employment in the age group sixteen to nineteen. By 1984, however, the black unemployment rate had nearly quadrupled, while the white rate had increased only marginally. This was not due to a major change in black values or black culture; this dramatic shift was the result of deindustrialization, globalization, and technological advancement.
>
> The economic collapse of inner city black communities could have inspired a natural outpouring of compassion and support. A new war on poverty could have been launched. Economic stimulus packages could

have sailed through congress to bail out those trapped in jobless ghettos through no fault of their own.

Education, job training, and relocation assistance could have been provided so that youth of color would have been able to survive the rough transition to a new global economy and secure jobs in distant suburbs.[24]

In 1954, 85.2 percent of working aged black males actively participated in the labor force.[25] The same statistic for white males was practically identical at 85.6, and had been since the start of the twentieth century. But starting in the mid-1960s, black male LFP began to drop much more rapidly than white male LFP. By 1977, black LFP stood at 73.8, white LFP at 79.5 percent. This widening gap was much more pronounced amongst Blacks and whites aged 16–17. In 1955, 48.0 percent of white 16–17 year-olds were participating in the labor force, as were 48.2 percent of Blacks. By 1970 however, a gap 14.1 percent existed between the two groups, with white employment at 48.9 percent and Black at 34.8 percent. In 1980, LFP for whites was 53.6 percent, and 31.9 percent for Blacks.[26]

In short, black male LFP went from 85.2 percent in 1954 to 73.8 in 1973, to 31.9 percent in 1980. The twelve-point drop from 1954 to 1973 occurred before globalization and deindustrialization began. Also important to note is that LFP for older black males remained the same throughout the period in question.[27] If the factories were all sent overseas by the profit-whoring, capitalist white men, these older gentlemen—who I think would be more likely to have a factory job than a "youth of color" would be—should of had the same, if not a worse, decline in LFP. And remember what we saw with the unemployment rate for 16–17 year-olds more than doubling from 12.1 to 27.8 percent. This was during the period when factory jobs were "plentiful in urban areas" according to Alexander. Yet from 1970–1990, the period when globalization and free trade really took off, the unemployment rate amongst 16–17 year-old black males only increased from 27.8 to 38.9 percent—nowhere near the more than 100 percent increase seen from 1950–1970. And amongst Blacks aged 18-19, the unemployment rate only increased 5.1 percent from 1970–1990.

So just why did the employment picture begin changing for younger black males in the mid 1960s? Alexander says the answer has nothing to do with a change in "black values or black culture."[28] I agree. To an extent.

In the early 1960s the American left began speaking of something they called "structural poverty."[29] Books like *The Other America* by Michael Harrington, spoke of poverty as being entrenched in America's economic system. The structuralists believed the system (capitalism) was at fault and expansion of the overall economy through growth would therefore not eradicate poverty. They claimed that America needed to radically change its system and engage in what they dubiously termed 'redistribution of income.' Poverty was no longer the individual's fault or problem. It was society in general, and capitalism in particular, that made people poor. And since society was not as enlightened as these forbearers of the clique, they would look to the government to solve this 'problem.' Never mind the facts that poverty had been with human beings as long as prostitution and that most people eventually worked their way out of it. Because, as two noted authors said, "In a nation as rich as the United States, it is an utter moral scandal that even the slightest remnant of poverty should remain."[30]

This would eventually become the only respectable way to view the issue amongst the elite. The consequences of this new way of thinking unfortunately became more prominent amongst Blacks because 1) The proportion of the black population that was in poverty was much larger than that of whites, 2) More so than any other discriminated against ethnic group in America, Blacks had a bevy of real grievances in their past that could—and at times should—justify such "It's society's fault, not yours," ways of rationalization, and 3) Politicians discovered they could win elections based on their stated intentions regardless of their results. Black values and culture were not about to change on their own; the government was about to subsidize and thus promote the change, much to the detriment of Blacks themselves and society as a whole.

In 1968, the National Commission On Civil Disorders released the very partisan Kerner Report.[31] President Johnson put this commission together to find the cause of the 1960s riots. Predictably, their findings were in lock step with the new de rigueur, Rousseauian "society is to blame" explanation for poverty. And if rioting in the street could be rationalized as having been caused by white racism, as poverty being caused by capitalism was—by a government commission no less—surely not working could be rationalized as well. After all the Kerner report did say that the riots were a predictable response to "the racial attitudes and behavior of white Americans toward black Americans." These prevailing notions of the time were readily accepted even though most of the cities where the rioting occurred were not nearly as destitute for Blacks as were other cities where no rioting occurred. (The riots in Detroit were especially puzzling considering Blacks there had an unemployment rate of 3.6 percent which was lower than the national average for whites at that time.)[32] All of these direct and indirect adoptions of Rousseau's "blame it on society" vision affected black's attitudes toward work. But much more blame should be placed on the government's changing of the constraints and incentives related to having a job.

Whether it was Stokely Carmichael, Dr. Martin Luther King Jr., or anyone ideologically in between, Blacks in the 1960s had a wide array of people (some reputable, some not) telling them their problems were caused by the 'system' and/or the white man. And in many cases these people were telling the truth. But they were wrong and counterproductive in claiming that drastic, revolutionary change was required in order for Blacks to gain economic equality with whites. Americans of Chinese and Japanese ancestry have very few of 'their own' in government yet have had higher incomes than whites for some time. Nonetheless, the Student Nonviolent Coordinating Committee in Chicago declared, "we must fill ourselves with hate for all things white."[33] Stokely Carmichael said black power meant "building a movement that will smash everything western civilization has created."[34] And H. Rap Brown claimed Blacks needed to "wage guerilla war on the honkey white men."[35] Most of the people proclaiming these views were good at oratory, college educated, and wore really cool leather jackets. In other words, kids corning of age in the 1960s and 1970s had a much different group of leaders and role models than their parents or grandparents had.

Think about it like this: You are a black teenager. Your great uncle was thrown in jail for walking down the 'wrong' side of the street after 6:00 p.m., or supposedly violating some other ludicrously racist law. The government, by the way of the Kerner report, just said that Blacks rioting in Detroit (where your cousin lives and has a decent job) were to be expected because of the racism directed at them by whites. And if the riots were to be expected because of external conditions over which the rioters had no control, they were justified and therefore blameless.

Then along come these really cool brothers with their righteous talk and defiant demeanor. They talk about black folks in a way you never heard before. They talk about Franz Fanon and other righteous brothers they read about in college. Momma always said, "If you're smart, you go to college," so you conclude these cats are speaking the truth. They say the whole system's messed up, and it ain't worth trying to fix. They say the white man will never give a brother a decent job.

You suppress any knowledge of the fact that Blacks in Detroit have a lower unemployment rate than whites in all the United States. Why? Because mundane facts like those do not make your brain release the dopamine-spiked cocktail of feel-good chemicals like the righteous talk of those black, leather-clad, righteous brothers does. So you say to yourself, why work? That is a game for suckers and Uncle Toms. Before long, such a black teenager will develop a much different attitude towards work than the one held by his father or grandfather.

Not just radical students and members of racialist groups were telling Blacks directly and indirectly that working a job in the white man's world was pointless. In 1965, if not sooner, the Office of Economic Opportunity (OEO) was directing its employees to trumpet the structuralist's view of poverty, in order to convince people that being on welfare was acceptable.[36] Through pamphlets, discourse, and proselytizing, the government workers from the OEO were able to convince many that being on welfare would not amount to a black eye on their reputations. Some even went so far as to say welfare was a right.

In 1966 George Wiley created The National Welfare Rights Organization (NWRO). Only a year later, the NWRO had become popular enough to hold a convention in Washington, D.C. no less.[37] And as their name implies, they were not encouraging people to seek employment relentlessly. In *Regulating The Poor: The Function Of Public Welfare*, Frances Fox Piven and Richard Cloward detail how community organizers worked to make the poor adopt the clique's new-fangled stance on the permissibility of welfare.[38] Children would come home from the community center and tell their parents about how the college-educated community organizers were telling them that welfare was a right. It was difficult for parents, who always told their kids college graduates were to be emulated, to now tell them they should not be listened to. These notions of welfare as a right, and Blacks having a blank moral check because of white racism, combined to make quite possibly the worst backdrop imaginable for the generation of Blacks entering the workforce.

The federal government engineered the relationship between an increasing receptivity to welfare and a declining LFP rate amongst Blacks. In 1962, the Aid to Families with Dependent Children (AFDC) program was significantly altered. Under its original provisions in the New Deal, AFDC was only available to widows with young children.

Removing the stipulation that the mother be a widow extended aid to families with unemployed fathers. Before long, twenty-five states adopted this alteration. In 1968, the Department of Health, Education, and Welfare ceased investigating recipient worthiness via surprise home visits. Lawyers were also filing challenges to eligibility proscriptions. In 1969, the Supreme

Court ruled that requiring welfare recipients to be residents of a particular state for one year before being eligible was unconstitutional. [39] In less than one decade, long held beliefs and laws regarding welfare changed radically.

In the late 1960s, the structuralists at the OEO wanted desperately to prove that giving the poor additional income in the form of wealth transfers would not weaken their will to work. In 1968, 8,700 people became subjects in a study called the Negative Income Tax (NIT) experiment; with structuralists everywhere hoping its results would prove and illustrate their convictions.[40] After ten years however, what the NIT actually produced was more evidence that widening the scope of welfare payments reduces LFP.

In Seattle and Denver, test subjects who were husbands showed a 9 percent decrease in "desired hours of work." Test subjects who happened to be wives showed a decrease of 20 percent. These reductions were not due to workers giving up overtime or choosing to work just a little less. They were "due primarily to reduced rates of entry to employment." The numbers for young men were alarmingly worse: A reduction of 43 percent for those that were not heads of households and 33 percent for those who became married during the experiment.[41] The time spent unemployed also increased amongst the test subjects. For husbands the increase was 27 percent to nine weeks without a job. For wives it was much worst at 42 percent and fifty weeks.[42]

The effects of these welfare payments in the NIT experiment were catastrophic for most families involved. In Seattle and Denver, the break up rate for white families was 26 percent higher than that of the control group. For Blacks receiving the NIT payment it was 42 percent. In New Jersey there was no difference amongst white families but a 66 percent difference amongst black families who received the free cash and those that did not. Amongst families whose primary language was Spanish, the family break up rate was an astounding 84 percent higher. Countless researchers reviewed the figures repeatedly, and in the end, no matter how many times they tried to massage the variables and data produced by NIT, the fact remained that the welfare payments had a disastrous effect on practically every measurable outcome. [43]

But what about Alexander's calls for "job training" programs and "economic stimulus packages" "so that youth of color would have been able to survive the rough transition" to what she calls a "new global economy?"[44] If so many Blacks are unskilled "through no fault of their own," why not give them training that would make them just as employable as whites or Asians? Why not take some money from all these rich white people and return it to its "rightful owners" via taxpayer-funded jobs that will produce benefits for the people? All of this has been done, and it has failed spectacularly!

In 1950, the federal government was spending around $11 billion (in 1980 dollars) on social security, AFDC, and unemployment insurances.[45] America had about 45 million people living below the poverty line at the time, which meant each poor person was receiving a little less than $250.00 (1980 dollars) a year. In 1968, four years after the first war on poverty bill was passed, the percentage of Blacks living below the poverty line stood at 30 percent.[46] Numerous laws providing for food stamps, medical care, job training and the like were passed during the 1960s under the banners of the War on Poverty and the Great Society. The funding for those programs however did not begin in earnest until the late 1960s to early 1970s. From 1969 to 1980, before President Reagan and his "minions" (as President Obama called them) began doing their evil deeds in Washington, the funding for those anti-poverty programs quadrupled. This produced an astonishing drop in the black poverty rate of: one percent. That is, from 30.9 percent in 1969 to 29.9 percent in 1980.[47]

This was after well over a decade of the types of programs Alexander claims would have helped "youths of color survive" and they were funded with four times their initial allocation of taxpayer money. Indeed. From 1950 to 1980, welfare spending increased 20 times over while the population only increased by 50 percent.[48] Between 1964 and 2010 the federal government spent $13 trillion 'waging war' on poverty.[49] Today, the government has 122 different anti-poverty programs that cost the taxpayers $591 billion a year. This means that taxpayers annually spend $14, 849 on every poor individual in America — a far cry from the $250.00 spent in 1950. Yet the U.S. Census Bureau said in 2010 that 27.4 percent of Blacks still lived below the poverty line. So after spending $13 trillion America was rewarded with a minuscule 3.5 percent reduction in the poverty rate of it's black citizens. The overall poverty rate for Americans in 1968, when funding really kicked in, was 12.8 percent. In 2011, it was 15 percent and expected to rise. During the $13 trillion spending spree, the poverty rate has never dropped below 10 percent.[50] It should, however, be kept in mind that the poverty rate amongst black children was 62 percent for those in female headed households but only 13 percent in two parent households.[51] Unfortunately, as we saw earlier with the NIT experiment, welfare payments normally increase the rate of family breakup exponentially.

Also discouraging is that only about 30 cents of every dollar confiscated and transferred to the poor actually gets to the individual. And just what does it mean to be poor? For starters, 80 percent of people living below the poverty line have air conditioning. This is something that less than 50 percent of Americans had in 1970. Almost 75 percent of the poor own a motor vehicle and 30 percent actually own more than one. About 98 percent of the poor have a color television, with a majority of them having either cable or satellite service. Over 75 percent own a VCR or DVD player, and over 90 percent a microwave oven.[52]

In *What Government Can Do*, authors Page and Simmons tell us that European countries do a better job of providing for their poor.[53] However, at least when it comes to housing, the average 'poor' person in the U.S. has a larger living area than the average middle class person in London, Paris, and may other European cities.[54] They also assert that food is a 'right' and cite a report that says in the 1960s "ten million Americans suffered from hunger and malnutrition."[55] The authors claim that government programs solved this problem for the most part, but that in the 1990s 5 percent of U.S. households "did not have enough to eat."[56] But many studies of the poor show their diets are no more lacking in nutritional content than those of the middle class.[57]

Also, a larger percentage of the poor are obese, making it difficult to believe hunger is a legitimate concern.[58]

THE PROBLEM WITH REGULATIONS

Minimum wage laws are merely one of the various ways government has limited the employment opportunities for non-whites in America. In his indispensable book on this subject, *Race and Economics*, esteemed Professor Dr. Walter E. Williams of George Mason University makes a point-by-point case against government as being the only hope for non-white economic prosperity. Dr. Williams argues that, "Free market resource allocation, as opposed to allocation on political grounds, is in the interest of minorities and/or less preferred individuals."[59] The reasons for this are simple. A minority is by definition, someone who will have trouble winning over the majority in order to receive some desired outcome. Whereas in a market the minority does not need to seek the favor of anybody, because his dollar is no different than the dollar a member of the majority can offer. For example, if you want to buy a particular car in which another individual is also interested, you can convey your greater interest by offering more money. In politics, you have but one vote. This does not allow you to 'register the intensity' of your desire for a particular item.[60]

Dr. Williams offers a comparison between Public schools and consumer goods:

> If one tours a low-income black neighborhood, he will see people wearing some nice clothing, eating some nice food, driving some nice cars, and he might even see some nice houses — but no nice schools. Why? The answer relates directly to how clothing, food, cars, and houses are allocated through the market mechanism. Schools, for the most part, are parceled out through the political mechanism. If a buyer is dissatisfied with the goods distributed through the market, the individual can simply "fire" the producer by taking his business elsewhere. If the buyer (taxpayer) is dissatisfied with public schools, such an option is not, in a black neighborhood, economically available to him. He has to bear the burden of moving to a neighborhood with better schools. Interestingly, if one does see high quality schools in poor or moderate-income neighborhoods, they tend to be private institutions, such as Ivy Leaf in Philadelphia, Marcus Garvey in Los Angeles, or Marva Collins Prep in Chicago.[61]

One of the many facts of slave life in the American South that has been left out of *Roots, Twelve Years A Slave,* and other conventional depictions was the method of self-hire. As early as the 1700s, some slaves were making their own money by "servicing ships as rope makers, coopers, and shipwrights."[62] Other slaves possessing the requisite skills even managed to find work "silversmithing, gold beating, and cabinet making." On most occasions, the slaves gave some of what they earned to their owners in exchange for slightly more liberty. Unfortunately, it did not take long for those who preferred complete control over their slaves to find fault with this practice. Planters in Virginia claimed that self-hire allowed some to live "free from their master's control,"[63] while others said it permitted Blacks to trade stolen merchandise. In reality, their real concern was with having to compete with Blacks willing to work and sell goods for less than they would, thereby reducing economic opportunities for whites.

Even though the southern states passed laws to prevent slaves from selling or trading "any commodities whatsoever"[64] there was "considerable property ownership among slaves in both the upper and lower south" bought and paid for by self-hire. The colonial era saw 44 out of 100 slaves in Virginia's Northampton County purchase their freedom by 1644, with some obtaining land. In the Charleston District of South Carolina, former slave James Pendarvis was the owner of 3, 200 acres of land and 113 slaves. Jenn Gough, a cabinet maker, was the landlord of several buildings in Charleston and the coastal south as well. And by 1819, free Blacks in Charleston were represented in thirty different occupations such as tailoring, carpentry, shoemaking, and even hotel ownership.[65] In New Orleans, free Blacks "owned some $2 million worth of property and dominated skilled crafts like bricklaying, cigar making, carpentry and shoemaking."[66]

Liquor, grocery, and general stores constituted the majority of the black-owned small businesses in New Orleans. Larger businesses included real estate brokering and cigar manufacturing. One successful black real estate dealer, Thorny Lafon, died with assets valued at $8 million in today's money. The "New Orleans registry of free negroes" listed 22 black-owned factories. Although one man operated most of these, some, like the one belonging to George Alces, employed 200 workers. Interesting to note is that even though most Blacks in New Orleans were unskilled laborers, their ratio of skilled to unskilled workers was actually higher than that of Irish and German workers. The 1850 census claimed New Orleans as home to "355 carpenters, 325 masons, 156 cigar makers, 92 shoe makers, 61 clerks, 52 mechanics, 43 coopers, 41 barbers, 39 car men and 28 painters." There were also 15 blacksmiths, 18 butchers, 19 cabinetmakers, 25 cooks, 11 overseers, 6 ship carpenters, 9 stewards, and 8 upholsters.[67]

Because of all this success in the private sector, Blacks were able to set up charities, orphanages, and schools—in spite of, not because of—the government. The free market allowed this at a time when 'society' was certainly not as tolerant as it is today.[68]

In the North, freed Blacks did just as well if not better than their peers' in Charleston and New Orleans. In Philadelphia for example, a register listed 57 different trades that were being practiced by Blacks in 1838. They included, but were not limited to, bankers, blacksmiths, and carpenters. Black women were also mentioned in this registry as "dressmakers and tailoresses, dyers and scourers, and cloth fullers and glass/ paper makers." Blacks also owned various businesses in Philadelphia, several of which were "very prosperous." Two Blacks, Stephen Smith and William Whipper, owned one of the city's biggest lumber and coal yards. There were also nineteen sail making enterprises with the largest one employing 40 laborers, black and white.[69]

The catering business in Philadelphia was "dominated" by Blacks. Two gentlemen, Peter Augustine and Thomas Dorsey, were so successful they garnered international notoriety for their work. A man who started out as a waiter before launching his own catering business, Robert Bogle, actually had a song written about him ("Ode to Bogle") by one of his customers who happened to be President of the Bank of the United States. Also very successful in the catering business in Philadelphia were Henry and Sarah Gordon. They amassed so much wealth they felt compelled to donate $66,000 (over a million dollars today) to charities.[70]

When it came to real estate, Blacks in Philadelphia owned fifteen "meeting houses and burial grounds adjacent, and one public hall."[71] Together these were worth $12 million in today's currency while Blacks personal property was valued at well over $12 million in today's money.[72]

Many other cities above the Mason-Dixon line also saw black-owned business prosper. In Providence, Rhode Island, a former slave opened the first oyster and ale eatery in 1764. Blacks also owned and operated several restaurants in New York City where they catered to the Wall Street crowd. In Boston, the foremost catering business along with a clothing store worth half a million dollars were both owned by Blacks. And in Chicago, a prosperous black tailor accumulated an estate valued at $100,000 by the time of his death.[73]

In short, when President Obama says a market economy with little to no government intervention has never worked, he is lying. Not only did it "work" for hundreds of years, it worked for free Blacks, albeit to a lesser extent, in an era when whites on average had much lower opinions of them as a race.

None of this means everything was fine and dandy for Blacks until the government interfered with the economy. Far from it. Obviously the civil war was a massive government intervention into the economy of the South and without it black slaves would have remained in bondage. And as late as 1940, a point in time in which Blacks had been free for over half a century with a fairly free market, 87 percent of Blacks were still living below the poverty line compared to 41 percent of whites.[74]

My point is that Blacks were able to find plenty of "employment opportunities" in America when whites were surely more likely to discriminate against them then they are today. As Dr. Williams puts it: "The fact that whites sought out Blacks as artisans and workers, while patronizing black businesses, can hardly be said to be the result of white enlightenment. A far better explanation: market forces at work."[75]

In prison, even non-whites who admittedly have never looked for a job will often say they believe white employers will not hire them because they are racist. I once asked a 23-year-old black inmate, who we will call J.G., "What kind of job did you have before you got locked up?" He replied, "I ain't never much look for no job." I asked him further about when he got out, if he would look for a job then. The look on his face showed my line of questioning genuinely puzzled him. I then gave him a hard time about "working for these white folks" (prison guards) for free, since he had once had a job in the kitchen.* I told him convicted felons could work in the oil and gas fields and sometimes bring home six-figures in a year. But he could not have been less interested. We went back to talking about the Texans and their chances in the playoffs.

I found our conversation odd because J.G. was a sharp kid. His IQ was 112. (They list IQs on the printouts we receive when we are written up for disciplinary cases.) This puts him 20 points above the average inmate and twelve points above the national average. Even though I never saw his grades from high school, I am sure he did well. He was always the go to guy when one of the inevitable arguments over some mundane matter broke out between other inmates. (A go-rilla cain't whup no tiger.) Whether it was science, geography, history, or whatever, J.G. normally could not be stumped.

So why would he not give serious consideration to trying to find a job? Because not working is accepted by his peers, including many potential mates among them. The clique's successful propagation of their fallacious narrative plays a key role in fostering this attitude.

J.G. could not offer up a long list of jobs for which he and his friends had been turned down (due to discrimination) because they never bothered applying for any. They just decided to skip the whole morally degrading foregone conclusion of being rejected by "them white folks" and became criminals. After all, why be a mark? Why be a chump? Why would they go against the wisdom they no doubt heard in countless rap songs telling them working for minimum wage is for fools, or in the "Conscious" rap songs telling them such work is "exploitation?" Why join the military when they are told in *Boyz in the Hood* by Laurence Fishburne's otherwise very admirable character, that there is no place in a "white man's army for a black man?"

With all of that swirling around their heads, how could they not rebel against this racist, capitalist, full-of-whiteness (a tautology for clique members) nation, and instead become "real ass niggas?" At least then they

---

* Even though the vast majority of the guards on the prison unit where J.G. and I are incarcerated are Hispanic and Nigerian, I still hear them referred to as "them white folks!"

get the respect of their peers and convey to women they are tough enough to defend them and their potential children, thereby increasing their attractiveness as potential mates. To put it into economic terms, the clique's narrative has screwed up the constraints and incentives for non-whites, and the consequences have been disastrous.

Most people believe the government does not pass laws anymore that restrict the economic opportunities of non-whites. Champions of government will point out that it was that particular institution that outlawed discrimination and created the many varied bureaucracies charged with policing it in society. But these are the same people who embrace Noam Chomsky's view that collateral damage in the form of innocent civilians being killed in U.S. air raids, is no different from what the Muslim terrorists did on 9/11. That is: results count, intentions do not. And if results are all that counts, then the government is right now, still today, discriminating against black folks—if you use the clique's own 'disparate impact,' results only, intentions need not apply, standard.

Disparate impact allows claims of discrimination to be proven on mere statistical "overrepresentation" or "underrepresentation." And no, Asians, Hispanics, and whites, you cannot sue the NBA or NFL because your groups are underrepresented. Former U.S. Attorney General Eric Holder has already asserted—with no evidence whatsoever—that discrimination laws were written for "[his] people." The disparate impact standard says, basically, that if a business in Houston, Texas, where two-thirds of the city's population is non-white, has more than 33 percent of its workers listed as white, non-whites can sue for discrimination. Even if only whites had applied for the jobs, it would not matter. The fact that you have no evidence of actual bias is immaterial to proving "discrimination" when disparate impact is your standard. Obviously, this criterion is sacred to the clique. They consider its implementation one of their crowning achievements.

But for some reason—that being the clique considers the government beyond reproach when it is attempting to help the victims of white men—they fail to see the disparate impact that the government's laws and regulations have upon non-whites when it comes to economic opportunities. They assume that anytime the government levels a tax on businesses, or raises the licensing fees for entrance into a particular occupation, it is taking money away from privileged whites and redistributing it to the downtrodden masses. The problem with this is that the higher the costs for starting a business or entering a trade become, the more prohibitive these activities become for the oppressed masses those in the clique claim to be so concerned about.

Since the federal government finances the U.S. Department of Housing and Urban Development (HUD), any project it undertakes is subject to the Davis-Bacon Act. If you will remember, Davis-Bacon was a piece of legislation Congress passed to keep southerners—especially those who hired black labor—from getting contracts and jobs by mandating that a prevailing minimum wage be paid for any government contract. As we saw earlier, this kept Blacks and others who were less preferred from getting jobs by eliminating their ability to work for a lesser wage. This took away their most powerful weapon in their competition with the preferred white Yankee workers.

Now for a few modern examples of Davis-Bacon discriminating, if disparate impact is the standard, against non-whites. In Chicago, Illinois, there is a public work association called Bethel New Life Inc. Its supervisor, Mary Nelson, knows first-hand how Davis-Bacon can exclude unskilled workers who are often black. She says the act is responsible for increasing her cost of doing business, which for her is renovating projects, by 25 percent. And since she has to pay a prevailing, government mandated wage regardless of what she hires someone for, she is often unable to hire the young, low-income, unskilled Blacks who live in these housing projects she is repairing.[76] Not only will fewer Blacks get jobs because of Davis-Bacon, the law will also keep more projects where the oppressed live, from being restored.

Also in charge is Elzie Higginbottom, a low-income home builder who's business, and it's potential employees, is often affected by Davis-Bacon, "I've got to start a guy at $16 dollars an hour to find out if he knows how to dig a hole. I can 't do that," says Higginbottom. And since the labor department defines carpenters as anyone who causes a hammer to collide with a nail, and Davis-Bacon mandates that carpenters be paid $23 an hour, Higginbottom is kept from hiring unskilled workers because they do not have an economic output of $23 an hour. This forces him to hire actual skilled carpenters, the majority of whom happen to be white, instead of the young unskilled, mostly black workers who desperately need jobs.[77]

The president of a company that works with HUD on housing projects, Ralph L. Jones, has had similar problems with Davis-Bacon. After agreeing to renovate 200 run-down apartments, Jones decided to hire some of the apartments occupants as laborers for $5 an hour. He figured they could do some cleaning up and help the skilled craftsmen renovate the complex. But the government—which is mostly comprised of lawyers, not businessmen like Mr. Jones—requires through this Davis-Bacon act, that all "laborers be paid $14 an hour." This of course dictated that Jones only hire skilled workers, most of whom were, you guessed it, not black, nor from the apartment complex.[78]

Davis-Bacon and the Fair Labor Standards Act (which codified the federal minimum wage) are not the only government interventions in the economy that in theory were supposed to help the 'little guy' but that in reality harmed him. The government also regulates access to many trades and professions by requiring those who wish to participate in them to attain licenses. These licenses of course cost money, which makes them more difficult for people with low-incomes to acquire. In some states, as many as 800 jobs require a license.[79]

The stated rationale for licensure laws is of course to safeguard the public. Obviously, nobody wants someone presenting himself or herself as a brain surgeon unless that person is actually qualified to operate on a brain. In reality however, the effects of regulation have very little to do with protecting the public and are much more inclined to protecting those who are already practicing a particular vocation.[80]

Common requirements for obtaining a license are: a high school diploma or GED, passing scores on proficiency exams, graduation from government sanctioned schools, or training programs, and being above a certain age—all of which are very reasonable. Unfortunately, there are many requirements that are anything but. Take, for instance, the exam aspiring barbers in California have to pass. It includes questions about the chemical make up of bones and the particular structure of the hyoid bone.[81] Your guess is as good as mine as to what any of that has to do with cutting hair. A majority of states require education on the biology of skin, nails, nerves, and also their diseases.[82] It is not hard to imagine a poor non-white, who grew up in the barrio or the ghetto and went to a sub-par school, having a more difficult time on these tests than the average white person.

The tests are not racist or culturally biased. That is, they do not intend to discriminate, but I would be willing to bet non-whites are less likely to pass them than their white peers.

The commissions that come up with these laws are dubiously constructed. Although most of those sitting on a particular board are elected, the voters are people already participating in the trade or profession. These people have little to no incentive to let others become licensed. In fact, they have all the incentive in the world to keep them from becoming so. The fewer people there are who can do what they do, the more they can charge for plying their particular trade.[83] Take a wild guess at what color these incumbent practitioners' skin most often is?

In addition to the educational requirements, some licenses require the would-be practitioner to buy expensive equipment.[84] A purchase of authorization from someone already participating in the particular occupation can also be required. Many of these certificates are very expensive. For example, when the interstate trucking industry was excessively regulated, a new entrant would be charged millions of dollars for such a certificate.[85] At the time I'm writing this, it costs $600,000 to become a taxi driver in New York City due to licensure laws.[86] Another obstacle to entry, in addition to the expensive certificates and equipment, is that some occupations only have a finite number of licenses available for its practitioners.[87]

The story of Monique Landers, a fifteen year-old student in Kansas, is a perfect, real life illustration of how licensure laws hurt black people more than they do whites. Ms. Landers became involved with the National Foundation for Teaching Entrepreneurship (NFTE). She entered a contest put on by the NFTE—submitting a business plan for braiding hair. She won and was awarded a $750 grant for her business, which she named "A Touch Of Class." She began charging $15–$20 per head and was well on her way. In fact, she did so well she was summoned to New York in order to be recognized as one of five "Outstanding High School Entrepreneurs" by the NFTE. A newspaper back in Kansas ran a story about Landers being honored, and then the trouble began.[88]

After reading this story, hair stylists and cosmetology school operators began complaining to the Kansas Cosmetology Board that Landers' business was illegal because she was operating it without a license. An official notice was sent to her, telling her that if she did not cease and desist her for-profit hair braiding, not only would she be fined, but she would also be thrown in jail. The director of the Cosmetology board, Nancy Shobe, said that if Landers wanted to become licensed, she could enroll in a government certified cosmetology school. This of course means that if disparate impact is our standard, Shobe—through government created power—discriminated against Landers. White teenagers are not operating hair-braiding businesses at the same rate as Blacks if they are doing so at all.

The professed reason for shutting down Lander's business was of course to protect the public. But the real reason was undoubtedly to protect the profits of licensed cosmetologists. Think about it: Hair braiding is not illegal. Hair braiding for a profit without a license is. The fact that money is exchanged does not make any of Landers' clients more likely to get some sort of infection.

Black folks have been braiding each other's hair for a long time and their rates of lice or anything similar are no higher than those of whites. The whole "we're protecting the public" claim goes right out the window.

Cosmetology school in Kansas, as is the case in most states, takes a year or more to complete and costs around $5,000. Landers did not have $5,000 to spare and was too young to enroll anyway. The black and Hispanic populations are on the average younger than the white populations. So here is another 'economic opportunity' taken away from a young black female by the government. Dr. Williams sums up the problem:

> Restricted entry through licensing places disadvantaged people at a severe handicap without necessarily improving the quality of services received by the consumer, the ostensible beneficiary of the regulation. In fact, one study showed that there is a significant relationship between occupational licensing and the number of accidental deaths by electrocution: the more stringent the states electrician licensing examination, the fewer the electricians and higher the prices for an electrician's services; therefore the greater the willingness of amateurs to undertake electrical wiring tasks and risk electrocution in the process.[89]

Whether by high entry costs restricting them from a given trade, or less competition among service providers increasing their costs as consumers, government regulations harm the disadvantaged more, and many of them are non-white. Where is the clique's otherwise omniscient moral outrage at this government discrimination?

THE PROBLEM WITH LABOR UNIONS

Labor unions were for generations notoriously racist towards non-whites. Samuel Gompers, the first president of the American Federation of Labor, once said, "Caucasians are not going to let their standard of living be destroyed by negroes, chinamen, japs, or any others."[90] (Gomper's image has of course been rehabilitated by the clique much like they did with Margaret Sanger and Che Guevara.)

Racial discrimination in the trucking industry was especially virulent. The International Brotherhood of Teamsters was an enormous obstacle to non-white participation in the trucking industry. Early on, before whites believed trucking wages were worthy of their time and effort, Blacks dominated the industry, as it was said to be a 'Negro job.' As the work became more lucrative, unfortunately for Blacks, it also became more unionized. Although there were Blacks in the Teamsters union, they had different seniority rules that made their ascension more difficult than that of whites. For example, if a black person was working as a dock man or local driver and wanted to get on the more preferred over-the-road labor list, he could not carry with him any seniority earned from his current or previous jobs as whites could. This forced Blacks to start at the bottom of the list and practically stay there, because every time a white person got on the list they would invariably be ahead of anyone black since their seniority was transferable. This stripped Blacks of any incentive to leave the jobs they had for more lucrative ones; a round of layoffs would affect those with the least seniority the most.[91] Another way the unions would discriminate against Blacks was by issuing ultimatums to local trucking companies: hire whites or else — the 'else' being large-scale labor upheaval.[92]

Since this discrimination went unchecked for so long, the passing of the civil rights act in 1964 had little to no effect on the trucking industry's racial composition. Most of the new workers came from the recommendations of drivers and union members who were mostly white. Fortunately for the black folks, deregulation of the trucking industry was finally on the way.[93] In "Deregulation And The Prevalence Of Black Truck Drivers," John S. Haywood and James H. Peoples state that black participation in the "traditionally lucrative for-hire sector" of the trucking industry, jumped from 21 percent to 27 percent in the late 1970s after deregulation began. The authors also point out that in 1981, 48 percent "of the minority certifications in force" were awarded prior to 1978. The majority, 52 percent, "had been granted in the two and one-half years following deregulation." The number of minority owned common carriers certified by the Interstate Commerce Commission soared from 314 in 1981 to 936 in 1992.[94]

In addition to increasing employment opportunities for non-whites, deregulation also lowered the prices of the myriad goods truckers haul all over the country by increasing competition. In 1980, there were approximately 18,000 carriers; by 1981, there were 33,548. This increase in shipping options for manufacturers lowered their costs, causing them to lower the prices of their goods or risk losing their market share to their competitors. This translated to an actual savings of 5 to 20 percent for consumers.[95] An amount of savings much more helpful to the low income family than that of "the rich" or "privileged."

Employment Disparities

Dr. Williams points out an additional benefit for those of us concerned about the cohesiveness of society:

> Deregulation has been valuable in another important way. It has increased black participation in the trucking industry without depending upon controversial measures that have caused so much divisiveness in our society, namely, quotas, and racial preferences.[96]
>
> If we retain these restrictive laws and regulations, *maybe* a case *can* be made for racial preferences as a "second best" solution. The "first best" solution, in terms of equity, efficiency, and morality is to eliminate restrictive laws and regulations. When this course is pursued, it ameliorates the injustice and brings the side benefit of doing so without the rancor and divisiveness of racial remedies.[97]

In short, by 1970 the government and intelligentsia had drastically changed the poor's (especially poor Blacks) economic opportunities and their attitudes towards those opportunities. They accomplished this by 1) Raising the minimum wage to price unskilled (mostly non-whites) out of the labor market, 2) Passing laws to strengthen racist labor unions (the largest contributors to President Obama's campaign), 3) Creating licensing and regulation fees that make the cost of entry to a given field too high, which disproportionately impacts non-whites, and, 4) Telling non-whites they deserved welfare payments and that work was a game for suckers caught up in the white man's plan. By issuing out a welfare payment that when combined with food stamps allowed most recipients to live as well as they did when they worked a minimum wage job, the government was able to make it more economical for the poor to take this path as opposed to working.

If you think lying about economic opportunities for minorities has no consequences, I would like for you to consider the case of Freddy's Clothing Store in Harlem, New York. In 1995, the owners of Freddy's, who happened to be Jewish, decided to discontinue leasing a portion of their store's space to the owners of a record store who happened to be black. A boycott immediately ensued, led by Morris Powell who was in charge of the Reverend Al Sharpton's 'Buy Black' committee. Powell appeared at radio station WWRL in New York to promote the boycott and say, amongst other racial, incendiary things, that the owners of Freddy's were, "Crackers." As he led one of the actual protests, Powell and others yelled to pedestrians, "keep [going] right on by Freddy's, he's one of the greedy Jew bastards killing our people. Don't give the Jew a dime...Freddy the Jew has to go, one way or another." One protester screamed "Fuck White People. Fuck

The Jews."[98]

Another threatened violence, "we're going to come back with twenty niggers and loot and burn the Jews." Not to be outdone, someone else yelled, "I will be back to burn the Jew down. Burn, burn, burn."[99] Never to miss out on just such an opportunity, Reverend Sharpton himself said on a radio program "we will not stand by and allow them to move this brother so some white interloper can expand his business on 125th street." He also claimed, "There is a systematic and methodical strategy to eliminate our people from doing business on 125th street... One of our brothers... is now being threatened."[100]

The tension and animosity mushroomed. Then, on December 8th, 1995, one of the protesters, Roland Smith, walked into Freddy's and told all the Blacks inside to leave. He then pulled out a gun and began shooting, hitting three whites and one Guyanese Indian. He proceeded to set the store on fire, which ended up killing seven innocent people and himself.

And despite his role in this, the Tawana Brawley hoax, the Duke Lacrosse hoax, and countless others, MSNBC still gave the Reverend his own television show.

CHAPTER 4

EDUCATIONAL EQUALITY

The third strand of the narrative asserts that Blacks do not have "access to...educational equality." Devout clique member President Barack Obama is fond of saying America needs to invest more in education, in spite of what the nation's past and current returns on this "investment" have been. In particular, he claimed that the Bush administration's signature legislation No Child Left Behind, "left the money behind." In addition to this supposed lack of funding, many in the clique also complain that non-whites are being taught a Eurocentric curriculum and therefore are doomed to fail. President Obama, in his first memoir "Dreams From My Father," speaks admirably of a high school guidance counselor named Assante Moran who believes that black students would be much better off if they had not been taught "someone else's history. Someone else's culture."[1] Especially since it is "the same culture that's systematically rejected them."[2]

Regardless of what one thinks when it comes to the overall equity of the educational system, it is beyond argument that America has not "left the money behind" when it comes to funding for its schools. In 1964, no federal funding existed for disadvantaged students in elementary and secondary schools. However, by 1966, funding for these students had jumped to $3 billion (in 1980 dollars). And from 1965 to 1980, over $60 billion (in 1980 dollars) was spent directly on trying to improve the education of disadvantaged kids.[3]

Spending in general had ballooned from $5, 671 per student in 1970 to $12, 922 in 2008. That is an increase of 128 percent. In 2010, the Department of Education (DOE) had $63 billion heaped upon it. This doubled the amount it received in 1977 even though the school population did not come close to doubling during that period. In fact from 1970 to 2008, America's school population only grew a measly 8 percent. What has grown however, by ten times the rate of student enrollment, is the number of jobs in public education. Contrast the 8 percent growth in students with a 61 percent increase in the number of teachers and the 12-fold increase in public education bureaucrats with titles like "instructional aide" and it becomes clear where all the money has gone. In 1955 there were 27 students for every one teacher. In 2007, the ratio was 15:1.[4] In other words, the gospel of "the students need more individual instruction in smaller classes" has been heeded.

Many will complain that when it comes to teachers, quality is much more important than quantity. And therefore, by extension, the taxpayers should pay teachers more so as to attract the most talented people to this all-important occupation. The problem with this argument however is that the average teacher makes $53,230 a year. Which means that if two teachers marry, their household income would be in the top 20 percent of all earners.

In *What Government Can Do*, Page and Simmons claim that expanding programs like Head Start and enrolling more children in pre-school are necessary in order to attain educational equality.[5] But Head Start in particular has had over $166 billion spent on it since 1965 and a majority of studies have shown it to be largely ineffective.[6] As for preschool, it must not help either because enrollment there has skyrocketed "from 11 percent in 1965 to 53 percent in 2008,"[7] while test scores and proficiency measurements have declined or remained the same. Money cannot be the problem here. One estimate even puts the amount spent since 1965 on disadvantaged children at $2 trillion.[8] (Yes, that is a 'T.')

Many will claim the problem is the allocation of the funds instead of the actual dollar amount allocated. They will argue that schools where the majority of students are non-white receive less funding than those that are majority white, as Jonathan Kozel does in his book *Savage Inequalities*. But during the 2002-2003 school year, Washington D.C.'s mostly black students had $16,344 allocated for each of them while students in Iowa and South Dakota, who are mostly white, had less than half of that spent on them. In spite of this, only 12 percent of the 8th graders in D.C. could read at grade level, and just 7 percent of them could do 8th grade math. In Iowa and South Dakota, over one-third of 8th graders could read and do math at eighth grade levels.[9]

After examining the differences in spending per-student, the National Center For Education Statistics found that spending increased according to the percentage of minorities in a school district.[10] In districts where the students were mostly non-white, spending was actually 15 percent higher than in districts where non-whites made up less than 5 percent of the student body. School location, as in cities versus suburbs, also defied the narrative. During the 1992-1993 school year, Atlanta's public schools got 20 percent more in funding than suburban schools in Dekalb County. The same was true in Hartford, Connecticut and many other places.[11]

SOMEONE ELSE'S HISTORY. SOMEONE ELSE'S CULTURE

Considering the views he expressed, I am hoping Assante Moran, the high school counselor President Obama describes in *Dreams From My Father*, is a complete fabrication like the 'Big Fight' Obama had with his white girlfriend after she asked him, why are "black people so angry all the time?"[12] And I certainly hope Mr. Moran is not a "composite" of all the counselors out there, although it would explain where many of your school's problems come from. When Obama introduces this man to the reader, he describes him as wearing an "African print" and an "elephant hair bracelet." He also mentions Mr. Moran's office as being decorated with, amongst other African-themed articles, posters of "Africa's Kings and Queens." Mr. Moran told Obama, "The public school system is not about educating black children. Never has been.... They're operated as holding pens—miniature jails, really. It's only when black children start breaking out of the pens and bothering white people that society even pays attention. Just think about what a real education for these children would include. It would start by giving a child an understanding of himself, his world, his community."[13]

Mr. Moran goes on to say that this 'understanding' is the beginning of any legitimate education process. "From day one" Blacks are taught white culture—a culture which has "systematically rejected" them and "denied" Blacks their "humanity." At no point does Obama voice any sort of opposing view to Moran's claims, leaving most readers to assume, in light of similar things Obama professes, that the President agrees with Moran. Towards the end of their meeting, Moran throws in for good measure, "I expose students to African history... I teach them that Africans are a communal people." He then mentions that his "European" colleagues feel "threatened by this."[14]

Mr. Moran is not alone in his belief that teaching black students about Africa is a prerequisite to a "real" education. School districts in Atlanta, Detroit, Washington, D.C., Baltimore, Indianapolis, Milwaukee, Pittsburg, Richmond, Philadelphia, and others, began implementing curriculums rooted in what they claim is African culture as early as 1990.[15] In this revised program of study, Egypt is portrayed as the birthplace of civilization. The most important and momentous works of philosophy and science are said to have been produced by Blacks and then stolen by whites. For example, Dr. Yosef Ben-Jochannon claims that Aristotle stole the theories and insights that became the underpinnings of western philosophy from a library in Egypt whose shelves were filled with books written by Blacks.[16] There is a problem with this however. That particular library was built 50 years after Aristotle's death. But the clique has never let the facts get in the way of an emotionally satisfying argument, and so by 1996, 12 of Detroit's schools were 'fully African centered', and officials were in the process of implementing Afrocentric curriculum in "all 261 schools."[17]

In Washington D.C., taxpayer money was used to pay Abena Walker $164,739 to design an Afrocentric curriculum for students and to teach "African-centered methodology" to teachers. These teachers were trained at Pan-African University—the unaccredited institution of higher learning founded by Walker herself. Note Walker's teaching credentials: A master's degree from her own university—the only degree ever issued by this 'University.'[18]

Another tenant of Afrocentrism, proffered by Professor Leonard Jefferies, is that the 'sun people' (Blacks) are superior to the 'ice people' (whites) because they have melanin in their skin. Professor Jefferies is no fringe kook. In 1989, he was selected to be the chief consultant to a commission charged with shaping school curriculum in New York by Thomas Sobol, the state commissioner of education. Another mainstream education bureaucrat, Kwame Kenyetta, said while serving on the Detroit school board, "For over 400 years, African-Americans and other people of color have been seen through the eyes of Eurocentric education and have been mis-educated." And, that children "of African descent shouldn't be infused with a different culture."[19] Apparently Mr. Kenyetta believes culture is heritable and programmed into black peoples' DNA.

In *Visions For Black Men*, Nairn Akbar claims that French general Napoleon Bonaparte desecrated statues in Egypt by shooting their noses off in order to alter their original black-African appearance. Schools in Milwaukee taught, "...black Egyptians once had wings and flew freely around the pyramids until the Europeans arrived and killed off all the natural fliers."[20] And, a teacher of African-American studies at Temple University, Karanja Keita Carrol teaches that Blacks are a 'spirit-focused' people, while whites are a 'material-focused' and 'patriarchal' people.[21]

Add all of this up. It appears that what Mr. Moran calls a 'real education' has been taught in major cities across America since the early 1990s. This means that Mr. Moran's hypothesis—that black children will do better if they are taught an Afrocentric curriculum—is testable. If Mr. Moran's assumption is correct, then we should see black students in Washington D.C. and Detroit getting better grades and test scores now that they are learning under an Afrocentric program.

Statistics show the opposite. In Detroit, just 3 percent of fourth graders managed to secure a rating of 'proficient' on a recent National Assessment of Education progress test. Only 28 percent merited a score of 'basic' and 69 percent scored 'below basic.' A score of 'below basic' means that a student is "unable to demonstrate even a partial mastery of knowledge and skills fundamental for proficient work at their grade level." Eighth graders are not doing any better: 4 percent 'very proficient,' 18 percent 'basic' and a staggering 77 percent 'below basic.'[22] These scores caused Michael Casserly, the executive director of the Council on Great City Schools to say, "There is no jurisdiction of any kind, at any level, at any time in the 30 year history of NAEP that has ever registered such low numbers."[23]

Although Detroit's public schools are considered the worst, Washington D.C.'s are a close second. This is the case in spite of the fact that the school district's teachers make $61,195, which is well over the national average of $53,230, and the students are taught an Afrocentric curriculum.[24] In spite of all this, since 1988, black test scores have actually worsened.

The Journal of Blacks in Higher Education, in 1995, compiled a list of reasons to explain why black's SAT scores were dropping. One was that, "increasing emphasis on Afrocentric studies in predominately black schools has reduced study in core math and reading programs." While another stated "school reform movements… are increasingly teaching black students to feel good about themselves instead of concentrating on teaching them reading and mathematics."[25] So once again, a proposal by the clique has not only failed to deliver its promised benefit, it has actually made the very problem it was supposed to remedy, worse.

Why not teach kids of all colors real, factual achievements of Blacks right here in America? Amongst many, there is Bronzeville, the all black business district where the first successful heart surgery of any kind was performed by black surgeons and nurses; the discovery of blood plasma; and the modern filament to the light bulb that made Thomas Edison's invention much more practical. The reason none of these facts are brought up as often as flying-black Egyptians spouting Greek philosophy before it was Greek, is because doing so would weaken the clique's treasured—yet simultaneously tenuous—argument: that Blacks never would have accomplished anything in America without the help of the government. As you saw in the last chapter, especially from an economic standpoint, this notion simply does not jibe with the facts. Wade Nobles, a black teacher from Oakland, said in response to being asked about the practicality of teaching black kids about Egyptian writing and cleansing rituals, "When we educate a black man, we're not educating him for a job, we're educating him for eternity."[26] Perhaps then we should wait until eternity arrives before judging Afrocentric curriculums.

Another stirring notion for the clique is that black students are culturally and biologically different from white students and therefore should be taught differently. Charles V. Willie, a professor of education at Harvard University claims "...in social organization there always are at least two norms, the norm of the dominant people of power[,] and the norm of the subdominant people of power." Because of this, professor Willie believes that the reason black children do not test well is because the tests are culturally biased, meaning they only work for whites. Dr. Asa Hilliard, a professor of education at Georgia State agrees that black children should not be held to what he believes are white standards.[27] In particular, when it comes to speaking English, "vocabulary is not standard, even when people use the same word"[28]—meaning, you should not criticize a black child for speaking incorrect English like you would a white child.

President Obama's "former" pastor, the Reverend Jeremiah Wright claims black children think with a different part of their brain than white children. Al Jezeera's Soledad O'Brien, who like my own daughter has a white father and a black mother, called the speech in which Wright said this, "Great." And according to Jawanza Kunjufu, an educational consultant, "African-American students and European-American students have very different learning styles."[29]

Professor Willie, Dr. Hilliard, and Mr. Kunjufu, like the Afrocentrists above, make claims that are testable. If black students are unable to learn because their "norms" as the subdominant people preclude them from doing so, this should be the case with other "subdominant," non-white people. If black children are genetically different, that is, their brains are a Mac while white brains are P.C.'s, then there should be no reason to expect black students to do as well as white students since they require different syntax and/or instructions. Non-whites have to be taught one way, whites another. But this has never been the case in the past or the present.

Educational Equality

In the 1890s in Washington D.C., there was an all-black high school where the student's test scores equaled or exceeded those of white students. This means the teachers at this particular school either had the correct method for teaching the genetically non-white or, Dr. Hilliard and Jeremiah Wright are full of you know what.

The school in Washington D.C. was called the M Street School throughout the late 1890s and later renamed Dunbar High School in 1915, after the black poet Paul Laurence Dunbar.[30] Dunbar High did not have a mostly upper, or even middle class student body, as has been claimed by those who fear the reality of Dunbar's success and all that it entails. During the 1892-1893 school year many of the jobs held by the students' parents were recorded. Among them were "51 laborers, 25 messengers, 12 janitors and one doctor."[31] So the success of Dunbar's students cannot be attributed to them being some anomalous group of privileged Blacks.

Nor were the students at Dunbar any more likely to be mulatto or less genetically African than the students at any other black high school.[32] Simply picking up a yearbook from Dunbar's past for comparison will prove this. These children were black, and they were equaling and outdoing whites on standardized tests when white people were much more racist.

Certainly we need to explore what type of teaching methods allowed black students to perform as well as those at Dunbar did. But before we do that, we must first get a better appreciation for the breadth of Dunbar's success in educating its black students.

In 1903, well before affirmative action policies, the first of several Dunbar graduates was accepted to Harvard University. Between 1913 and 1923, Dunbar alumni received 25 Ivy League college degrees. Dunbar graduates eventually came to be held in such high regard that they were not required to take the "entrance examinations to be admitted to Dartmouth, Harvard and some other selective colleges." One Dunbar graduate, Robert M. Mattingly, was accepted to Amherst in 1902 whereupon he received college credit for freshman mathematics and physics; thus helping him graduate in only 3 years with Phi Beta Kappa honors.[33]

The first black graduate from the U.S. Naval Academy came from Dunbar. Likewise the first enlisted black soldier to become a commissioned army officer. Dunbar also produced the first black woman to earn a P.H.D. from an American university. Another female graduate of Dunbar, Allison Davis, became "the first black full professor at a major American university." Dunbar also produced the first black federal judge, general, cabinet member, and amongst others, the doctor who discovered the function of blood plasma. The great jazz musician Duke Ellington worked on his musical talents at Dunbar.[34] And at a time when black military officers were scarce, Dunbar could claim as alumni, "many captains and lieutenants, nearly a score of majors, nine colonels and lieutenant colonels, and one brigadier general."[35]

So just how were all of the above academic and professional achievements accomplished by Dunbar and its students? As Dr. Sowell often says, this is a question seldom asked, much less answered. Were the students taught with archaic and esoteric teaching methods specifically designed by the black Egyptians to teach black students? This would have to be the case if Reverend Wright and Dr. Hilliard are correct.

However, Dr. Sowell himself, a black man who has done extensive research on Dunbar in particular, and education in general, says flatly, there was no "curriculum especially designed for Blacks" at Dunbar.[36] They were not taught an African-centered curriculum. In fact, while there was one day a year reserved for honoring Fredrick Douglas, and a week set aside for Negro history, Dunbar's students were not taught the Afrocentric delusions so many black students are taught today.

Edward Brooke, a senator and Dunbar graduate, recalled the following:

Negro history week was observed and in American history they taught us about the emancipation of the slaves and the struggle for equality and civil rights. But there was no demand by students for more, no real interest in Africa and its heritage. We knew about Africa as we know about Finland.[37]

Dunbar's students were taught with methods, and learned from a curriculum no different from that of whites. Today, minority-majority schools like Marva Collins Preparatory School in Chicago get extraordinary results with a "no-nonsense, back-to-basics curriculum that is centered on phonics and memorization for the younger students and higher-level reasoning and literary analysis for the older ones." Other mostly non-white schools like Cascade Elementary in Atlanta and the Kipp academies in Houston and New York have achieved the same type of success with similar "old fashioned" teaching techniques and unwavering discipline.[38]

Unfortunately, these proven methods are at odds with the popular opinions of America's teachers unions and education bureaucrats. It is currently believed that teachers are supposed to be "facilitators" standing behind students so they can "discover" and "create" knowledge. Students are basically being forced to participate in experiments (without being compensated) while attending school. The originators of the Kipp academies, Michael Fienberg and David Levin, took an incredibly unorthodox approach when developing the curriculum and teaching methods they would use in their schools: They studied other successful programs, gathered the most effective techniques and implemented them. In particular, they got low-income, non-white students to devote 67 percent more time to the classroom than the average public school student does. Upon arrival each morning, Kipp students are given "a worksheet of math, logic and word problems" to complete during their free-time that day.[39]

The teachers at Kipp receive wide latitude when it comes to plying their trade. They are however, explicitly required to succeed in educating the children. Whatever they do, it must work. If they fail, they are replaced, as is the case in all private sector jobs. The parents of Kipp students can expect home visits from these teachers in which they will discuss what each party needs to do. And lest they forget to bring something up during these visits, the teachers stay equipped with cell phones (that have toll free numbers no less) that parents can call even after school is out.[40]

Maybe you think all of this is a little far-fetched. Or, perhaps you think it would cost too much to implement such a program nationwide in public schools. On the contrary, Kipp is just one of several schools, many of which are public, that have involved, day-to-day routines for students, teachers and parents; and they also spend less money per pupil than Washington D.C. or Detroit. One such school is Bennet-Kew Elementary in Inglewood, California. There, the principal went against the establishment's conventional wisdom and got results similar to those of Kipp. Bennet-Kew's students are mostly poor and non-white. And even though the school is 52 percent Hispanic, the principal rejected modish and compulsory 'whole language' and 'bi-lingual' methods of instruction. She insisted upon her teachers using phonics and teaching only in English. This catapulted the children's reading scores from, "the third percentile to the fiftieth percentile in just four years." Instead of being rewarded for such an achievement, the principal was threatened with having her school defunded because she "taught exclusively in English." Her results could not have meant less to the education bureaucrats threatening her. This story does however have a happy ending. The parents of the newly successful students at Bennet-Kew elementary "bombarded these officials with protests that caused them to relent and let this principal continue to succeed in her own way, instead of failing their way."[41]

So once again we have a case of human beings succumbing to the feel-good chemicals their brains release when they develop a belief and create a wall to block away evidence to the contrary. Analysis and verification are vetoed in favor of a shot of dopamine.[42] When the clique asserts its identity as defender of the white man's victims, it proposes that keeping more Hispanics speaking Spanish is somehow a way of thumbing their noses at the gringo—even though the white conquistadors who conquered the natives in Mexico spoke Spanish. How else can you explain the wisdom in encouraging a group of mostly poor immigrants to speak a language that 85 percent of the people in the country they immigrated to do not speak? What would be more efficient: buying 10–20 million copies of Rosetta Stone for all non-English speakers coming to America, or buying 270–300 million, times however many different languages there are, Rosetta Stones for everyone already living in America?

Dr. Sowell sums up the problem with the clique's choices of teaching methods and curriculum:

> Documented results are not allowed to override the prevailing educational dogmas—which pervade the schools of education, the teachers unions, and state and federal education bureaucracies—none of whom pays the price for failure of these dogmas. Neither do their children, who are typically enrolled in private schools. What they would have to pay a price for would be widespread demonstrations that the methods to which they are committed produce educational results that are grossly inferior to those produced by the methods they oppose. Should these revelations become widely known among parents and voters, this would threaten not only their careers but also their agendas, which include the use of public schools to promote fashionable beliefs and attitudes—political correctness—rather that to equip student's minds with knowledge and develop their capacity for independent use of logic and evidence.[43]

In *Why People Believe Weird Things*, professor and science historian Michael Shermer points out that "Europeans are an intermediate hybrid population of 65 percent Asian genes and 35 percent African genes."[44] Evolutionary biologist Jared Diamond often mentions the fact that Australian Aborigines, thought by some to be "primitive," have been taught to fly airplanes. And as we saw above, low-income, non-white students have been doing just as well if not better that their "privileged" white counterparts since at least the 1890s.

Despite these facts, Adolph Hitler's 'Race Experts' tried, and President Obama's former pastor Jeremiah Wright continues, albeit for different reasons, to try to convince people that black brains are different from whites. Hence, Blacks either cannot learn as whites do (Hitler), or they learn differently than whites do (Wright). But whites and Blacks, especially in the United States, share at least 35 percent of their genes. The Jeremiah Wrights of the world might argue that the 65 percent of genetic material that is different between Blacks and whites is where the brain/learning disparities are to be found. The problem with this however is that Asians, while more similar to whites from a genetic standpoint, do better than whites on standardized tests and in school. If Reverend Wright, Dr. Hilliard and the rest are right—that Blacks cannot learn as well as whites because their brains and culture are not like those of white people—then Asians should only do a little better than Blacks in school. The Reverend's and Doctor's logic would dictate that Asians do 30 percent better than Blacks and 35 percent worse than whites. The inconvenient truth, however, is that Asians of Taiwanese, Japanese, and Chinese descent do better than whites in America's 'Eurocentric' schools.

There are a few documented anatomical differences between the so-called races. A study done by researchers from the historically black Howard University and Duke University has shown to a large extent that elite sprinters and swimmers can thank their success to their body's proportions. An elite sprinter will have longer legs than an elite swimmer of the same height while the swimmer will have a longer torso than the sprinter. That is, a six-foot tall swimmer has a greater proportion of his six-feet devoted to his torso, while the six-foot tall sprinter has a larger share of his height in his legs. When you are swimming, you are trying to float and propel yourself across the top of the water. A larger torso and shorter legs are more buoyant than the inverse.

When running, you are putting yourself in a controlled fall forward. Longer legs and a shorter torso are easier to balance and allow the sprinter to cover more ground with each stride than if he had shorter legs. For whatever reason, white people have, on average, evolved with more of their height apportioned to their torsos. Blacks on the other hand have evolved with more of their height devoted to their legs. This is why most gold medal-winning swimmers are white and most gold medal-winning sprinters are black.[45] (Though for the clique, it is much more gratifying from an emotional standpoint to believe all whites are rich and have swimming pools in their backyards and therefore have an advantage over Blacks; or whites are lazy and therefore not good at running.) But this particular difference obviously has nothing to do with mental ability.

Another difference might. Different ethnic groups have varying abilities to answer questions dealing with abstract problems of logic, time, and assorted non-verbal factors.[248] African and Jamaican children have trouble solving problems that deal with "three dimensional conceptions of space."[47] A study done in England demonstrated that boys from the city did better in questions dealing with abstractions than their counterparts from the countryside. In America, white children living in secluded mountain populations also did poorly on questions of 'abstract comprehension.' Likewise, the same has been observed with Indian youngsters in South Africa, and lower income children in Venezuela.[48] In Hong Kong, Chinese youth happened to be better at abstract problem solving than whites but were outperformed on those same questions by Eskimos.[49]

There is scientific evidence connecting differences in a person's body chemistry with his or her ability to solve problems dealing with abstractions.[50] At least for the purposes of our discussion, the question then becomes, do these differences in body chemistry preclude some groups of people from learning in the manner in which American schools teach. And more importantly, how does an inability to perform well on questions of abstractions affect ones chances of success?

Jewish children have typically done poorly on these types of questions. Yet in America, they are, along with Americans of Chinese and Japanese descent, more likely to attend college and earn incomes above the national average than any of the 'privileged' white ethnic groups.[51] Jewish families in America earn 172 percent of the nation's average family income. American families of Chinese descent, who do very well in reasoning in the abstract, earn 112 percent of the average family. So apparently, reasoning in the abstract is not a prerequisite for success since Jews are more successful than Asians.[52] And judging by the fact that Jews are 'overrepresented' at most Ivy League colleges, there seems to be no need to change the curriculum in the public schools because some kids are better than others at solving abstract problems.

Fortunately for America and its future, the formula for successfully educating minority students has been around since the 1890s. Current demonstrations of this can be seen at the Kipp academies, David Robinson's Carver Academy, or any of the other many outstanding minority-majority schools. One of the few common denominators amongst these varied schools is that they do not concern themselves with teaching a non-white child "his world, his community" as Assante Moran did. Nor do they teach black children differently because their non-white brains would have them "crawling on their desks" as the esteemed neuroscientist Jeremiah Wright claims.

In prison, for most inmates here in Texas at least, we have several educational opportunities ranging from getting your GED to earing a bachelors or even in a few cases a masters degree. There are also a dozen or so vocational trades most inmates can take. I personally completed a little over 60 credit hours of academic college before the last round of budget cuts closed down the college program on my unit. The name of the school I attended was Coastal Bend College. The actual campus is in south Texas near the prison in which I reside. The vast majority of the teachers from Coastal Bend who came to teach here were Mestizo (part native American, part European), Hispanics just like the prison guards.

With the exception of one, all the teachers leaned to the left politically and always—even in computer science class—found a way to interject their left-wing ideology. I hear this is not unusual for college professors.

One night in my sociology class, the teacher, who I will call Mrs. S, decided to aid and abet the narrative. With her master's degree, she was seen as an authority. I cannot remember how the subject of crime came up, but Mrs. S told a class made mostly of 'youths of color' that "when the cops show up, if there's Blacks there—they're going to jail. They're getting locked up." I winced slightly; the 'youths of color' nodded their heads in agreement. She made no mention of the fact that black males make up about 7 percent of the American population yet in some years commit over 50 percent of its murders, 40 percent of its rapes, and 60 percent of its robberies.[53] She made it sound as if Blacks are put into prison because they are black instead of because they committed an imprisonable crime.

When people with Mrs. S's credentials endorse conspiratorial nonsense about the 'white man's' justice system being rigged, they may be giving 'youths of color' a much appreciated indulgence, and at the same time endearing themselves to these oppressed political prisoners, but they are hurting them by robbing them of much needed feedback. Instead of learning, as the Irish did when their incarceration rates were sky-high, that they are doing something that is causing them to be locked up, Blacks and Hispanics are told the problem is not their rates of crime, but the justice system itself and its discrimination towards them.

The actual textbook, *Principles of Sociology*,[54] was even more incendiary and detached from reality. It was full of oddly named regurgitations of Marxism that were supposed to explain why American society is so awful with the word 'theory' bastardized, and placed at the end.* These pseudo 'theories' are such because they cannot be tested, as the theory of gravity can be. They are presented as either/or propositions—each one with good guys and bad. Oppressors and oppressed. America is a zero-sum society full of rich villains and the innocent victims they dispossessed, with white men—not the rule of law in charge of it all. There was no mention of the fact that many of the disparities in outcomes amongst the different racial and ethnic groups in America could be explained by mundane facts such as what the group's knowledge and abilities were when they arrived in America. Not a word about how Jews were good at being middlemen and financiers because they had not been allowed to work more traditional jobs wherever they had been because of discrimination.

After reading the text and listening to Mrs. S, any 'youth of color' with any sense would not only reject America but also choose to disengage entirely from its culture, which had "systematically rejected them." Because they are being told no matter how hard you try, the cops can always show up and arrest you for no reason at all, simply because they do not like your skin's color, non-whites might as well not even try. Your textbook, which is without question an authority because people with college degrees like Mrs. S. wrote it, is telling you that American society is set up for you to fail. You cannot make it. "Conflict theory" even proves it. We will discuss how this debilitating mindset affects the non-white crime rate in the next chapter.

One black person who might disagree with Mr. Moran and President Obama on what constitutes 'real' education for black children, is the founder of Black Entertainment Television and former owner of the NBA's Charlotte Bobcats, black billionaire Robert Johnson. In the May 25th issue of *Sporting News*, Johnson said the most beneficial class he took in college was European Diplomacy. He said it taught him about the "balance of power, politics, and how leaders make decisions."[258]

Johnson is a very successful American. Do you really think he would have taken a class titled European Diplomacy if he had Asante Moran as a guidance counselor in high school? Or what if Johnson had attended Stanford University and heard Reverend Jessie Jackson chanting, "Ho, ho, ho, western civ has got to go?" He might not have taken the class he

---

* It has always bothered me that Sir Richard Dawkins and other scientists I admire are quick to criticize the improper use of the word theory when it is put with "Intelligent Design" but not when it comes to it's equally improper usage in the social sciences (e.g. "conflict theory" or "critical race theory").

now claims was most beneficial to him and could have possibly been less successful. Had this been the case, many of the jobs Johnson has created over the years through his business ventures that provided employment for all Americans including non-whites, might of never been created. Clique members would do well to note that Johnson did not say 'black studies' was the most beneficial course he took. I am certain Johnson has a deep, personal understanding of the unique journey black Americans have made. But his own personal journey would not have been possible if he believed the system was rigged, and that the cops would snuff out his success at any given moment simply because he is black.

Also in my sociology textbook, was an inset titled "Unpacking the Invisible Knapsack: Exploring Cultural Privilege."[56] It was written by a woman named Peggy McIntosh, an American of Irish descent. McIntosh says she always wondered why she was not as aware of her race as her black friends were. So, she made a list of things she could "take for granted because of her whiteness." Amongst other things, McIntosh claimed:

1) If minorities fail as leaders, their race is blamed.
2) When she goes shopping, store detectives do not follow her.
3) All people on TV and in newspapers look like her.
4) When she studies America's history, she sees people who look like her often, who are portrayed in a positive light.
5) To protect her children, she does not have to teach them to be aware of racism.

To her first contention, that minority leaders have their failures blamed on their race: President Obama, a minority leader, has failed to deliver on practically all of his campaign promises except for health care. However, if Americans were blaming his poor performance on his race, assuming that he could not accomplish an agenda because he is black, they would not have placed Herman Cain—who has two black parents—atop the polls for the Republican Party's presidential nomination.

Next she claims that store detectives follow black shoppers around but fails to mention the higher rates of theft and robbery committed by Blacks compared to whites. While the majority of black people are certainly not thieves, our brains have evolved to look for patterns. This is why I receive looks of condescending astonishment from Blacks, especially here in prison, practically every time I play basketball in front of those who have never seen me play before. They *know* "white folks can't hoop."

McIntosh's third claim, that all people on television and in the newspaper are white is demonstrably false. An entire cable network is devoted to black folks (BET). Television shows feature majority black casts (Meet the Browns), and hundreds of black-owned and operated newspapers dating to before the civil war exist. A similar misconception is that Blacks are overrepresented as criminals on television shows. A study done by Brian C. Anderson showed that "only 8 percent of prime-time criminals were black..."[57]

While Blacks make up about 13 percent of the population and actors in television shows, they are depicted as only committing 10 percent of the violent crimes in those shows. This is a percentage much lower then the 52 percent of crimes they commit in the real world. When it comes to murders in particular, black actors are only responsible for 3 percent of the homicides committed on the small screen. This translates to Blacks being approximately 18 times less likely to commit a homicide on television than in reality. White people are shown committing 90 percent of all murders in television shows while in real life they are actually responsible for about half that number. This led to ABC's vice-president of motion pictures and television saying, "almost every villain you see [on TV] is a WASP... in their desire to avoid stereotyping, I think broadcast standards and practices sometimes go to an absurd extreme."[58]

That third claim by McIntosh makes me question her existence as a flesh and blood human being. If she is in fact real, her friendships with black people cannot be. I can remember walking into the houses and apartments of my black friends when I was a kid in the 1980s and 1990s. There were copies of Jet, Ebony, Essence, or any of the other numerous black periodicals lying in the customary places. In Houston, the Forward Times probably has the largest circulation of the black-owned and operated newspapers though it is not the only one. My friends and I, black and white, all watched the Cosby show, the Fresh Prince of Bel-Air, and my all-time favorite, Martin, religiously. In light of all this contradictory evidence to McIntosh's claim, we have to assume, again if she is a real person (she could be an abstract "composite" like President Obama's white girlfriend in *Dreams From My Father*) that her friendships with black people are at best superficial, existing only for the express purpose of allowing her to see herself on an island of moral high ground surrounded by an ocean of lesser whites who just do not "get it." Were any of her friendships with black people of substance, she would have at least visited their homes and learned what the Jet "beauty of the week" is.

McIntosh also says that when she "studies our national heritage" she sees white people represented in a positive manner, insinuating that non-whites are portrayed negatively. This is another head scratcher. From grade school to college, I have never seen a history textbook that did not mention the shortcomings and moral failings of the founding fathers and presidents. Yet, I have never read anything negative about Fredrick Douglas, Dr. Martin Luther King Jr., or W.E.B. Dubois even though Dr. King and Dubois certainly had their faults.†

Lastly, McIntosh tells us that she does not have to teach her children about racism in order to protect them from it. Depending on her definition of racism, she might want to check the crime statistics on inter-racial crime. While the vast majority of crimes occur intraracially, when crimes do occur between Blacks and whites, 89 percent of those acts are black against white. When it comes to hate crimes, the FBI has reported that 63 percent of all such crimes are "anti-white."[59] This of course does not mean that white kids should be taught to avoid black kids, but does call into question McIntosh's belief that black children need to be warned about racism from whites to protect them. After all, white criminals only choose black victims 3 percent of the time according to the FBI.[60] A more in depth discussion of this will take place in the next chapter.

McIntosh's half-baked attempt at showing she is a 'good' white person, hurts 'youth of color' by adding fuel to the fire that divides us. But for the sake of argument, let us say that McIntosh is 100 percent correct in her pronouncements. Just what does this privilege actually do? Much to the chagrin of Beau Sea, who wants desperately to take rank with the victim set, Americans of Japanese and Chinese descent have incomes and levels of educational attainment higher than those of whites even though they do not have a cable station, magazines, and newspapers like Blacks. In other words, we should save our collective sorrow for Asians if we go by McIntosh's standards for being underprivileged.

THREE DEFICIENCIES GOVERNMENT CANNOT REMEDY

Different cultures—sometimes in different countries, sometimes in the same country—have time and again demonstrated differing

---

† Dr. King is said to have cheated on his wife with women half her age and DuBois put swastikas on the cover of the magazine he edited to show his support for Hitler's National Socialist party.

attitudes towards education. Although most people articulate a desire for learning, their actual willingness to forfeit more immediate gratification — which often gets hidden beneath their proclamation — is of much more consequence when they are trying to become educated.[61] For example, Jewish and Irish immigrants in the early part of the twentieth century lived in the same type of slum housing and attended the same overcrowded, rundown schools. Yet, "Irish youngsters in New York finished high school at a rate less than one-hundredth of that of youngsters from a German or Jewish background." This was the case even though the Irish had much more political power than the Jews and, at least up until World War I, scored higher on intelligence tests than their Jewish peers.[62]

Many will be tempted, especially those who read the late Howard Zinn's *A Peoples History of The United States*, to say that the Irish students were stereotyped and discriminated against. But the country of Ireland had little to no intellectual history. Celtic culture was said to be "hostile to literacy." Of all the notable western European nations, Ireland was the only one not to "build a single university during the middle ages."[63]

Jews however were taught, largely by their religion, to pursue intellectual pursuits beginning with comprehension of their complex religious books like the Talmud. Jewish mothers urged their daughters to marry educated men regardless of their income level.[64]

The Jewish people embraced the public schools and libraries in New York. "A survey of public libraries in the Russian-Jewish tenement neighborhoods in New York in 1912 showed that 53 percent of the books borrowed were non-fiction, and the bulk of the fictional works were by such authors as Tolstoy, Dumas, and Dickens. Frothy best sellers 'remained dusty' on the shelves.[65]

In short, the Jews did better in school than the Irish because they had a culture more geared towards learning, not because the Irish were oppressed. It was not a case of the Jews owning the books, the land, or the means of production. They were immigrants just like the Irish.

There was no Jewish-centric curriculum holding back little Tommy O'Brian. This absence of a scapegoat was a boon. Unfortunately, as was the case with the Irish, the government does not have a proven program that will improve the attitudes of 'youth of color' towards education. Mr. Moran's Afrocentrism has been tried in many cities and failed to improve the level of educational achievement amongst black students. The evidence from Detroit and Washington D.C. in particular, shows that these curriculum changes have made things worse.

Educational Equality

Another shortcoming the government cannot legislate out of existence is the lack of student motivation. In a column titled "Why One School Reform After Another Falls," left-leaning economist and Obama supporter Robert J. Samuelson said, "The larger cause of failure is almost unmentionable: Shrunken student motivation. Students, after all, have to do the work. If they aren't motivated even capable teachers may fail."[66] Raise your hand if you think telling non-white children they were kings and queens before white men came around will help motivate them to learn what happened in 1776? As Samuelson says:

> Motivation comes from many sources: curiosity and ambition; paternal expectations; the desire to get into a good college; inspiring or intimidating teachers; peer pressure. The unstated assumption of much school "reform" is that if students aren't motivated, it's mainly the fault of schools and teachers.[67]

In the past, students had Sputnik or the Soviet threat in general to motivate them to learn. This is not the case today. Students are also not taught that America is worth preserving, and that doing so requires that they become educated. If you believe that America is the only place slavery and conquest occurred, why would you want to work hard to compete with students in other countries where you assume they never had these crimes against humanity? Patriotism serves many purposes. Through the societal cohesiveness it encourages, it can directly motivate people, including students, as well. Teaching a false, agenda driven and perspective lacking version of America's history undermines this vital process. Those in the clique, peddling the narrative, are responsible. Something else the government cannot create with a majority vote in congress is a competent parent.

Thomas Friedman, a Pulitzer Prize winner like Pitts who writes for the New York Times, says, "Some new studies are showing we need better parents."[68] Shocking. Friedman says that a study done by the Organization for Economic Cooperation and Development reports that "fifteen-year-old students whose parents often read books with them during their first year of primary school show markedly higher scores...than students whose parents read with them infrequently" and, that there is an advantage to be had "regardless of the family's socioeconomic background."[69]

These results were duplicated in a current study done by the National School Board Association Center For Public Education and printed in The American School Board Journal by Patte Barth. The study found that "monitoring home work; making sure children get to school; rewarding their efforts and talking up the idea of going to college" were the only types of parent involvement that helped improve "attendance, grades, test scores and preparation for college." Barth found all of this "somewhat surprising," while I imagine most parents, myself included, would have found anything different surprising.

Dr. Sowell said that when he began studying the history of slavery around the world, he was puzzled by the fact that some slaves were actually paid to do certain jobs. This is hard to imagine of course because slave masters have the power to take their slaves lives at any given moment. But some jobs required judgment and/or talent, and the only way to find out which slaves had enough of both was to incentivize them to disclose their abilities. The point? No matter how much power and control you give the government and education bureaucrats, they will not be able to make our children into good students. Regardless of what the teacher's unions tell you, there is only so much they can do no matter how much you increase their pay and shrink their class sizes. Peers, parents, and patriotism must incentivize students. Power and force have their limits.

CHAPTER 5

CRIME, RACE AND THE JUSTICE SYSTEM

The final prong of Michelle Alexandre's abridged version of the narrative claims "Blacks make up a disproportionate portion of the prison population."[1] Former Senator and Secretary of State Hillary Clinton agrees, saying that America's criminal justice system is a "disgrace" because it "incarcerates so many more African-Americans proportionately than whites."[2] The subtitle to Pitts' May 6, 2012 column read, "Leonard Pitts Jr. says African-Americans erroneously believe that black people are more likely to commit criminal acts than other races." Pitts has also said on numerous occasions that the justice system is racist because it "funnels" Blacks into prisons. And in *The New Jim Crow*, Michelle Alexander says that America's justice system is responsible for "perpetrating racial hierarchy in the United States" through its war on drugs which she claims has led to "mass incarceration" of non-whites.[3] In other words, the criminal justice system is racist because it locks up a larger percentage of the non-white population. And because of this, according to Alexander and many others, non-whites are being relegated to a second-class citizenship like Blacks were in the Jim Crow south.

We will examine these claims in detail in Part I of this chapter. In Part II, we will focus on crimes as they occur between the different races and how the perceptions of these crimes affect race relations and the progress of non-whites.

PART I —
THE QUESTION OF RACISM IN THE JUSTICE SYSTEM

In 2006, approximately one in every thirty-three black males in the U.S. was incarcerated. This statistic contrasts sharply with the corresponding figures for Hispanics, 1 in 79 and whites, 1 in 205. Amongst black males aged

20–34, the figure is over 1 in 10.[4] For those in the clique, these numbers are more than enough evidence to indict the criminal justice system on charges of aggravated racism and capitol oppression. Remember we live in the era of the "disparate impact" standard, which says that discrimination can be proven regardless of intent. That is, if a business requires its perspective employees to score above a certain level on a skills test and whites happen to score above that level more often than non-whites, thereby causing a larger number of whites to be hired, that business can be sued for using a "discriminatory" test because it has a "disparate impact" on non-whites. This is of course a drastic departure from the former disparate treatment standard, which required a plaintiff to prove that there was an actual intent to discriminate.

However, in order to prove that the justice system discriminates against non-whites, we need to see statistics showing that white criminals are being arrested, convicted, and sent to prison at lower rates than non-white criminals. I stress white criminals, because assuming all groups commit crimes at the same rate is like assuming all groups produce professional basketball players at the same rates. Deeming the system racist merely because a larger proportion of the non-white population is locked up than that of the white population would force us to set our "racial justice" sights on the NBA long before the justice system. From a proportional standpoint, the NBA is much more askew than the prison population.

Alexander and Pitts like to believe that when it comes to drug crimes, they have verifiable evidence that proves all the races commit drug crimes at the same rates. However, we will see they derive their premise from a survey that does not tell the whole story.

Crime and crime rates are recorded and measured through several different mediums. The most common are police reports, victim surveys, and self-reports. Police reports consist of the number of crimes reported to the police. The obvious weakness with them is that many crimes are never reported to the police. In fact, estimates from the National Crime Survey (NCS) suggest that about 50 percent of all serious crimes are never reported.[5] Victim surveys are a much better measuring device, especially for our purposes here. Since 1973, the Bureau of the Census has conducted interviews of sixty thousand American households inquiring about rapes, robberies, assaults, burglaries, larceny, and car theft. Victim surveys could over-report or under report crimes depending on the honesty and memory of the person being surveyed. As we will see however, the data taken from these surveys, especially when it comes to the race of the perpetrator, often match arrest records. Perhaps the least reliable of these methods are self-reports. Amongst many other problems, self-reports are notorious for over-reporting minor offenses and underreporting major ones. We will return to the reliability of self-reports when we consider Alexander's foundational claim, that Blacks and whites use and sell drugs at the same rates.

Since most crimes committed by Blacks are against other Blacks, meaning the people calling the police to report black criminals are normally not white, we should be able to determine whether or not the police are purposefully locking up Blacks in order to oppress them. In 1993, the NCS reported that amongst Blacks who had been the victims of violent crimes, 79.7 percent of them said that their victimizers were black. When it came to robberies and assaults, black victims blamed black criminals in 67 and 88 percent of the cases. The total number of crimes committed against Blacks by black criminals was 1.3 million in 1995.[6] The same survey also showed that 54 percent of black criminal's victims were white. Of the 1.7 million interracial crimes, 89 percent of them were committed against whites by black criminals. In other words, no matter how you slice the data, Blacks are offending at higher rates than whites. Even uber-liberal Michael Tonry, who Alexander often quotes approvingly in her book *The New Jim Crow* has said, "Black incarceration rates are substantially higher than those for whites…[because] black crime rates for imprisonable crimes are substantially higher than those for whites."[7]

The NCS from 1974 was used in a study that goes straight to the heart of this matter. That particular survey reported that 62 percent of its robbery victims claimed to have been robbed by a black criminal. That same year, the percentage of Blacks arrested for robbery was 62 percent. So unless the robbery victims, a large percentage of whom were black mind you, are lying, in order to protect white criminals, there is substantial reason to believe Blacks commit robbery at a higher rate than whites. Numerous other NCSs have shown that Blacks are about 40 percent more likely to have their homes burgled, and 100 percent more likely to be robbed than the typical white person.[8] In order for these figures to be correct, either Blacks are committing crimes at higher rates than whites, or Jessie Jackson, Spike Lee, and President Obama have been lying to us all these years when they have claimed whites are scared to go into black neighborhoods. Apparently, they have not only been going into these neighborhoods, they have been jacking once they get there!

Another piece of evidence comes in the form of homicide statistics. In 1980, arresting the killer solved 72 percent of all murders. Like most crimes, perpetrators of homicide shared the same race as their victims. The year 1980 saw a total of 24,278 murders. Thirty-five percent of those killed were black.[9] This means that Blacks were murdered at more than six times the rate that whites were. Again, since most homicides are committed by people who are from a similar demographic, and know their victim personally, we can safely infer if a large number of black males are being murdered, a large number of black males are doing the murdering. More recently, in 1995, 50 percent of all homicide victims were black, and 56 percent of those arrested for murder were also black.[10] This is exactly what you would expect to see if most Blacks are killed by fellow Blacks. The percentage of Blacks arrested for murder would be much higher than 56 percent, if racist whites consistently called racist white police departments and falsely reported that it was a black person who killed someone they'd just seen murdered.

Also in 1995, when Blacks made up 12.6 percent of the U.S. population, they accounted for over 42 percent of those arrested for rape; 59 percent of those arrested for robbery; 38 percent of those arrested for aggravated assault; and 38 percent of those arrested for weapons violations.[11] In 2005 the black murder rate was more than seven times that of whites and Hispanics combined. Between 1976 and 2005, Blacks committed over 52 percent of all homicides. In 2006, black criminals made up 39 percent of all those arrested for violent crimes: 56 percent of robbers, and 34 percent of aggravated assailants while accounting for 13 percent of the population.[12]

In his excellent book, *The Myths That Divide Us*, John Perrazzo makes a very effective argument against the notion that a larger percentage of Blacks are locked up because the justice system is racist. Perrazzo first points out, as we saw above, that NCS data given by crime victims matches that of arrest records in regards to the perpetrator's race. Next, he mentions that most property crimes (burglaries, auto theft, etc.) are committed without witnesses.[13] And therefore:

> ...if police racism were indeed responsible for the comparatively higher overall arrest rate of Blacks, we should expect to find a greater racial imbalance in arrest for property crimes than for violent personal crimes. Such is not the case however. The racial gaps for property crime and arrest are significantly smaller. Correcting for the unequal population sizes of black and white Americans, the black-white arrest ratio for burglary is 3.92 to 1, for larceny theft 3.97 to 1, for auto theft 4.01 to 1 and for arson 2.96 to 1. To put it another way, the average black is approximately three to four times more likely to be arrested for property crimes than is the average white. By contrast, the black-white arrest ratios for personal

crimes (where police have almost no room to allow their own prejudices to influence their arrest patterns) are 6.76 to 1 for murder, 6.66 to 1 for rape, 11.950 to 1 for robbery and 5.06 to 1 for aggravated assault.[14]

If a racist white police force just wanted to lock Blacks up in order to "keep them down," they could arrest them for crimes like burglary more often than robbery because the victim of a burglary can rarely identify the race of the burglar. It is the complete opposite when it comes to violent crimes. Racial identification is more likely. Yet Blacks are arrested at a much lower rate for non-violent crimes.

Mr. Perrazzo explains what the statistics show. Blacks are arrested at higher rates for crimes even a racist cop would have the most difficult time arresting them for—crimes with witnesses. Unless a cop could convince a person who was robbed by a white male that instead a black male was guilty, it will remain almost impossible for a cop to arrest a black guy for the crime and get him sent to prison. With the complaining witness saying their robber was white, a white male will be arrested.

This should render moot the argument that cops are the modern day version of plantation overseers. It should also demonstrate that when Pitts chose the subtitle to his May 6, 2012 column stating, it is erroneous to "believe that black people are more likely to commit" crimes than other races, he is misrepresenting the facts. Blacks made up 13 percent of the population but 39 percent of arrestees for violent crimes in 2006.[15] Whites make up 70-80 percent of the population but do not commit even 70 percent of violent crimes. Blacks commit crimes at three times their percentage of the population. This means the average black person you encounter on the street is much more likely to have committed a crime than someone of another race—especially if they are a black male between the ages of 15 and 35.

JENA JUSTICE

While campaigning for the presidency in 2008, then senator Barack Obama, on Martin Luther King Jr. day no less, said that Blacks and whites "are arrested at very different rates, [and] receive very different sentences for the same crime." Further, he claimed there is "Scooter Libby justice for some and Jena Justice for others," implying that Blacks are treated more harshly by prosecutors and jurors than whites are.[16] However, a study done using prosecutions that took place in 1992, when the crime rate was

America Apart

higher than it is today, 20 plus years later, showed the opposite outcome for most crimes. Using data from the seventy-five largest counties in the U.S., researchers found out that of 14 distinct crimes, Blacks were more likely to have their cases dismissed or end in acquittal than whites in all but two of fourteen categories—felony traffic violations and a miscellaneous felony category.[17]

Percentage of cases ending in acquittal or dismissal by race and crime in 1992:

Crime	Black	White
Murder	24	23
Rape	51	25
Robbery	38	35
Assault	49	43
Burglary	25	21
Felony Theft	27	25
Drug Dealing	24	14
Other Drug Offenses	32	23
Other Crimes Against Persons	48	28
Other Property Offenses	27	26
Public Order Offenses	32	32
Weapons Charges	32	22
Felony Traffic Violations	4	10
Other Felonies	14	22

A study done in 1997 by criminologist Janet Laurtsen and Robert Sampson refutes another of Obama's claims about the justice system. After combing through reams of data on prison sentences and the charges that brought them, the pair determined, "large racial differences in criminal offending"—not racism—was the cause of Blacks making up such a large percentage of the prison population. In 1993, another criminologist adored by the media, Alfred Blumstein, said Blacks were actually underrepresented in prison for murder according to their prevalence in arrest reports. And in 2012, law professor Sonja Starr and economist Marit Rehavi studied 58,000 criminal cases and determined race was not the cause of the disparities in black and white sentences.

Shawn Loiseau was an undrafted, rookie linebacker for the National Football League's Houston Texans. He appears to be Caucasian. When he was 17 years old, he came home one evening and was challenged to a fight by what he called "two gang members." According to Loiseau, one of them hit him in the forehead with a pipe, causing him to fall to a knee. He then 'tackled' one of the gang members "to the pavement and punched him." The guy Loiseau hit ended up in a coma. Loiseau ended up in jail, charged with assault and battery with a deadly weapon. He was told the ground was the deadly weapon, and that he went above and beyond self-defense. Loiseau himself required 26 stitches, but his assailant was not charged with anything. While sitting in jail, Loiseau was told by his lawyer he could potentially be looking at life in prison.[18]

I bring up the story of Shawn Loiseau not because he played for the best football team in Texas, but because many in the clique like to believe that Blacks are the only ones ever treated unfairly by the justice system. Pitts in particular said, referring to the Trayvon Martin tragedy, that had Zimmerman been black, "he probably would not have been sent home by prosecutors who declined to press charges." Because, as he puts it, "whiteness still has its privileges."[19] Ignore the fact that Zimmerman is only half white. No, what matters is that Zimmerman was **treated** like he was white. As Pitts puts it, "White denotes not race, but the privilege of basic rights."[20] In other words, if you are black you will get the shaft by the white supremacists who only honor the rights of people who look like them. But less than a few months after Trayvon Martin was killed, a black man named Pernell Jefferson shot and killed a white man in Tulsa, Oklahoma, and was not charged with murder because the police believed Jefferson—a convicted felon—had acted in self-defense.[21]

In 2012, Carl England got a call from his daughter saying that Jefferson had threatened her and tried to kick in the door of her home. England and the girl's boyfriend searched for and found, Jefferson. Then, Jefferson made a move to attack England, but England hit him with a stick, causing Jefferson to fall to the ground. Jefferson then pulled out a pistol and shot England, killing him. He then ran away from the murder scene—unlike Zimmerman who stayed and cooperated with the police. He was not arrested until authorities found him at a hospital.[22]

This happened in one of the reddest of the red states, Oklahoma. To the uninitiated, all white people in red states are even more racist, patriarchal, exploitative, etc., than whites in states that vote for Obama. So how is it possible Jefferson, a black convicted felon, who made the first move on England, got off? Pitts and the rest of the clique will dismiss Jefferson's successful self-defense claim as an exception to the rule and point out that he was charged with attempted burglary and a weapons violation. Never let the facts get in the way of your emotionally rewarding vision.

Charles Rangel, a Democratic congressman from New York, claimed, while on MSNBC's Martin Bashir Show, that "if the police had gotten a black [George] Zimmerman, the question would be whether they would have beat him to death," echoing Pitts' claim.

Yet in Phoenix, Arizona, on April the 3rd, 2012, Daniel Adkins, who like Zimmerman has a white father and a mother of Native American ancestry, was shot and killed by Cordell Jude, a 22 year old black male. Adkins, 29, was walking through the parking lot of a Taco Bell when he stepped in front of Jude's car which was transporting him and his pregnant girlfriend. Jude slammed on the brakes to keep from hitting Adkins, who yelled, "Watch it!" at Jude. Jude claims that Adkins then swung something at him, a pipe or a bat. Jude then reached into his pants and pulled out a pistol and shot Adkins in the torso. No bat, pipe or weapon was ever found. Jude claims he did not drive away from Adkins because the dog Adkins was walking was in his way. Jude told the police he was in fear of losing his life and that of his girlfriend and their child still in her womb. But later, while talking to investigators, Jude revealed he did not think Adkins would have killed him, but that he was trying to injure him.[23] Jude was never arrested. Congressman Rangel stands corrected.

Again, this happened in what clique members have to consider one of the most racist, whiteness filled states in the union. Not only did Arizona not vote for Obama; they even passed legislation to enforce immigration laws the federal government has refused to enforce. Where is the white privilege for the Adkins family? If the 'whiteness' concept is such a certainty, why have at least two black males gotten off after killing one-and-a half privileged white men? The case against Jude seems much stronger than the one against Zimmerman. Where are the protests and calls for justice in Phoenix?

In 1995, statistician Patrick Logan examined the court records of 42,500 offenders and concluded there was, "no evidence that, in the places where Blacks in the United States have most of their contacts with the justice system, that system treats them more harshly than whites."[24] A similar analysis of 11,000 convicts in California "found that the severity of sentences depended heavily on such factors as prior criminal records, the seriousness of the crime, and whether guns were used in the commission of these crimes. Race was found to have no effect whatsoever." Important to keep in mind is that the rates at which Blacks are arrested in cities like Washington D.C., where the police is majority black, are no different than the rates in cities where the police force is majority white.[25]

Also, there are several states in the south where the gap between white and black arrests is smaller than the national average, even though there are larger percentages of Blacks in the south than anywhere else in America.[26] To sum it all up, Blacks do not make up a "disproportionate portion of the prison population" because unfortunately, just like the Irish when they first immigrated to America's big cities from rural origins, they commit crimes at a rate that dictates an above average percentage of them, will be incarcerated.

None of the above is an attempt to bash black people. An above average incarceration rate for any group of Americans is an American problem. But trying to improve upon this problem by crying racism is like giving someone with the flu chemotherapy and expecting them to get better. You are in fact making them worse. Chemotherapy is a necessary means to combating the problem of cancer, comparable to pointing out racism when that particular type of discrimination is occurring. You cannot however tell people problem X is someone else's fault and expect the situation to improve, if in reality improvement depends upon their own actions. Doing so often worsens the problem by making the undesirable behavior even more acceptable. Diseases are rarely cured when they are improperly diagnosed.

THE NEW JIM CROW

January 13, 2012: Pitts writes in his syndicated column that he is going to hold a drawing in order to award 50 people a prize. In order to become eligible, all you had to do was send him your name and promise to use this prize should you be lucky enough to win it. The prize was an autographed copy of what is one of the most misleading and inflammatory books I have ever read: Michelle Alexander's *The New Jim Crow*. Pitts says that in this book, "Alexander promulgated an explosive argument. Namely, that the so called war on drugs amounts to a war on African-American men and, more to the point, to a racial caste system nearly as restrictive, oppressive and omnipresent as Jim Crow itself."[27] Pitts then resorts to the same type of fallacious, incendiary analogies used by Alexander throughout her book.

For example, she writes, "It's as if George Wallace were still standing at the schoolhouse door."[28] Yes, you read that right. Pitts equates the rule of law, and how it applies to common criminals—who come in all colors—to the exclusively color based Jim Crow laws and their racist supporters like

Wallace whose sole purpose and focus was to oppress black people because of their skin color.

In the book itself, which Pitts tells us has won several awards,[29] Alexander claims that 1) "mass incarceration" is merely the latest in a long line of racial caste systems created to control Blacks in America; 2) the war on drugs unfairly targets Blacks, sweeping them into the justice system where inadequate legal representation dooms them to lengthy prison sentences; 3) a "formerly race-neutral criminal justice system" can imprison large numbers of non-whites even though they are "actually no more likely to be guilty of drug crimes and offenses than whites"; 4) the caste system continues oppressing non-whites even after they leave prison; 5) there are many similarities between the legalized discrimination of Jim Crow and mass incarceration; and, 6) nothing short of a "major social movement can successfully dismantle the caste system."[30]

Before we begin with Alexander's first claim, allow me to interject some perspective into some of her book's more blatant historical distortions. In a section titled "The Birth of Slavery" in Chapter 1, Alexander claims that plantation owner's beliefs in white supremacy 'rationalized' the systematic enslavement of Africans.[31] Nowhere does she mention that Arabs and other African tribes had already enslaved rival tribes for thousands of years before white people even set foot in America.[32] In West Africa for example, where the Kunte Kinte character in Alex Haley's *Roots* came from, Africans had been enslaving and selling one another in slave markets they themselves constructed long before any white man laid eyes upon them.

East Africa was no different. The Masai tribe attacked and enslaved other African tribes by themselves and in combined raids with Arabs. Even at the height of the Atlantic slave trade, African slave traders kept more African slaves for themselves than they sold to the Americans. Black slaves were brought to America because they were the most cost effective to obtain — not because of their skin color or white supremacy. The reason they were easier to obain was because Arabs and other Africans — not Europeans — had long ago set up slave networks on the coast of Africa.[33] So when Alexander says slavery was a "system of racialized social control," it is simply not true. Slavery was a thriving institution in Africa and the rest of the world long before any particular "race" decided to control another.

Alexander also makes the mistake, very common amongst clique members, of claiming, "slaves were defined as three-fifths of a man, not a real, whole human being. Upon this racist fiction rests the entire structure of American Democracy."[34] The three-fifths comment is a favorite of clique members specializing in the melodramatic, which is to say most if not all of them. But as any historian worth his weight in mule dung will tell you, the three-fifths fraction applied to how slaves were to be counted for representation purposes in the House, and had nothing to do with trying to classify slaves as some subhuman species. The southern states were actually the ones who wanted to count slaves as they did citizens because it would allow them to have more representatives by allowing them to claim a larger population. The anti-slavery congressmen were against this because they knew it would permit the southern states to perpetuate slavery even longer through their increased power in the U.S. House of Representatives. Striking the three-fifths compromise therefore actually helped black slaves.

As for the "entire structure of American Democracy" resting "upon this racist fiction" claim, I can think of little else more myopic. American democracy is built upon the many hard-fought triumphs and abominable failures of western civilization. All people, of every color and culture, on every continent, had been conquered and enslaved several times over before the United States Constitution was ever written. And democracy, American or otherwise, was a system of government conceived of long before white Americans decided to be racist towards Blacks.

Alexander also tells us that "the current stereotypes of black men as aggressive, unruly predators can be traced" to the era after slavery ended and when whites were concerned about a possible insurrection by Blacks.[35] I find this statement astonishing.

She offers no evidence whatsoever for the actual tracing part. Nor does she give examples of white people today taking their cues from whites who lived 150 years ago. It seems as if Alexander never even considered the possibility that whites who do stereotype are cognizant of the fact that Blacks are 11 times more likely than whites to commit robbery, and 6 times as likely to commit rape or murder.[36] After all, at least one poll suggests Blacks may be aware of this: In 1991 a University of California poll found that 59 percent of Blacks said they thought black people were in general "aggressive and violent" compared to 52 percent of whites.[37] And according to government statistics, Blacks are five times as likely to commit aggravated assault as whites.[38] But Pitts and the rest of the clique will dismiss the University of California poll as self-hate foisted upon Blacks by Eurocentric white men even though the Irish and white southerners were "stereotyped" in the same way.[39]

CLAIM 1: MASS INCARCERATION

The first strand of Alexander's thesis claims that supporters of "racial hierarchy," after creating slavery and then Jim Crow, have now "birthed yet another racial caste system in the United States: Mass Incarceration."[40] She says they have accomplished this largely by appealing to the "racism and vulnerability of lower class whites,"[41] and that 'conservative whites,' after Jim Crow ended, started looking for a new "formerly race neutral" system that would allow them to keep Blacks oppressed while not appearing to be racist.[42] They found it, she claims, in the words 'law and order.'[43]

Alexander invokes the time-honored left-wing tradition of arguing that when whites say they are tough on crime, they really mean, "I hate black people." She points out that plenty of segregationists supported tough-on-crime policies and opposed civil rights laws.[44] As a result, the questions that need to be addressed are: Was there a legitimate reason to believe the crime rate was getting out of control? And, do longer sentences unfairly target Blacks while creating a racial caste system?

From 1961 to 1980, the average number of murders per year increased 122 percent; forcible rapes 287 percent; robberies 294 percent; aggravated assaults 215 percent; while burglary, larceny, and auto theft all increased 189, 159, and 128 percent respectively.[45] But Alexander only pays lip service to these frightening explosions in crime, calling them "fairly dramatic." She also says there was "significant controversy" about the "accuracy of the [crime] statistics."[46]

Inaccuracy in the numbers may very well exist, with one glaring exception: Murder. Although you may be able to run your car off into a river and claim it was stolen, it is much more difficult to fake a dead body and distort the homicide statistics. A 122 percent increase—especially, without the benefit of the hindsight we have today—is not "fairly" dramatic.

During this period of skyrocketing crime rates across all races, the black rate increased more for some reason. In 1960, presumably before racist white men conspired to create 'mass incarceration,' black males aged 13–39 were being arrested at ten times the rate of same aged whites.[47] But from 1965–1970, the black arrest rate for violent crimes increased seven times as much as the white rate, which was also on the upswing.[48] In a study done on a large group of schools during the 1974–1975 school year, researchers found that Blacks were responsible for 75 percent of the violent crimes on campus even though they only made up 29 percent of the population in the cities in which the schools were located. When it comes to robberies in particular, over three-fifths of the cases involved white students being robbed by black non-students. In cases in which the robber and the robbed were both students, 50 percent of the time the former was black and the latter was white. [49] Keep in mind that Blacks only made up 29 percent of these city's populations. These same lopsided numbers for robbery were practically identical to those for simple assault, aggravated assault, and larceny.

So regardless of how many racist politicians and 'lower class whites' there may have been conspiring or wishing for a 'new racial caste system,' the increase in crime was a real verifiable problem. Obviously, some of the politicians campaigning on a 'law and order' platform were racist. This does not incriminate the lawmakers who actually paid attention to the crime statistics and had good reason to be concerned. Remember, they did not know the crime rate would eventually level off in 1991 and continue down as it has. They may have assumed that unless they changed course, the murder rate would go up another 122 percent over the next decade. And who knows, stiffer sentences may have contributed to the drop.

Our second question asks whether or not increasing the length of prison terms unfairly affects Blacks and puts them in a racial caste system. The answer to this question largely depends on one's definitions of the words 'fair' and 'racial caste system.' When it comes to the word fair, Pitts and many other seekers of 'social justice' do not believe that having the same set of laws and rules for everyone constitutes fairness. That is, they do not believe in the traditional definition of the word; which is, according to my Random House Webster's Dictionary, "free from bias, dishonesty, or injustice." [50]

Members of the clique believe that any outcome in which non-whites do worse than whites must be inherently unfair. This is why the racial makeup of the prison population bothers them, but the much more out of proportion demographics of the NFL or NBA does not. What the clique really seeks are pre-arranged outcomes that fit their vision and favor their preferred group — not fairness. They believe words, especially those in the U.S. Constitution, should malleable.

They know however that most people do not support the idea of centrally planned outcomes for favored individuals due to the histories of the Soviet Union, China, Cuba, et. al. This is why they make Orwellian changes to the meanings of words like "fairness" — because everyone is in favor of "fairness." Just like they know everyone is in favor of "justice." Therefore, when they give a speech about the justice system or how much money people make, they can claim a result they do not like, for whatever reason, is "unfair" or "unjust"—instead of simply not to their liking. The uninitiated, listening to, say, President Obama, only hear the words unfair or unjust. They do not have time to dive into crime statistics. They think to themselves, "Well, no matter what his politics or mine, I definitely want things to be fair." In short, the people on the left often change the meanings of words in order to camouflage their beliefs because they know most voters will not support contrived, potemkin-village outcomes.

Alexander and the rest of the clique do not like the results of the criminal justice system. So, she claims it is unfair and akin to slavery and Jim Crow, things everyone condemns—as well they should. Jim Crow laws were specifically designed to isolate and oppress a group of people because of their skin color, which of course is something they had no control over. The criminal justice system operates, albeit far from perfectly, under the rule of law, not under a racial caste system.

Criminal cases have been prosecuted for centuries in America. Some of the harshest penalties for the most common of crimes, hanging for the stealing of horses for example, were introduced not only before the end of Jim Crow, but before the ending of slavery; and at the time, visited in some parts almost exclusively on whites. William H. Bonney, better known as Billy the Kid, was sentenced to death for cattle rustling. In fact, he even had a lynch mob sent after him as more whites than Blacks did.[51] Tough sentences have always been around. Like slavery, they were not invented after white people first encountered black people. Alexander herself states "The American colonies passed laws barring criminal offenders from a wide variety of jobs and benefits, automatically dissolving their marriages and denying them the right to enter contracts. These legislators were following a long tradition, dating back to ancient Greece."[52] If these types of practices were followed before Blacks were even living amidst whites, it becomes more arduous to argue that harsh sentences were invented to oppress Blacks.

Another fact that makes it more difficult to believe the U.S. criminal justice system has been turned into a racial caste for oppressing non-whites is the declining of clearance rates. A crime is said to be "cleared" when its perpetrator has been arrested. The FBI uses clearing data to calculate the likelihood of an individual offender getting away with a particular offense. Between 1955 and 1960, the odds of not getting arrested for a string of five robberies were 15 to 1. Between 1965 and 1970, they plummeted to 5 to 1.[53]

This means a criminal was 300 percent more likely to get away with a robbing spree in the mid to late 1960s, as he was just 10 years prior. From 1960 to 1980, the clearance rate for murder declined 22 percent, for rape, 34 percent and for aggravated assault, 24 percent. Burglary and auto theft clearance rates dropped from 53 to 49 percent.[54] Despite the number of crimes practically doubling within the same 20-year period, the number of people incarcerated per 1,000 arrests was almost cut in half, from 232 in 1960, to 124 in 1980.[55]

After considering what these numbers mean, it becomes easy to imagine someone in a night club hearing a criminal brag about getting away with an armed robbery and then deciding to attempt one himself. In 1960, there were 981,000 total arrests for murder, robbery, rape, and aggravated assault, what are collectively referred to as the 'index crimes.' The total number of state and federal prisoners in 1960 was 212,957. In 1980, the number of arrests for all index crimes had more than doubled since 1960 to well over 2.5 million, while the number of prisoners had increased less than 50 percent to 314, 272.[56] This means that while the newest racial caste system was supposedly taking off, the police were managing to arrest and imprison criminals at a lesser rate even though the number of crimes was more than doubling.

At the end of 2006, there were 858,000 black people locked up in state and federal prisons, and county jails combined.[57] If this were the number of Blacks in the free world and the rest of the 40 some-odd-million Blacks in America were incarcerated, Alexander would have a case. But a racial caste system that only manages to encapsulate 2 percent of its targeted victims is anything but. Another problem with her argument is the vaguery of her villains. Although she repeatedly mentions the names of several segregationist politicians, whom I assume are the 'proponents of racial hierarchy,' she never tells us specifically what they did to make Blacks commit crimes at much higher rates than whites. And remember, per arrest, the number of Blacks in prison was declining.

CLAIM 2: THE WAR ON DRUGS

Next, Alexander tells us that the justice system does not work as it is portrayed on the TV show "Law and Order." (Scripted TV dramas are not reality? Who knew?) "These television shows," she says, "especially those that romanticize drug-law enforcement, are the modern-day equivalent of the old movies portraying happy slaves, the fictional gloss placed on a brutal system of racialized oppression and control."[58] Ludicrous attempts at analogy like this are commonplace in *The New Jim Crow.*

I find it most appalling that real victims of oppression like the slaves are so thoughtlessly placed on the same moral plane as common criminals. However, this is common in today's non-judgmental, never-feel-shame society. Alexander says that "Full blown trials of guilt or innocence rarely occur." She also tells us that people are forced to take plea bargains "to avoid harsh mandatory sentences."[59]

What she fails to mention however, is that plea bargains benefit the criminal much more often than not — especially drug criminals. Possession of drugs is easy to prove. Most cop cars come equipped with cameras that record the cop tossing the car and finding the dope. Therefore, most drug cases do not require a trial. Plea bargains are an enormous help to drug criminals because most of them are caught red-handed. And if not for the ability to strike a plea agreement with the prosecution, they would end up doing much more time. If someone wishes to go to trial because they are innocent, they can. Will innocent people be convicted or plead guilty when they are factually innocent? Of course. All systems are prone to errors and the American Justice system is no different. But even if the defendant is innocent, they still receive the benefit of not having to serve as much time because of plea bargaining.

Clique members howl that this is not 'justice.' What they really mean is that it is not perfect, and they do not like the results. An innocent person going to prison is unjust, but we must live in reality. No society, in the history of humanity, has ever achieved a mistake-free justice system. The Pitts of the world have to remember there is a reason why they see so few statutes erected in honor of critics: They and their criticisms are a dime a dozen. Solutions, or even productive tradeoffs, are much harder to come by, as is evidenced by the complete and utter lack of them in Alexander's book — notwithstanding her occasional Marxist platitude about "social movements" restructuring the economy.

In an attempt to prove the war on drugs is mainly responsible for black's high rates of incarceration, Alexander resorts to half-truths and verbal slights of the hand. She claims "Drug offenses alone account for two-thirds of the rise in the federal inmate population and more than half of the rise in state prisoners between 1985 and 2000." "...nothing has contributed more to the systematic mass incarceration of people of color in the United States than the war on drugs."[60] The key words in the first sentence are 'rise' and 'federal.' Alexander cannot claim drug crimes account for two-thirds or half of any prison's population, state or federal. So, she lambasts the proportion of the **rise** in the prison population

First of all, Alexander never mentions in the entire 248-page text that federal inmates only make up 12 percent of the U.S. prison population. Eighty eight percent—1.2 million convicts like myself—are housed in state prisons. In the period from 1980–1990 in which the prison population increased the most, state prison populations grew 36 percent because of violent crimes and 33 percent because of drug crimes. The ensuing years saw drug criminals account for even less of the increase: from 1990–2000, violent crime caused 53 percent of the increase and all of it from 1999–2004.[61] In 1980, before the war on drugs began, Blacks made up 34.4 percent of the federal inmate population and 46.6 percent of inmates in state prisons. In 1994 after waging over a decade of the war on drugs, Blacks made up 35.5 percent of the federal system, a miniscule increase of 1 percent.[62]

It was much the same story in state prisons. In 1993, the percentage of black inmates in state prisons was 49.7 percent, an increase of only 3 percent since the beginning of the war on drugs.[63] Is 3 percent evidence that the war on drugs birthed 'a racial caste system?'

More recently, in 2006, black criminals accounted for 37.5 percent of all state prisoners. If you would have discharged every single black inmate locked up for a drug crime, you would have lowered that figure to 37 percent. No, that is not a typo. By releasing all the black "political prisoners" incarcerated for drug crimes, you would only reduce the overall percentage by 0.5 percent. This is because most Blacks in prison, regardless of what Alexander wants everyone to believe, are there for violent crimes. In 2004 for example, 53 percent of all offenders were locked up for violent crimes while 21 percent were in prison for property crimes. Drug criminals only made up 20 percent of the entire prison population. Amongst federal inmates in 2006, 47.6 percent were incarcerated for drug crimes.[64] A large percentage indeed. However, remember, federal inmates only make up 12 percent of all those incarcerated. Moreover, in 1994, during the height of the drug war, releasing just 855 black inmates would have lowered the proportion of Blacks in federal prison for drug crimes to the level of whites.[65]

In the same chapter, Alexander writes at length about law enforcement and their ability to search and seize. She gives colorful, story-like accounts of the police (the villains) asking for, and getting consent to search several black males (the victims/heroes).

America Apart

As I read through these cases, I kept thinking to myself, *Okay,* **this** *will be the* one *where the cops plant dope on the guy, and we later find out the cop and his partner were secret members of the Klan—or at least big fans of Rush Limbaugh*. However, such a story never came. In every single case, the people actually possess drugs when they are searched.* Her beef is that the cops had no probable cause to search these individuals—not that they were factually innocent.

I do not want to see the constitution's protections eroded any more than they already have been; yet a hawkish interpretation of the fourth amendment's scope is only a problem if you are carrying drugs or some other contraband. Possessing something you know to be illegal is a choice, whereas being born black in the Jim Crow South was not. Alexander's anecdotes are all disturbing examples of law enforcement officers stretching, and at times trampling on, the bill of rights. To her and Pitts, those are cases of discrimination because a larger than average proportion of those searched are non-white.

But to those whose judgment is not clouded by their ideology and emotions, these are instances of human beings abusing their power—something that, unfortunately, is going to happen regardless of the system type, or the number of bureaucrats monitoring that system. This is not to say that no one should attempt to make improvements upon this or any other system. It is to say, however, that these defects were not invented to oppress black people, as Alexander and the rest of the clique would have you believe.

You can rest assured that the whites who worked for Al Capone in the North and moonshine makers in the South were not always afforded their fourth amendment rights either. Everyone involved in the justice system—prosecutors, cops, judges—should have less immunity and more skin in the game. But corruption and abuse of power have been with us as long as flatulence, and I fear, have just as much staying power. The adding of more monitors to monitor the monitoring bureaucrats is of course subject to the law of diminishing returns. America's bureaucracy joins those the world over who have proven this repeatedly.†

---

* In another part of the text Alexander does mention the Tulia case and some people claiming actual innocence, but not nearly as often as she does drug criminals who are factually guilty.

† "Knowledge and Decisions," by Dr. Thomas Sowell, has a great· explanation of the law of diminishing returns as it applies to monitors.

Racism in the Justice System

Sentencing Distortions

Alexander also complains that "mandatory sentencing laws [have] forced judges to impose sentences for drug crimes that are often longer than those violent criminals receive."[66] This is another example of Alexander misleading her readers. First, mandatory minimums are only guaranteed for federal offenders. Some states have them, but even those that do, often do not apply them to first time offenders. And remember, as we saw above, federal inmates are a small percentage of the overall prison population. What really matters, for our purposes here, is how the sentences are calculated for parole eligibility.

In the state of Texas, for example, most non-violent criminals are given what is commonly referred to as 'non-aggravated time' when they are convicted. Violent criminals however are sentenced to 'aggravated time.' A non-aggravated sentence—what drug criminals usually get—requires you to do a quarter of your sentence before you are eligible for parole. But because of the credit an inmate can receive for 'good time' and 'work time,' he or she will most likely come up for parole before they complete their 25 percent. A friend of mine, S.H. was sentenced to 45 years for his third drug crime conviction. Because he managed to stay out of trouble, he came up for parole after only doing 4 years and 6 months. His parole was denied, but he will be brought back up in a year.

Another friend of mine, who goes by 'Gut,' got 10 years for his second conviction involving crack cocaine. He was sentenced to 10 years, and made parole after barely doing 2 years on that 10.

S.H. is white. 'Gut' is black.

An aggravated sentence requires that the offender do 50 percent of his time before he or she is eligible for parole. Aggravated offenders get no benefit whatsoever from 'good time' or 'work time.' If you rob a Seven-Eleven and are given 30 years for doing so, you will do 15 years, day-for-day, before you are eligible for parole. But if you are a drug criminal sentenced to 99 years or 'life,' you will be up for parole after serving just 6 years of your sentence.

I know a guy who was given two life sentences for some powdered cocaine and made his first parole after doing only six years. In other words, while it is certainly possible for a drug criminal to get a sentence that is numerically larger than one a violent criminal might receive, it is highly unlikely that the drug offender will spend as much time behind bars as the violent one will. Their sentences are calculated completely differently.

Analogous reasoning should be an integral part of a comprehensive argument on discrimination for obvious reasons. However, the comparison must be valid. Pears must be compared to pears. When this is done correctly, especially when trying to show biased treatment of one group by another, you often have devastatingly effective arguments. Alexander compares pears to grapefruits in yet another shameful and incendiary attempt to show racial bias in the justice system, when she tries to draw the picture of equivalence between selling crack, and driving drunk.

Alexander informs us that drunk drivers "typically [get] two days in jail for a first offense and two to ten days for a second offense," but possessing "a tiny amount of crack cocaine" gets a "mandatory minimum sentence of five years in federal prison." She mentions that drunk driving kills more people than overdosing on illegal drugs and the violence surrounding them, combined.[67] She also tells us that a "Yale historian" and other "scholars" have documented a disturbing though unsurprising pattern—punishment becomes more severe when drug use is associated "with people of color but softens when it is associated with whites."[68]

A near perfect comparison of the sort Alexander so desperately seeks is readily available. Why did she not opt for it? Only because it obliterates her entire claim that white's drug crimes are treated less harshly than Black's.

Even though you don't hear anyone in the media complaining about the sentencing guidelines for methamphetamine, they are exactly the same as those for crack cocaine. If you are caught with five grams of meth, you will be subject to a mandatory minimum sentence of five years in federal prison—a term identical to that for possessing 5 grams of crack.[69]

The primary reason this information undermines Alexander's contention of racial bias is the fact that only 2 percent of all federal inmates doing time for meth are black. Instead, 98 percent are either white (54 percent) or Hispanic (39 percent). And the total number of people in federal prison for meth is greater than that for crack: 5284 for meth, vs. 4495 for crack.[70]

The production of these drugs is also treated much differently. Have you ever heard of someone being arrested for "manufacturing crack" because they were caught with a box of baking soda and a pot of boiling water? Of course not. There are however numerous people (mostly white) who are doing life in federal prison (where there is no parole like state prison) because they got caught with batteries and red phosphorous. There is a good reason for this. Normally, crack houses do not blow up from making crack, whereas 'meth labs' often do because of the dangerous chemicals involved in manufacturing methamphetamines. With the exception of manufacturing, meth and crack offenders are treated equally. This actually targets mostly white meth offenders much more harshly than the group of mostly black crack offenders supposedly discriminated against.

The Media Exaggerated the Crack Problem

Today, many in the clique are attempting to rewrite the story of crack cocaine and the destruction it brought with it. Alexander says the media made "claims that have now been proven false or highly misleading" about crack being "instantly addictive" and "extraordinarily dangerous." U.S. District Judge Clyde Cahill apparently agrees, claiming "Legislators unconscious racial aversion towards Blacks, sparked by unsubstantiated reports of the effects of crack, reactionary media prodding, and an agitated constituency, motivated the legislators... to produce a dual system of punishment." The clique's 'paper of record' also got in on the action with an article that said, mischievously, "Images—or perhaps anecdotes—about the evils of crack, and the street crime it was assumed to stoke"—obviously suggesting that the crack problem was overblown by stereotyping.[71]

After getting a conviction against a crack dealer who raped and killed ten crack users from 1987–1998, Los Angeles prosecutor Robert Grace remarked, "[The] crack epidemic was one of the worst things that happened to the black and brown community." Also in the Los Angeles area, Matthew Kennedy, the manager of a notorious public housing project in Watts, recalled that during the crack epidemic, children were scared to go to school for fear of being shot. And said consequently, when that happens, "You've just lost that generation." Concurring with Mr. Kennedy, Lawrence Tolliver, the owner of a barbershop in south central Los Angeles said, in reference to all of the crack related shootings, "Sometimes it was so bad you had to scout the horizon like a gazelle at a watering hole in Africa."[72]

L.K., a good friend I made while working in the laundry here on McConnell, is one of the few inmates I have ever met that will admit he used crack. Everybody likes to claim they sold it. Finding people who will admit they were smoking it however, is much more difficult than it should be in light of all the people who were supposedly only selling it. After reading The New Jim Crow and thinking about the few friends I had in the free world who sold crack, and how these two different sources painted divergent pictures of the same world, I decided to ask L.K. to answer a few questions. Below are my questions, and his responses, unedited. They are included with his permission.

LEXTER KENNON KOSSIE #700661

D.O.B. 11/16/54; BLACK MALE, FROM HOUSTON, TX.

1. List all the drugs you have ever done.

    "I started drinking real heavy when I was about 12 or 13 years old. At that time I was also using marajuana practically every day. I then started popping pills such as Reds, Yellow Jackets, Trees, Blue Heavens, Valiums, and Qualuudes. All of my young friends were doing these drugs on a regular basis. [At age 17] I began to do speed as black mollies, preyludes, window payne acid, orange sunshine acid, and a little purple mierojite. I started messing around with heroin...[but was] actually able to cold-turkey heroin. In 1987 I started using cocaine...By august of 1987 I had become addicted to the devil crack cocaine."

2. Was crack instantly addictive?

    "One day a girl named Brenda showed me how to work the fire when smoking it. From that day I was addicted to the high it gave me. Two years passed before I realized that shit had taken over my life."

3. Was the high stronger than any other drug you had ever used? What about powder cocaine?

    "I had used so many different types of drugs in my life going back to when I was 12 or 13 years old and none had taken control of my life the way crack had. I had done cocaine in the powder form by sniffing it and by intravenous use which was no comparison to crack. Crack dominates."

4. What changes to your personality/demeanor did crack cause?

    "When I was on crack it changed my entire life. I remember how I would get my paycheck and get all the way to the drive way of my house then something would start talking to me, 'man go get you one rock!' I knew if I went to get one or even two rocks I would be gone the entire weekend until I had spent my entire paycheck. It was always two voices talking to me. One voice telling me that I owe it to myself because I worked for that money and it was mine. Then the other voice telling me that I know what happened last weekend when I tried to do that – 'you never came back home.' For some strange reason [that] bad voice always won because I would back out of the driveway and wouldn't return for days

Racism in the Justice System

later after I was broke. My wife put up with this crap and tried everything in her power to get me help but the drug addiction was just [too] strong. I had a good job. I was a lab optician and my job is probably what kept me afloat for such a long time. Not neccessarily my job, I'll say my profession because I lost [one] job after another. But because of my profession I was able to get jobs real easily.

5.   Did you ever commit crimes before using drugs?

"Yes. I've committed crimes since I was 9 or 10 years old."

6.   Did you commit more daring/ violent crimes after discovering drugs?

"In 1979, I went to prison for 3 counts of aggravated robbery and attempted capitol murder of a peace officer. I was sentenced to 20 years and made parole in 1986. When I got out crack cocaine was terrorizing the neighborhoods. I felt like I had tried every drug on the planet before experienceing crack [so] I thought I could handle it. Before I realized what had happened I was out there full steam robbing and doing just about anything to get more crack. I wasn't planning any of the robberies I was just running into stores and sticking them up because the craving was too strong for me to resist. I had never experienced a drug so powerful in my life. I believe that if I was put in a position to kill somebody for crack back then I would have. What I noticed about crack was once I had smoked it is when the craving took over my mind. I wanted more and more.

7.   Did you commit your most serious crimes while on crack?

"I would say I committed my most serious crimes when I was on crack but if I had not gotten caught I probably would have killed somebody for crack."

8.   How did crack dealers and their way of conducting business differ from that of all the other drug dealers you ever dealt with?

"Whenever I bought heroin I would usually go to a nice club and meet a dealer. We would then go out to his car and I would get in and check out the balloons. It never was as hostile an environment as with crack. Whenever I bought crack I would drive up to a corner and dudes would run up to my truck trying to sell me a rock. There would be 10 to 15 dudes at a time trying to make a sale. Most of them packed a gun because a crack addict might do anything to get crack. There were times when I would pull up on the corner to buy crack and have fake money or I would knock the dope out of the crack dealers hand while he was leaning over in my truck then I would speed off. There would be 2 or 3 dudes shooting at me as I sped off. Crack made me do some wild things where I would put my life in danger."

9. Did the fact that the high from crack was short lived compared to, say, heroin, influence the incidence and prevalence of crack transactions?

"Whenever a person smokes crack the rush from the high usually lasts anywhere from 10 to 60 seconds. I've never gotten lucky enough to get it to last no more than 15 seconds. This [is] what makes this drug so dangerous. Crack heads go to wild extremes to chase that rush. Dealers know that crack heads will be back in a very short period of time buying more crack until he has run completely out of money or means to get more money. With heroin the high lasts 2 to 6 hours so an addict isn't going to be ripping and running back and forth all night trying to buy more heroin. If a heroin addict had $2000.00 in his pocket, the next morning he will have probably $1900.00 left. If a crack head had $2000.00 in his pocket, the next morning he will probably have 19¢."

10. Because of that, does it surprise you that crack dealers get arrested more often?

"It doesn't surprise me that crack dealers get arrested more often than any other drug dealers because crack dealers deal with so many more people in a day's time."

11. Did you ever see any white people come to black ghettos to buy crack? If so how often? And in what neighborhoods?

"This is a very powerful drug. I remember seeing young white kids coming to some of the worst neighborhoods to buy crack. They weren't afraid to drive up with jewelry dripping off them in their expensive cars. I've seen them pull up at 3 o'clock in the morning to score crack. The only reason they didn't get robbed was because the dealers knew they would be coming back for more."

12. Did you ever see or hear of crack dealers getting their powder cocaine from white people? What about the CIA or FBI?"

"Most of the dealers that I bought crack from would score cocaine from Columbians and Jamaicans. Before crack came on the scene Blacks bought powder from white dudes but it wasn't used to rock up dope. It was used to snort. When crack came on the scene, that's when Blacks started buying kilos af powder to rock up and that powder mostly came

Racism in the Justice System

from the Jamaicans. I knew of some HPD laws that sold dope but no CIA or FBI."

13. Did you see an increase in violence because of turf wars over crack?

"When crack first came on the scene there were a lot of killings over turf. But after they realized that crack was selling so fast and in such a short period of time they realized they could all get paid. "

14. Did the police start to patrol areas where the violence happened more?

"Quite naturally the police started patrolling the areas where the violence was. In the beginning there were a lot of killings over turf. Later most of the killings were done by crack heads trying to get more money for crack. It wasn't nothing to read about an 85 year old woman found murdered in her home over a TV or VCR."

15. How many rehab/prevention type programs have you been enrolled in? Were they effective?

"I've been in several drug rehabs. I've been in St. Joseph hospital, Herman hospital, West Oaks hospital, and the Texas House, all to no avail. I don't believe that these drug facilities can help crack addicts. Crack isn't like heroin where your body physically fights it off into withdrawals. Crack is a mental drug and in order for a person to get off of it he has to want to and he has to be locked up. I know that's harsh but it's a fact. These 30 day drug rehabs are only in it for the money. A person that has become addicted to crack needs to be locked up away from the crack for at least 6 months. It's not a 2 week kick like heroin. Crack plays tricks with the mind. While I was in St. Joseph's hospital I met Marvin Gaye's second cousin. He was there because of his crack addiction. It was only a 30 day program that most insurance companies paid for. Anyway Marshall had been there about 27 days and he was ready to go. Well, at least he thought he was ready to go. He had done real good while in the program but I was really curious whether he was ready after only 27 days in. I decided that I was going to play a game with him on the day he would be discharged. I cut me some soap up in the sizes of $20 rocks. On the day he was to discharge I told him that I needed to talk to him later on in his room. He agreed. When I got to his room, I told him that my friend had come to see me and that he had left me two rocks, I pulled the rocks out and showed them to him. Before I could say anything else he asked me what we were gonna smoke them on. He started looking through his drawers trying to find something to smoke on. I just sat back and watched him as he looked and finally found an ink pen and said "this will work." I handed him the clear plastic bag with the rocks of soap. He opened the bag and when he realized that it was soap he looked like he had swallowed a lemon. He then told me, "man I really thought I was ready but: I'm not." Marshall ended up staying another 30 days at least because when I left after my 30 he was still there. He thanked me for making him aware that he was still sick. In most cases prison is the best remedy because as I said, a person has to be away from the stuff at least 6 months."

16. Do most of the crack users you know have similar experiences with the drug and crime?

"In most cases dudes that mess with crack have experienced the same effects I have from addiction. It's powerful and it causes a person to commit crimes to get more crack. A lot of them just haven't got caught but if they continue to use crack they will get caught and if they don't get caught they will probably O.D. one day."

17. What do you think would have happened to you if you had not gotten locked up?

"If I had not gotten locked up I would probably be dead right now. Either I would have O.D.ed or somebody would have killed me. I was taking serious risks to get crack. Crack was my life and nothing else mattered. My feelings were dead. Crack is the worst thing that could have happened to my life. This drug destroys lives by the millions and it doesn't matter if your rich or poor. I end up getting a life sentence behind crack. I walked into a Burger King not to rob it but to steal the money out of the cash register. I was high on crack. I ordered a fish sandwhich. When the fish sandwhich was ready I was going to drop the coins in my hand on the floor when the cashier had opened the register then I was gonna snatch the money out when she bent down to pick up the coins off the floor. It all backfired when I didn't have enough change to pay for the fish sandwhich. The cashier never opened the register. I started faking like I had something under my jacket. I never had nothing but my fist balled up. She opened the register and I snatched the money and ran. I was charged with aggravated robbery and sentenced to life in prison for $173.00. Well I did get a chance to smoke it all up in crack before getting caught riding around the next morning in the same car wearing the same clothes that I had worn that night. Heroin has never made anyone do the things crack has. This drug is more powerful than most people can imagine. It destroyed my life."

Perhaps my friend's story leaves those of you in the clique less than convinced. After all he does not have a college degree, nor does he blame

Racism in the Justice System

all of his problems on white men. He also never went into 'public service' as a community organizer. Fair enough.

But what about a doctor (several degrees) who works in inner-city hospitals and prisons (eschewing the greater pay of a private practice), and lives in Britain where they spend a great deal of time trying to accommodate non-white immigrants by giving them rights only a British citizen should have? There is just such a man. His name is Dr. Theodore Dalrymple. He has dealt with thousands of drug users and dealers. His experiences have formed the following "expert" opinion:

> Stimulant drugs such as crack cocaine provoke paranoia, increase aggression, and promote violence. Much of this violence takes place in the home, as the relatives of crack takers will testify. It is something I know from personal acquaintance by working in the emergency room and in the wards of our hospital. Only someone who has not been assaulted by drug takers rendered psychotic by their drug could view with equanimity the prospect of the future spread of the abuse of stimulants.[73]

The problems of the crack trade were not overblown. Saying they were is merely the newest way to say, "I am not racist" if you are white, and "I am down for the struggle" if you're non-white.

Pitts and many others believe legalizing or at least decriminalizing drugs would be preferable to putting drug offenders in prison. They talk about the high cost of incarceration, and point out that surveys show the percentage of Americans using drugs is about the same as it was before the war on drugs began.

I personally thought this was a good idea because, although I have never used drugs, I knew a few people who did, and thought that if not for the high cost of the drugs, their habits alone were not too much of a problem. And I knew if drugs were legalized, the cartels would not be able to charge their exorbitant prices and would therefore collapse overnight because they would not be able to prop up their infrastructure for lack of funds. Many other legalization/decriminalization advocates also claim that addicts only commit a large share of their crimes because they cannot afford their drugs. They tell us all of these crimes would vanish if addicts had drugs provided to them by the government.

In Amsterdam, most drugs are easily obtained with a doctor's prescription. But according to Dr. Dalrymple, Amsterdam "is among the most violent and squalid cities in Europe." He explains this contradiction of the current fashion by saying that people who sell drugs are not likely to seek respectable employment once their vocation is obsolete.[74] When it comes to the users, "look at Liverpool, where 2,000 people of a population of 600,000 receive official prescriptions for methadone: this once proud and prosperous city is still the world capital of drug motivated burglary..."[75] Drugs and the problems they cause should not be taken lightly and, as we have already seen, if the war on drugs is a failure because people are still using drugs at the same rate they were before the war began, than by that logic, we should "...abolish medical schools, hospitals, and departments of health" because medicine is not winning the war against sickness and death.[76] Dr. Dalrymple makes this point very well:

> If the war on drugs is lost, then so are the wars against theft, speeding, incest, fraud, rape, murder, arson, and illegal parking. Few if any such wars are winnable. So let us all do anything we choose. But to demand a yes or no answer to the question "is the war on drugs being won" is like demanding a yes or no answer to the question "Have you stopped beating your wife yet?" Never can an unimaginable and fundamentally stupid metaphor have exerted a more baleful effect on proper thought.[77]

Crimes caused by the drug trade are not the only reason drugs should be illegal. The damage drugs do to a person's motivation and capacity for responsibility can be total and irredeemable. When someone gets high, they artificially extract the very important feel-good chemicals from their brains essential for driving a person to accomplish things in life. It feels good to graduate from high school because your brain releases some combination of chemicals due to the accomplishment. If you figure out a way to get bathed in those chemicals without having to work for them, you eliminate the need for work, which makes it very difficult to achieve anything meaningful in life. And as my friend L.K. explained, crack consumed him, and he became interested in little other than getting more crack.

Reagan The Racist

Alexander likes to believe that cops have been able to lock up so many non-whites for drug crimes because President Ronald Reagan increased the funding for the war on drugs and incentivized law enforcement to arrest as many people as possible, regardless of their guilt or innocence. She claims Reagan's campaign for the Presidency was "built on the success of earlier conservatives who developed a strategy of exploiting racial hostility or resentment for political gain without making explicit references to race."

And that once in office, his justice department reduced the number of specialists used to ferret out white collar crime by 50 percent, shifting those resources to "street crime, especially drug-law enforcement." Alexander says this was done to win over voters who were unconcerned with drugs, yet very concerned about race in general and stopping the progress of Blacks in particular. She proclaims it was all a success because Reagan won the votes of 22 percent of all Democrats and 34 percent of those Democrats who believed civil rights leaders were moving too fast.[78]

In support of these claims, she begins with a fairly misleading statement about America's racial climate in 1968. Alexander says, "Richard Nixon and the independent segregationist candidate, George Wallace," won 57 percent of the vote.[79] This is supposed to signal to the reader that most of the whites voting then were racist because two 'law and order' politicians got a majority of the vote. However by 1968, Wallace was running on the American Independent Party ticket as a class-warfare Barack Obama -type populist, who definitely mentioned the words law and order, but had "recognized that southern-style segregation was a lost cause" and was now trying to "appeal to working class and lower middle class whites in [the] North and South."[80] More importantly, of that 57 percent, Wallace only got 13.5 of it. The rest went to Nixon, who despite accusations never pursued a "southern strategy" or attempted to repeal the Civil Rights Act or the Voting Rights Act.[81]

Alexander also says that in 1968, a Gallup poll showed that 81 percent of Americans agreed with the statement that "law and order had broken down in this country" and that most of those polled believed "Negroes who start riots" and "communists" were responsible.[82] However, 54 percent of the whites polled also said that when it came to dealing with the riots, they preferred "trying harder to improve the condition of the Negroes" as opposed to "build[ing] up tighter police control in the Negro areas," which only 16 percent favored.[83]

This of course does not mean that all was well. It does however suggest that while whites were concerned about the riots and lawlessness—as the statistics we saw earlier indicated they certainly should have been—a majority did not think black people were some incorrigible hoard that could only be controlled by dispatching a battalion of storm troopers into black neighborhoods to arrest and imprison the residents.

When discussing the election of Ronald Reagan, nowhere does Alexander mention anything about the 10 percent unemployment, the stagflation, or the problems with Russia and Iran that were certainly weighing on voter's minds. Nor does she mention the ineptness of President Carter and the fuel shortage that happened on his watch. That she ignores all of these problems and attributes Reagan's win strictly to racism by whites is dishonest and reprehensible. It was at this point in the book that I quit taking her seriously.

Alexander also tells us manpower was taken away from the law enforcement agencies who were trying to stop white collar crimes in order to target drug crimes, because doing so allowed the imprisonment of more non-whites. But if Reagan's aim was to win and maintain the presidency by appealing to the racism of whites via the 'mass incarceration' of Blacks, he should never have taken away "half the number of specialists assigned to identify and prosecute white collar criminals"[84] and sent them after drug criminals. Why? Because white collar criminals make more money, and if your goal is to "keep Blacks down," you ought to go after the Blacks making the most money.

You howl, "But Long, Blacks don't commit white collar crimes—whites do! That's why Reagan the racist eased up on them, you dumb white privileged racist!" Not quite.

In 1980, when Reagan was surely sitting in a smoke-filled room adorned with Swastikas and wearing a white satin robe with matching hood while he, Bush, Cheney, and a bunch of similarly clad wizards and dragons plotted on how to further oppress non-whites, I am quite certain he was cognizant of the fact that Blacks made up about one-third of all criminals arrested for fraud, forgery, counterfeiting, and receiving stolen property. They were also one fourth of those arrested for embezzlement.[85] And at the time, Blacks compromised just 10 percent of the U.S. population. This was before crack hit the streets mind you. And any good proponent of 'racial hierarchy' would have recognized that he could get more bang for his white-power buck by directing manpower towards the most profitable criminals. A few black or brown drug dealers in ghettos and barrios were not a threat to 'white supremacy.' Maybe Reagan the racist really was senile and indisposed back then, as everyone in the clique claims.

This makes me think of Herman Cain when he was running for the Republican Party's Presidential nomination in 2012. The clique's pundits said white people only supported Mr. Cain because he was "a black man who knew his place," suggesting the emotionally satisfying notion that all whites who are not in the clique are racists and those who identify these whites as such are heroes.

The problem with this, however, is that Herman Cain made his career and money telling white people what to do with their companies and assets. He directed them in hiring and firing, merging and acquiring, and eventually took over a white-owned company and sold it when he got ready—making himself a multi-millionaire in the process. He also worked with the late congressman Jack Kemp on the Reagan tax cuts and was hired by the U.S. Navy to instruct them on the proper trajectory at which to launch their missiles.

If I were a white supremacist, I would much rather black citizens model themselves after Barack Obama, community organizer, than Herman Cain, CEO, rocket scientist, pastor and gospel singer. The former would not be much of a threat filing frivolous lawsuits, voting "present," and writing fictional memoirs to convince white people they should feel guilty.

In 1995, near the crime rate high of the early 1990s, Blacks accounted for 54.4 percent of all criminals arrested for murder and non-negligent manslaughter; 59 percent of those for robbery, and 42.9 percent of those arrested for forcible rape.[86] Yet when it came to drug crimes, Blacks were only 36.9 percent of those arrested. After more than a decade of warring on drugs, 'proponents of racial hierarchy,' with all the advantages of 'whiteness' at their disposal, were unable to arrest Blacks at the same rate for drug crimes at which they managed to arrest them for other crimes.

Lastly, the dealers and users of drugs are not the benign lot Alexander and the rest of the clique make them out to be. A study involving addicts from Philadelphia, Phoenix, Washington D.C., and San Antonio showed that on average, addicts committed 26 crimes a month—which translates to 312 a year per addict. Other studies have shown that murder is often the number one cause of death among addicts—responsible for one-fourth of all addict deaths in one study, and two-thirds in another. A study conducted in Wayne county Michigan, where Detroit is located demonstrated that well over half of "all the homicide victims were drug users or involved with drug dealing." Another study done with addicts from multiple cities showed that male drug addicts got between 25 and 50 percent of their illegal income from committing violent crimes. From the criminal's perspective, this was the logical thing to do since crimes against people produced, on average, $187 versus only $59 for property crimes.[87] All of this means taking drugs and those who use them off the street will lower the crime rate. This is what Reagan wanted.

Lastly, if support of drug laws is enough to tar and feather the great Renaldus Magnus a racist, Alexander must also condemn both Vice

President Joe Biden, who as a senator in 1982 coined the benevolent term 'drug czar' for the head of the office of National Drug Control Policy, and the Congressional Black Caucus for pushing the Anti-Drug and Abuse Act of 1985.

CLAIM 3: DRUG-CRIME BASED INEQUALITY

The most important premise in *The New Jim Crow*, indeed the entire book hinges upon it, is found in Chapter 3. Alexander says that studies prove whites and Blacks use and sell drugs at the same rate and therefore because a larger percentage of Blacks are locked up for drug crimes, the justice system is racist.[88]

As we have already seen, the black crime rate is much higher than the white crime rate for practically all offenses. Alexander says that crime rates are an attractive explanation for the high rates of incarceration amongst Blacks because they reinforce racist stereotypes about Blacks "dating back to slavery."[89] In other words, statistics that she believes prove her contentions are valid; while those that prove the contrary are merely the manifestation of racist white people's prejudice. So convenient.

She says, "...rates of drug crime do not explain the glaring racial disparities in our criminal justice system because people of all races use and sell drugs at remarkably similar rates."[90] Finally, a statement by Alexander I actually agree with—to an extent. Drug crimes do not explain why so many Blacks are in prison. Violent crimes do. The second part of her statement, that rates of drug trafficking are the same amongst all races, is a non-sequitur. Blacks and whites play football and basketball at the same rates, yet Blacks make up the vast majority of professionals in the NFL and NBA even though the white population is about six-times the size of the black population.

Nevertheless, I had someone send me the 2010 National Survey on Drug Use and Health (NSDUH) from which Alexander got her numbers. On page 14, it had a yearly chart dating from 2003 to 2010, showing the percentage of those aged 12 or older who used drugs in the last month, broken down by race. In every year reported, Blacks were only slightly more likely to have used illegal drugs in the past month than the other races. Even the year with the widest gap between Blacks and whites, 2010, showed only a 1.6 percent difference—with 10.7 percent of Blacks and 9.1 percent of whites, using illicit drugs in the past month. I then went through the other 67 pages of this study and came back to page 43;

"Appendix A: Description of the survey." This is where they explain how they gathered their data and put the study together. These surveys had been conducted in households with persons living in houses/townhouses, apartments, condominiums; civilians living in housing on military bases etc. and persons in non-institutional group quarters. Half-way houses were included; correctional facilities were not.[91]

The problem with this survey is that 'households,' or the people that occupy them, are all similar and only reflect people living in such arrangements. It should not be a surprise that people living in fairly stable conditions use and sell drugs at the same rate. This survey however fails to capture many of the high rate offenders, those most likely to end up in prison for drug crimes, who are often in their state's youth commission or living a transient lifestyle. These are the offenders who sell and use drugs often enough to get caught and show up in prison population statistics. To go to prison for drugs, you will usually need multiple drug cases or some other offenses on your rap sheet. These other offenses often put youths in places that prevent them from participating in surveys like the NSDUH.

Studies based on self-reports conducted in junior high and high school also fail to record high-rate offender's crimes because these offenders are often in reassignment school, have been expelled, or have quit altogether before these surveys are administered. Another problem with self-reports is that people with low levels of verbal intelligence, a hallmark of offenders who end up in prison, are very likely to have trouble answering questions accurately, causing them to "under report delinquent acts."[92] These are precisely the individuals whose crimes these surveys need to record in order to give us a realistic picture of criminal offending.

Blacks and whites in general have different scores on verbal intelligence tests, and offenders are no different. In 1976, the gap between black and white college bound high school seniors was 119 points. By 1995 it had shrunk to 92 points, with the average score for whites 448 and for Blacks 356.[93]

One study demonstrated that students who did well in English and did not have police records "were twice as likely" to complete self-report surveys than were "poor students of English with police records."[94] A study done by J.C. Hackler and M. Lautt showed that black youngsters in general were more likely to underreport their crimes than white youngsters were.[95] Lie detector tests and third parties have also proven that self-reports are given to under/over reporting.[96]

One particular study showed that in reality over 50 percent of white boys who said they had been arrested had "no police record." Another self-report study conducted among male college students showed a significant number of them lied about starting a fist fight.[97]

All of this calls into question the validity of Alexander's premise, because it is based mostly on self-reports/surveys. If her premise is false, and I contend it is, her conclusions are bogus.

Along with self-reports *The New Jim Crow* also uses the "number of drug related emergency-room visits"[98] to bolster the claim that Blacks are overrepresented in prison for drug crimes. However, whites make up over 70 percent of the U.S. population and should therefore, even if they are using drugs at the same rates as Blacks, account for most drug-related visits to emergency rooms.

Emergency room records are more reliable than self-reported data. So are the results of a urinalysis test the New York Telephone Company gives its prospective employees. These tests, which are a required part of the physical examination, have shown that 15 percent of Blacks and 4 percent of whites "who applied for a job had traces in their urine of either heroin or the substance (quinine) typically used to dilute heroin."[99] So in this case, Blacks were using heroin at almost 4 times the rate of whites. We should be more inclined to trust the hospital records which Alexander believes support her contentions, and urinalysis tests, which support mine, over self-reports.

In Chapter 3, Alexander repeats her claim that "violent crime is not responsible for the prison boom." She says that the reason there are so many violent offenders in prison is because they get "longer prison sentences" when compared to drug and property crime offenders, somewhat contradicting her earlier statements that the inverse is often the case. Once again, she uses the alarming figure attributing "61 percent" of the rise in the federal prison population to drug law enforcement. She then points out that only 4 percent of the growth in the federal prison population comes from homicide offenders and that "less than 3 percent of new court commitments to state prison typically involve people convicted of homicides."[100]

This is verbal sleight of hand. As I explained previously, the "61 percent" increase claim is in federal prisons, which only hold about 12 percent of the country's inmates. When it comes to homicide, the vast majority of murders are prosecuted in state courts. So that 4 percent figure is understandably small.

Likewise, her statement that only 3 percent of newly convicted criminals headed to state prison are serving time for murder creates a false picture, all in an attempt to prove that violent crime has not contributed to the increase in the prison population as much as drug crime has.

Just why did Alexander choose murder as her representative for violent crime? Because it occurs the least of all violent crimes! If you want to make violent crime seem as insignificant as possible, choose the one that occurs at a fractional rate of all others.

In 1960, for example, there were 5.1 murders per 100,000 people in the U.S. In 1990, that number jumped to 9.4, almost doubling. When it came to other types of violent crimes, 1960 saw 9.9 rapes, 60 robberies, and 86 aggravated assaults per 100,000 people. In 1990, the numbers soared to 41.2 rapes, 257 robberies, and 424 aggravated assaults per 100,000. In fact in no year since at least 1960 have murders even come close to occurring as often as rape, robbery, or assault.[101]

In 1960, when there were a total of 732 violent crimes per 100,000 people, murders only accounted for 1.2 percent of them.[102] Something accounting for a scant 1.2 percent of a collection cannot be used to represent the entire collection. That would be like saying that the 2 percent of incarcerated Blacks represent the entire black population.

Alexander cites a study from Seattle that is supposed to prove that black drug dealers, crack sellers in particular, do not conduct their business in a manner that would cause them to get arrested more often than white drug dealers.[103] But as my friend L.K. explained, the rush and subsequent high from crack does not last as long as heroin or prescription pills. Also it is easier to go undetected as a drug dealer if you are stealing Xanax pills from your dad, the psychiatrist, and selling them to your friends than if you have all sorts of people coming to your house at all hours to buy crack. Again, what we have is a clique member angry that the justice system is not perfect. Dr. Sowell says this is a desire for "Cosmic Justice," because no society has ever constructed a system that operates as if a god-like figure were in control of it; and able to exercise, at all times, his omnipresence and omnipotence to make sure there are no exceptions to the rules.[104]

And as I said before, white and black people play sports at the same rates. Yet it is never argued (as well it should not be) that whites are discriminated against in the NFL and NBA even though, according to the clique, whites are severely "underrepresented" in both of these professions. Statistical representations are just that.

CLAIM 4: SHAME AND STIGMA OF PRISON

In Chapter 4, titled "The Cruel Hand," Alexander "considers how the caste system operates once people are released from prison" and "argue[s] that the shame and stigma of the prison label is in many respects, more damaging to the African American community than the shame and stigma associated with Jim Crow."[105] She then quotes Fredrick Douglas when he was addressing the National Colored Convention in 1853 in an attempt to ally her cause with a man whose character and objective were beyond reproach. This is a favorite technique of the clique. (Today, they often attempt to do that when they compare illegal aliens and gays with black Americans and their virtuous struggle for first class citizenship.)

Although I do not have any of Douglas' writings in my possession in which he expresses his opinions about crime and punishment, I have a hard time believing he would compare the historic plight of black Americans in his day to black criminals in today's justice system. And unlike the late Howard Zinn who "conscripted" the views of the Arawak and Cherokee natives along with black Americans for his "history textbook,"[106] I am not about to ascribe anything to an American hero like Mr. Douglas unless I have substantial documentation that can be verified.

Alexander explains how Blacks in Fredrick Douglas' day had no rights. They could be captured by slave owners and enslaved even if they had been born free. She then tries to draw a parallel between present day black criminals on parole and Blacks persecuted in the mid-1800s. Again, she takes something she knows everyone is against—slavery—and tries to say that the current justice system is no different: "lynch mobs may be long gone, but the threat of police violence is ever present [for Blacks]."[107]

In addition, "a criminal record today authorizes the forms of discrimination we supposedly left behind—discrimination in employment, housing, education, public benefits, and jury service. Those labeled criminals can even be denied the right to vote." Worst of all however is this gem of demagoguery: "hundreds of years ago, our nation put those considered less than human in shackles; less than one hundred years ago, we relegated them to the other side of town; today we put them in cages. Once released, they find that a heavy and cruel hand has been laid upon them."[108]

This argument fails to recognize significant differences between conditions in that time and today. Slaves and Blacks living in the Jim Crow South did nothing to bring their grievous predicament upon themselves.

Racism in the Justice System

On the other hand, unless a miscarriage of justice exists, convicted felons have done something that most people in our society detest. They broke the law, and depending upon the crime, they have probably hurt someone and/or deprived them of something, causing that victim or taxpayers to incur an unnecessary cost. Once again Alexander has made an unconscionable comparison. It only seems legitimate because of the authority she carries as an attorney and law professor.

Take a look at the quote about lynch mobs. She makes it seem, as she does with slavery, as if white racists specifically created lynch mob justice for black people. She ignores the reality that before the civil war, 90 percent of all the people lynched in the South were white.[109]

A study by the Tuskegee Institute says that from 1882 to 1968, in total, whites lynched 3,446 Blacks.[110] These facts are important to a racially heterogeneous society like America, because knowing the truth makes it more difficult for the S.W.R.D. Bandaranaike's out there to get elected.

As for police brutality, it happens. I can personally attest to this. But in 1997, the Justice Department released a study in which less than 1 percent of Americans who had a run-in with the police were even threatened with, much less actually subjected to physical force.[111] Alexander offers no alternatives to improve the system.

Until artificial intelligence and robotic capabilities improve to the point where cops can be replaced, police officers will continue to make the mistakes all people do. And yes, of course their mistakes can be more injurious than those of a baker or salesman. But the human condition is what it is, and the available alternatives to a police force must be less desirable, seeing as how most societies have had cops for quite some time.

Alexander claims racist white people discriminate against Blacks with criminal records just as they did in the Jim Crow South. But just what does it mean to discriminate? The $5.00 dictionary I bought from the commissary gives two definitions:

1) To make a distinction on the basis of prejudice; show partiality;
2) To note a difference; distinguish accurately.[112]

In other words, to discriminate is to choose.

When Alexander chose to marry her husband, she simultaneously chose not to marry Sean Hannity. That is discrimination. When she chose to write a book on drug crime, she discriminated against a book on violent crime.[113] I personally choose to root for only two NFL teams: The Houston Texans and whoever is playing the Dallas Cowboys—thereby discriminating against the NFL's other thirty teams. No one has a problem with these forms of discrimination. Why then, does Alexander have a problem with employers or property owners choosing whom they hire or accept as tenants?

This is as reasonable as the analogy between crack cocaine and drunk driving. The only way to find such an argument reasonable is to refuse to consider the costs to anyone other than the ex-con. People choose to avoid criminals for very specific reasons. The labeling and sorting that occurs in everyday life cannot be tossed aside suddenly because a large percentage of these criminals are black, and it is currently in vogue to have lower standards for Blacks.

Imagine going into a grocery store in which the canned goods have no labels, and all the other items are completely disorganized. Think about how much it would cost in terms of time and money to shop at this store for a single meal. The trial and error process that would be required for the canned goods alone would make people refuse to shop at such a store.

If a human being has a criminal record, he or she is either impulsive, defiant, and of below average intelligence or highly intelligent and calculating. The vast majority of criminals, regardless of race, possess these traits. The average employer or property owner probably has no clue when it comes to a criminal's personality traits. However, they know from experience, personal or vicarious, that criminals are less likely than non-criminals to make good employees or tenants. It is much easier then, when looking for prospective employees or tenants, to exclude those with criminal records. After all, subjecting someone to a personality test, which could be answered dishonestly, is risky.

Here is a typical account of the living conditions in a neighborhood with paroled or discharged criminals:

> They spoke of living a nightmare brought about by the non-stop crime, intimidation, vandalism and harassment inflicted upon them by their criminal residents. All spoke of their total failure to get local politicians, MPs/criminal justice officials, police, or indeed anyone to take any notice of their desperate situation.[114]

Alexander cannot write this off as cowardly white people stereotyping the black criminals in their community because this passage comes from white people observing white criminals in Britain.

There are no doubt ex-cons who can—if given the chance—make good employees or tenants. Of course, it is tragic when one who could prove to be so is not even given the opportunity. However, it is not the fault of the potential employer or property owner, who will incur the actual cost of dealing with the felon, that the criminal acquired the label. Nor should the other employees or tenants have their livelihood jeopardized by having a criminal in their midst. They also are not responsible for the criminal's felony conviction.

Alexander's criminal-centric vision of the issue is most disturbing because she makes it seem as if a criminal record just happens to someone—like a natural disaster, which no one can control. When she compares Blacks with criminal records with Blacks in the Jim Crow South, who she freely admits were discriminated against "on the basis of race,"[115] she cannot limit the source of discrimination to race. If you do not want a criminal record, you do not commit crimes; if you do not want to be black, tough. You have no choice in the matter.

She mentions a "forty-one-year-old African American mother" who cannot get into a public housing project because of a prior drug conviction. The woman says, "I deserve a chance. Even if I was the worst criminal, I deserve a chance"—and surely she does.[116] But does she (and Alexander) really think the public wants their tax dollars subsidizing a felon *instead* of a non-felon?

The waiting list for public housing is long and contentious, especially in light of the recent recession. There are so many people trying to get into so few apartments, why not restrict those (criminals) who, on average, will make far less desirable tenants?

I am certain there are ex-cons who function in society. I have personally known a few over the last seventeen years. However, the recidivism rate is 67.5 percent.[117] There are only so many taxpayer-subsidized apartments available. Why not give them to the people more likely to succeed as opposed to those who have already screwed up and have a propensity to do so again?

The *Houston Chronicle* (the clique's paper of record in the South) printed an article by Robert Stanton in July of 2011, which said that the Housing and Urban Development Department was sending out letters to public housing authorities telling them to use "discretion" in allowing felons to house. There were two types of offenders discretion could not be extended to. Sex offenders were banned for life.[118]

Very understandable. No one in their right mind wants to find out if Jerry Sandusky can still coach football and be a productive member in their community.

The other banned group? Surely it was crack dealers, if you are living in a racial caste system akin to Jim Crow after all, right? Apparently not. The second type of felon to be banned for life from public housing is anyone who has been convicted of manufacturing methamphetamine.[119] As we saw earlier, very few in this group are black.

In an attempt to illustrate just how difficult life is for someone with a criminal record, Alexander quotes someone named Jeremy Travis: "In this brave new world, punishment for the original offense is no longer enough; one's debt to society is never paid."[120] Nothing like an ill-conceived metaphor to confuse the masses.

Dr. Dalrymple eviscerates this popular absurdity with precision when talking about a woman who spent years in prison proclaiming she had "paid her debt" to society:

> ...Life is not a matter of double entry bookkeeping. No number of years in prison can be equivalent to the torture and killing of children: if it were, the term could be served in advance and the person who served it would be entitled to commit his crimes on his release.[121]

We must also consider this. Doing a prison sentence usually does not change the characteristics which caused a criminal to commit the crime for which he was imprisoned. If it did—if you could somehow zap the impulsiveness and other culpable traits out of a criminal's personality, you might then be able to make a case for no longer labeling and sorting criminals as ex-cons. However, the technology required to do this remains in the developmental stages at this point in time. And until this technology is proven, convicts, like canned goods and everything else in life, are best served with labels that explain what they are, or at least were, capable of doing.

Losing the right to vote and serve on a jury are unfortunately the furthest things from the average inmate's mind. In the 17 years I have spent in the Texas Department of Criminal Justice Institutional Division, I have never heard an inmate say, "I can't wait to get my right to vote back." I wish that were not the case, but this is often how reality works. As for jury duty, there are probably some law-abiding citizens who would be willing to take a felony on their record—if they could do so without having to serve time—in order to get out of jury duty. Not once does Alexander mention that white ex-cons return to the free world stripped of all the same rights lost by black felons.

Racism in the Justice System

In prison, over the years, I have seen numerous inmates get out and come back. In 1994, the Bureau of Justice began gathering statistics by tracking the lives of 272,000 state offenders who had been discharged that same year. Over the next three years, they found that 67.5 percent of these ex-cons were rearrested because they committed 744,000 new felonies and "serious misdemeanors."[122] These were not parole violations like missing an appointment with your parole officer because your car broke down.

This is disturbing in light of a study done by a liberal, anti-prison group that probably has Alexander and Pitts on their mailing list. The JFA Institute calculated that in 2007, a mere 3 percent of violent and property criminals ended up behind bars. And according to the Bureau of Justice Statistics, only an infinitesimal 1.6 percent of burglars were incarcerated in 2004.[123] This of course means that those 774,000 documented crimes were probably the tip of the iceberg, and the recidivists got away with many more crimes before they were caught.

A good friend of mine, who we will call T.B., did 20 years in prison from 1986–2006 for a robbery he says he did not commit. While doing that long, god-awful stretch, all of his relatives died and all of his 'friends' left him for dead. When he got out, he lived in a half-way house where he said more people were being raped and extorted than in the prison he had paroled from. He struggled 'mightily' at times. He found work with some lawyers even though he had no formal training.

All that time T.B. spent in the prison's law-library paid off. He then met a woman and got married. They found a house they could afford to rent—owned by someone who did not care that T.B. was a convicted felon. Then the lawyers paid him with some checks that bounced. He nearly lost the house. (Hate to stereotype, but lawyers seem to have a penchant for making promises they cannot keep.) But T.B. is a very resourceful cat, and last I heard from him he had a job working in the IT department at Sears Holdings.

He has constantly stressed to me, even during the recession, that here in the great state of Texas, you can find a job. Even a black, ex-con like T.B. had numerous options: from the ordinary, a night stocker as Costco, which started employees out at $15.00 an hour, to the hilarious, working for the enviro-nazis at Green Peace. T.B. says it's comical to hear someone say there are no jobs here in Texas.

A guy T.B. and I both knew—one of the two or three best basketball players on Connally—got out at about the same time. We'll call him G.O. He had a financially stable female friend with a home to which he paroled.

He also had a few family members and friends more than willing to help him readjust after doing 17 years in here.

G.O. got a job in a place that could safely be described as a factory making $14.00 an hour. Gregarious and upbeat, within 6 months he was a mid-level supervisor, making close to top pay at around $22.00 an hour. However, before a year passed, G.O.'s DNA showed up at the scene of a violent robbery where a couple of the victims were pistol-whipped. Last I heard from T.B., G.O. was sitting in county jail, with the D.A. offering him 80 years.

I truly wish it were not the case, but from what I have seen over the years, the circumstances to which an inmate is released do not matter nearly as much as the inmate's temperament and level of impulsiveness when it comes to whether or not they stay out or come back. T.B. and G.O. are both black. But I know plenty of white inmates that have come back. To a man, they have very extroverted and gregarious personalities like G.O.

One in particular, M.S., had his mother, a place to live, and a job waiting for him when he got out. Yet before he had even been free for six months, he was using drugs again, even though he spent the last six months of his eight-year sentence in a prison 'drug program.' He was a typical, restless, impulsive inmate. Prison and umpteen prison "programs" could not change him.

Think about G.O. He had a job paying a 'living wage' as Matt Damon and the rest of the cast of Ocean's 23 advocate. He had everybody's favorite outgoing personality type. No problem attracting women, therefore no self-esteem issues. He even had a place to stay and friends and family waiting on him when he got out. Yet none of that mattered. On the other hand T.B. had every reason to fail but managed to carve out a fairly normal life for himself. To sum it up, that recidivism rate of 67.5 percent is what it is for a reason.

Towards the end of Chapter 4, "The Cruel Hand," Alexander quotes the mother of a teenager who is locked up:

> All of your life you been taught that you're not a worthy person, or that something is wrong with you. You don't have no respect for yourself. See, people of color have—not all of them, but a lot of them—have poor self esteem, because we've been branded, we have been programmed that it's something wrong with us. We hate ourselves.[124]

Alexander uses this as a rebuttal to Bill Cosby and others who claim that Blacks in the ghetto 'have no shame.'[125] She says that the stigma caused by 'mass incarceration' has pushed Blacks "beyond shame to a place of self-hate."[126] (I find this fitting because I believe the narrative I am rebutting in this book makes white people hate themselves.) Over the last seventeen years, I have seen very few if any black inmates lacking in the self-esteem department. Alexander claims that people in the ghetto do not look at prison as a 'rite of passage.'[127] Well, they might say that in an interview with a left wing sociologist, but when they are down here getting a large neck tattoo that flaunts their gang affiliation and has the ever popular prison cell bars for a border, you tend to come away with a different impression.

Another problem with the self-esteem argument is that Blacks have always had substantially lower rates of suicide than whites. Back in 1978, when there was certainly more racism in America than there is today, the black suicide rate was 50 percent lower than the white suicide rate.[128] Those in the clique will write this off as Blacks being of heartier stock. I have met plenty of Blacks in the free world and in prison who believe that Blacks are superior to whites and that is why whites supposedly oppress them. It goes something like this: whites cannot jump, dance, fight, sing, or invent anything without stealing the original idea from the Asiatic-Africanic black Hebrew original man. And when it comes to white men in particular, they are especially inferior when it comes to manliness. White skin becomes pink skin, as in "them pink folks." Suffice it to say, there is no dearth of black self-esteem. In fact, recent studies have shown black school children have the highest levels of self-esteem even though their grades and test scores are the worst.

I find it ironic that Alexander's book and other forms of narrative-compliant multimedia, which criticize the above-average rate of incarceration for non-whites, actually contribute to the problem they set out to alleviate. In the case of 'mass incarceration,' they are essentially saying, "There's nothing wrong with being a convicted felon if you're non-white because either the white man sent your job overseas or created a war on drugs for the express purpose of placing you in a racial caste system." Once this becomes the explanation for the predicament a non-white inmate finds himself in, he has even less motivation to pursue the necessary personal improvements needed to make it on the outside. He also has a ready-made excuse from highly educated, prominent people like Pitts and Alexander. After all, those people never lie.

When I was a teenager, my mestizo-Hispanic friend L.T. told me that his sister literally cried tears of joy when he got out of a juvenile detention center, because while there, he kept his mouth shut and did not reveal the names of any of his co-conspirators in the robbery for which he was detained. It improved his status as well as hers in their neighborhood on the east side of Houston.

Over the years I have had several black inmates tell me that their own parents, beginning when they were young, told them that prison was where you went for "standing up to the white man." One individual told me that when he was a child his dad began telling him, "The cops are the bad guys, they want to hurt us." D.E.'s dad had been locked up in California and may have had good reasons for viewing certain cops as "the bad guys." But if it is wrong for white people to stereotype Blacks as criminals, I would think it is also wrong for Blacks to stereotype cops.

Growing up in Los Angeles, D.E. and his older brother, who I also met down here, were members of "the biggest gang in the city." Both were placed in the California Youth Authority as juveniles where D.E. did a little over a decade. He got out in his mid-twenties. He made some money performing in a rap group and came to Texas to do some studio recording. Almost immediately after arriving here, he 'caught' a murder case.‡ He had only been free a matter of months.

D.E. had an abusive father who beat him, his brother, and their mother, constantly. He and his brother were encouraged from a young age in their criminal pursuits by almost everyone around them. The odds were obviously stacked against them.

But it was not white racism that proportioned those odds. Contrary to what Alexander likes to believe, D.E. and many other non-white criminals are told directly and indirectly that America and its laws are not legitimate. Therefore, they should pledge no allegiance to her nor should they recognize her laws as an authority to abide by. When this is your reality, why would you feel any shame when you break from the norms or break the laws? Criminals and their families are not necessarily the innocent and virtuous pawns caught up in the white man's newest racial caste system, which Alexander wants them to be.

In addition, she needs to recognize that articulated beliefs sometimes bear no resemblance whatsoever to actual behavior. The stigma and scorn she believes is so detrimental to a criminal's progress could actually, when sufficiently intense, make them think twice about committing a crime. But

---

‡ In prison, most inmates refer to the crime they were convicted of as something they "caught." This false perception is very similar to Alexander's description of criminal records as things that just happen to people like infectious diseases. This is especially troubling because she professes a belief in free will.

when you come up like L.T. and D.E. did, there is no shame or stigma, only congratulations for "keepin' it real" in this "white man's world."

D.E. and others I have met with his background eventually figure out that their peers and even their parents were leading them in the wrong direction. Unfortunately, this normally comes after they have been sentenced to so much time they will in all likelihood take their last breath in a prison infirmary. Shame and scorn have been around a long time for a reason.

Claim 5: Illegitimacy Caused by War on Drugs

Alexander starts Chapter 5 ridiculing Bill Cosby, President Obama, and Louis Farrakhan for criticizing black fathers for abandoning their children at such high rates. She claims the reason over 70 percent of black children are born out of wedlock is because of a "massive federal program known as the war on drugs."[129] She is half right. The high rate of illegitimacy amongst Blacks may be traced to a 'massive federal program'—but not the war on drugs.

According to the U.S. Bureau of the Census, in 1960, only 22 percent of black children aged 18 or younger lived with a single parent. By 1970, this number had increased 8 points to 30 percent. By1980, it had risen to 44 percent. And in 1995, at the height of the war on drugs, 52 percent of black children lived with a single mother.[130] These numbers demonstrate that from 1960-1980—before the war on drugs began—there was a much larger increase—from 22 to 44 percent—than seen between 1980-1995, when the 'New Jim Crow' was presumably raging.

The percentage of black children living with only their mother doubled from 1960 to 1980, years in which unprecedented sums of tax-payer money were spent on government programs designed to address poverty, crime and racism. In contrast, the increase was only 15 percent between 1980–1995, the war-on-drug years during which Alexander claims black fathers "did not walk out on their families voluntarily; they were taken away in handcuffs."[131] So if the 20 years prior to the war on drugs/ Reagan administration saw an increase of 100 percent in single parent homes, and the 15 years after an increase of only 15 percent, logic dictates that America double down on whatever President Reagan was doing and get as far away as possible from what LBJ, Nixon, Ford, and Carter were doing if they wish to slow the rise of black single motherhood.

Alexander insists, "Racial minorities were always overrepresented among current and ex-offenders" but that the "criminal justice system was marginal to communities of color" until the war on drugs began.[132] This statement about racial minorities is misleading. As usual, she conveniently forgets Asians of Chinese and Japanese descent, and Blacks of West Indian origins, who have lower crime rates than whites. She also leaves out the fact that the Irish in the mid 1800s, had incarceration rates much higher than average even though they were white. As for the criminal justice system being less involved in poor neighborhoods, the fact that it was less involved when the crime rate was much higher than it is today ought to tell her something.

While he was serving as the general counsel for the NAACP, Thomas Atkins made the following statement about crime in black communities: "[It] destroys our businesses and hinders our ability to organize politically because people won 't come out at night. It drives down the value of the property in our communities and undercuts the possibility of economic development."[133]

Proportionally, no group of people was harmed more by the increase in crime than poor Blacks. In 1993, 86 percent of all murders committed by black criminals were against black victims. In that same year, 51 percent of black rapists and 53 percent of black robbers also chose black victims.[134] Since over a decade of War on Poverty and Great Society programs specifically designed to get at the root causes of crime had failed to even slow, much less stop or reverse the rising crime rate, it should come as no surprise that people were ready to try something different. Something different turned out to be more police involvement in 'communities of color.'

Alexander tells us: "To be a black man is to be thought of as a criminal... a social pariah... but as a white criminal you are not a racial outcast.... Whiteness mitigates crime, whereas blackness defines the criminal..." and "the conflation of blackness with crime did not happen organically, rather, it was constructed by political and media elite's as part of the grand project known as the War on Drugs."[135]

I have already related my personal experience which tells me Blacks aren't viewed as "social pariah[s]" once they obtain criminal records. A study involving adolescent offenders in a New Jersey penal institution "measured the expected value of crime to each inmate and the extent to which each one identified with leading a life of crime."[136] They found that:

> Even though black and white inmates were of about the same age and economic background and had comparable careers, they differed greatly

in the relationship between their own sense of self-worth and their criminal prospects. As the expected value of crime increases, the self-esteem of the black inmates also increased, but that of the white inmates decreased. The more the white inmates identified with the criminal class, the less self-esteem they had, but this was not the case for Blacks.[137]

The researchers reasoned that in order for whites to become criminals they "must traverse a greater moral and psychological distance than Blacks making the same choice."[138] To put it another way, black inmates felt far less inner turmoil when they considered committing a crime than white inmates. I believe the reason for this is belief in propaganda like that in the *New Jim Crow*. This book works to convince even the most determined black kid in the ghetto to give up and become my new cellmate because the white man will never allow him to succeed anyway.

The claim that the media and politicians conspired to make "blackness" synonymous with crime would be laughable if I did not know that it would trickle down to Lil' Red, Lil' Black, and Lil' Lil' through some movie or rap song and give them another reason to give up and become a criminal.

Dennis Prager makes a related point:

Nothing dulls the conscience quite like regarding oneself and/or one's group as victims. The vast majority of violent criminals believe they are victims of society, poverty, racism, etc. Islamic terrorists see themselves as victims of the West's alleged "war on Islam." Germans in the 1930s saw themselves as victims of the Versailles Treaty.[139]

The reason women sometimes clutch their purses when they see a young black male on the street is because amongst people under the age of 19, 67 percent of those charged with robbery are black; as are 58 percent of those charged with murder, and 43 percent of those charged with auto-theft.[140] The human brain evolved to solve the problems of hunter-gatherers like avoiding injury during the hunt. No matter how politically incorrect it is to say so, as was once the case with the Irish, black males commit three to six times the crimes as their percentage of the population dictates.

If Asian grandmothers committed 15 percent of all robberies, even though they were only about 3 percent of the population, women would start clutching their purses when they passed through China town or entered a sushi bar. Even Reverend Jackson has said "there is nothing more painful to me...than to walk down the street and hear footsteps and start thinking about robbery—then look around and see somebody white and feel relieved." I imagine being brutally assaulted and then robbed would actually be more painful but what do I know?

In short, 'blackness,' whatever that is, only defines the criminal because Blacks offend at much higher rates than everyone else, not because of some racist social construct created by the media and President Reagan.

"Studies have shown that joblessness—not race or black culture—explains the high rates of violent crimes in poor black communities," says Alexander. And also, "when researchers have controlled for joblessness, differences in violent crime rates between young black and white men disappear."[141] In the next chapter she adds, "If and when crime rates rise—which seems likely if the nation's economy continues to sour—nothing would deter politicians from making black and brown criminals, once again, their favorite whipping boys."[142] In 1967, LBJ's Presidents Crime Commission told us that, "'warring on...unemployment is warring on crime."[143]

These are all beliefs widely held by those in the clique. But as Stephen and Abigail Thernstom pointed out:

> Black crime exploded in the 1960s, a decade in which black incomes rose rapidly and black poverty rates dropped rapidly. If "a civil rights law is a law against crime," the landmark civil rights and voting rights acts of 1964 and 1965 certainly should have sent the crime rate plunging. Furthermore, Blacks received a disproportionate share of the benefits from the social programs of the great society because they represented a disproportionate share of the poverty population, but that did not stop the wave of black crime. Since the 1960s African Americans have continued to make progress on most economic and social measures; that progress has done nothing to drive their crime rate down to lower levels.[144]

When it comes to crime rates being the same amongst jobless white and black males, Alexander wrongly assumes that correlation equals causation. She fails to recognize that people who do not have the desire and/or ability to stick with a job—possibly because of an impulsive personality—are more prone to taking risks, which often come in the form of crimes. Alexander also thinks that crime rates will rise if the economy continues to 'sour.'

However, fellow clique member and columnist Richard Cohen wrote in a 2011 piece, "...crime is not committed by good people who lose their jobs. It is committed by criminals who never had a job in the first place.... Robbers don't rob because they're out of work; they rob because robbery is the kind of work they do." In support of these statements, Cohen mentions that robberies declined across the U.S. by 9.5 percent after the Great Recession, and that violent crime overall was reaching a 40 year low.[145]

Unemployment amongst young black males has been at all-time highs since 2008. Yet violent crime rates have dropped. So, "mass incarceration" has caused the crime rates to go down, and/or unemployment rates have little to do with crime. Neither of these facts bode well for two of Alexander's most important arguments. Moreover, I have never heard a fellow inmate say he chose a life of crime because he could not find a job. Never.

CLAIM 6: COLORBLINDNESS CAUSES HARM

Chapter 5 is titled, "The Fire This Time," which Alexander adapted from the similarly titled book by James Baldwin which she describes as "one of the most extraordinary books ever written."[146] In this chapter she claims that colorblindness is wrong, and that the criminal justice system "is better designed to create crime and a perpetual class of people labeled criminals, rather than to eliminate crime." Also, that only 3 to 25 percent of the reduction in crime can be attributed to "mass incarceration" in spite of it "costing nearly 200 billion annually."[147] And, lastly, Alexander tells us that, "The striking reluctance of whites in particular, to talk about or even acknowledge race has led many scholars and advocates to conclude that we would be better off not talking about race at all."[148]

Blinded By Color

Alexander says she is opposed to colorblindness because "the systematic mass incarceration of people of color would not have been possible in the post-civil rights era if the nation had not fallen under the spell of a callous colorblindness."[149] Instead of colorblindness, she says society should be committed to "color consciousness." This struck me as sounding a lot like the Reverend Jessie Jackson's "color aware" standard. Her reason for believing "race consciousness should be the rule in perpetuity"[150] is that, "for the foreseeable future, racial and ethnic inequality will be a feature of American life…" and "colorblindness will cause society to "look the other way and deny our public agencies the resources, data and tools they need to solve"[151] the inequality problem.

In other words, there are non-whites who are not doing as well as whites. This is the fault of whites. To remedy this problem we must treat non-whites as victims, and give large amounts of money to the government for redistribution.

This line of thinking runs into trouble very quickly. Americans of

Chinese and Japanese descent do better than Caucasians in practically every category used to measure success in America. They are more likely to have a college degree, be self-employed, get approved for a loan, and earn higher incomes than whites. The Blacks from the British West Indies look identical to American Blacks yet have rates of poverty and incarceration similar to those of whites.

Any sane person should recognize the large scale discrimination black Americans faced for centuries in America. Slavery and racism has hindered the black community's accumulation of wealth and its overall progress. However, how do we accurately determine which poor black people are poor because of discrimination and which are poor because of their own mistakes or attitudes? Should white people today be held responsible for things other whites did before they were even on the planet? Holding Caucasians responsible for slavery or something Bull Conner did, because they share the same skin pigment—through no fault of their own—is like saying that it is okay to lock up a black male for a crime he did not commit so long as the perpetrator was also black. No sane person would consider this fair.

Alexander and the rest of the clique endorse the politics of identity, yet they speak against racial profiling? The color conscious/color aware standard instructs us to see victims in need of reparations every time we see a black person. How is that different from an employer assuming that a convicted felon is probably not worth his time and money to train because recidivism is almost 70 percent? If we are to assume all Blacks are victims even though some are descendants of 'freed Blacks,' then why not assume all criminals are unworthy of a second chance since almost 70 percent re-offend anyway?

The philosophy that requires its followers to wrap themselves in a mantle of victimhood masks a limiting nature. Clique members believe that giving "people of color" a shared sense of community by way of vicarious suffering makes those victims more powerful. (And in today's hyper-politically correct society where you are taught not to question or criticize anyone who is a non-white male, they are partially right.) But this faux camaraderie is based on a vision, not actual shared suffering, which leaves it hollow and wanting; [152] an emotional house of cards from an artificially indignant deck.

So the clique is telling Caucasians, "Look at non-whites as being unequal to you. Look at them as being unequal because they were hurt or dispossessed of something." However, promoting this view, when an individual has not gone through the actual trauma, incentivizes them to identify as such, since they are receiving benefits (e.g. affirmative action) without having to endure the actual injustices. "The politics of identity in fact reaffirm difference at the very moment when we are trying to establish equality, and lead, in the name of antiracism, back to the old commitments connected with race or ethnicity."[153]

The very reason for the civil rights movement and all of its righteous struggle was to make sure Blacks were treated as equals. The color conscious standard reverses all the progress made towards that end and trivializes the bloodshed that progress required. So instead of viewing Blacks as inferior, you are now supposed to view them as victims, and award them damages ex post facto to arbitrarily selected heirs, according to the whims of "racial justice" advocates. This means every non-white baby born enters life with a collection of theoretical injustices[154] the clique will command him to capitalize upon.

If he does not take advantage of these inherited privileges? He is to be castigated as a sell-out, an Uncle Tom. And just as Blacks are stereotyped as victims under this clique-approved form of generalization, whites have been issued an identity as well: Privileged Oppressors.

So this is what we have: Permanent grievances that time will not be allowed to heal even slightly. Even though those wounds were opened long ago by another generation, they are constantly renewed artificially. Telling kids to be "aware" or "conscious" of their peer's skin color because their forefathers were enslaved by their classmates forefathers[155]—especially when you distort the history of slavery like Alexander does—is a recipe for disaster—unless you wish to live like I do. It encourages a tribal mindset by accentuating our differences, real or perceived. It increases polarization and ensures the arrival of ethnic political parties like we learned about in chapter one.

Alexander believes color blindness keeps 'public agencies' from getting enough taxpayer money to 'solve' the "problem" of different groups having different levels of success. She proffers no evidence in support of her claim that different races, having evolved in different parts of the world, should have achieved the same levels of success in different endeavors.[156] As we already saw in Chapters 3 and 4, the track record for government programs is abysmal.

There are simple, banal, though emotionally unsatisfying, explanations for the differences in group achievement levels. Consider the beer industry in America. Anheuser-Busch dominates it. German immigrants started the company. They did not come to America and "dispossess" some other group and then 'corner the market.' They merely made a product people came to prefer over the competition. They were able to do this because they came equipped with the skills necessary to farm and brew beer as they had been doing in Germany for centuries.

Other examples of certain ethnic groups dominating certain industries include:

- Scottish tradespersons making 80 percent of "the worlds sugar processing machinery" in the early 1900s;
- People of Japanese descent, holding "91 percent of all green grocers licenses in Vancouver, Canada;"
- Jewish people making up over 50 percent of all medical doctors in Hungary during the 1920's while only constituting 6 percent of the population.[157]

On the other hand, in the 1400s, on the Canary Islands, there were white people living at a "stone age level."[158] Another group of people that trailed in technological advancement because of their seclusion was sub-Saharan Africans.

Most societies advance by borrowing technology from other societies. But "in addition to having many geographic barriers limiting their access to the peoples and cultures of other lands, sub-Saharan Africans also faced internal geographic barriers limiting their access to each other. The resulting internal cultural fragmentation is indicated by the fact that, while Africans are only about 10 percent of the world's population, they have one-third of the world's languages."[159]

> Why are different groups so disproportionately represented in the first place? Perhaps the simplest answer is that there was no reason to have expected them to be statistically similar in the first place. Geographical, historical, demographic, cultural, and other variables make the vision of an even or random distribution of groups one without foundation.[160]

Alexander and the rest of the clique assume omniscience and declare all disparities have been caused by discrimination. However, even in racially homogeneous societies, where there was no discrimination, the same disparities—whether in income, education, or wellness—have materialized. This has long been the case between Eastern and Western Europe, where as recently as 2002, the majority of countries in Eastern Europe had per capita earnings 50 percent below their Western European counterparts.[161] This is a gap much larger than the one between black and white Americans.

We should ask, when considering the different levels of achievement amongst racial and ethnic minorities in America, what the particular groups would have achieved but for the discrimination. For instance, what else might the Chinese or Japanese immigrants have accomplished had they not been excluded by law and labor unions from so many jobs or been thrown into internment camps during World War II—causing many to lose their homes and employment. Although we know discrimination retarded their progress, Americans of Japanese and Chinese descent do better in most regards than the 'privileged whites' in America's supposedly insidious, Euro-centric society. They do not "own the means of production" or large tracts of land with mineral rights. Nor did they inherit all of their assets, as clique members wrongly believe all successful white people do. Like the Germans, the Japanese came to America with cultural elements that helped them succeed where others had failed.

So imagine if you will, sub-Saharan Blacks arriving in America as immigrants (not slaves) during one of the great immigration waves. They would have no ability to farm and brew like the Germans, or be middlemen like many Jews. They would have been coming from an arid culture that would have prepared them no better for life in America than Theodore Roosevelt's upbringing would have prepared him for living on the Serengeti. We know the discrimination faced by many Blacks throughout history has impeded their progress. Yet assuming racism is the cause of some groups doing better than others because of mere statistical disparities has become "the reigning non sequitur of our time."[162]

Throw Away The Prison, Not The Key

Next, Alexander tells us that the current criminal justice system is basically a waste of time. At best, she says it is only responsible for 25 percent of the current crime rate reduction. Also, she claims the law of diminishing returns is starting to kick in because we have reached a "tipping point." Neighborhoods are now unstable because so many men are locked up, leading to more crime. Prisons cost too much to operate and as a crime reduction strategy, have failed.[163]

Crime Rate Reduction

First of all, the evidence is overwhelming. Locking up more criminals for longer periods of time reduces the crime rate. This has been the case even in societies not tainted by 'proponents of racial hierarchy' and their diabolical schemes to oppress 'people of color.' For example, Australia and New Zealand both saw a reduction in their crime rates after an increase in their incarceration rates.[164]

Almost simultaneously, Britain experienced the exact opposite. They went from having one of the lowest crime rates in the world, to exceeding the notoriously high rate of crime in the United States.[165] Britain's criminal justice system had adopted many of the same notions about incarceration Alexander holds.

Not long after World War II, a young man from Singapore named Lee Kuan visited London. He was immediately struck by how well mannered and lawful the city's people were, which could not have contrasted more sharply with his homeland and its teeming crime and poverty. Years after this revelatory visit, Lee became a leader in Singapore. He implemented a set of rules similar to what he saw in London. This transformed his country, causing the crime rate to plummet and the economy to flourish. Indeed, towards the end of the 1990s, Singapore had 693 crimes per 100,000 people compared with England's 10,000 per 100,000 people.[166] Per capita, England had 14 times as many crimes as Singapore.

A multitude of studies have shown that in states where the likelihood of going to prison for a crime is high, the crime rate is lower than that of states where the inverse is true. In fact the connection between certain punishment and crime is better established than that between poor "economic conditions" and crime.[167]

Draft dodging, for example, was a problem during the Vietnam War. Just ask the 42nd President of the United States. The states in which draft dodgers were most likely to come to prison had lower rates of evasion. I use the example of draft dodgers because the effect of fear of the punishment on criminal behavior does not always show up in studies of less severe offenses. The government may decide not to prosecute low level criminals and because of this, the data can give a misleading impression.[168]

A study involving 2,000 prisoners from California, Texas, and Michigan had similar results. The inmates were asked if they thought they could commit the same crime again and avoid being apprehended. At the time, criminals in Texas were more likely to go to prison for a given crime than offenders in Michigan and California. Predictably, the California inmates, even though their crimes were actually more severe than those of the Texas inmates, were over twice as likely to believe they could get away with the same crimes were they to commit them again.[169]

A study involving spousal abuse showed the same pattern. Offenders who were arrested and put in jail (for only 48 hours or less) were not as likely to have the police call on them again as were offenders given counseling or other alternatives to incarceration.[170] This is very telling because the conventional wisdom on spousal abuse is the people become so angry and emotional that they cannot think; ergo, punishment will not have a deterrent effect on them in the future. This study proves otherwise.

In prison, the 'tough on crime' approach works. While I hate to give the administration any credit, their reform measures to reduce crime in here have worked. When I first got locked up in the late nineties, stabbings were much more common. What has changed? Today a virtual guarantee exists that you will have an additional sentence to serve, resulting in a much longer stay in prison, if you stab someone. Nowadays, even if they do not recover the weapon or have inmates willing to cooperate and testify against an assailant, he will probably be charged and offered a plea-bargain anyway. If he decides to go to trial, an eager-to-convict jury ready to believe anything any corrections officer with a pulse tells them, will be waiting to serve 'justice.'

Is that fair? Perhaps not. And no one, especially yours truly, wants to see someone convicted of a crime they did not commit. My point here is simply this. Once the certainty of prosecution increased, the number of stabbings decreased.

During the summer of 2011, I clearly remember the day when an inmate walked into the dayroom§ after attending a court hearing that Monday. He announced that he had just been offered 60 years for having a cell-phone on another unit. Guys went to howling in disbelief, saying they would never mess with cell-phones, the most sought after piece of prison contraband, again. For some, that will be enough. For others, the more impulsive inmates with shorter time horizons in particular, no amount of punishment will deter them.

The fact that incarceration does not work as a deterrent on all offenders gives the clique enough reason to scrap the entire system. They will never admit it, but they are looking for a panacea they will never find. Like the philosopher Edmund Burke and countless others have pointed out, there are

---

§　In the Arab world, they have 'the street.' In prison, we have the 'dayroom.' Inmates gather there to socialize, fight, watch TV, and slam—i.e. play dominoes.

no solutions to some of life's problems, only trade offs. This does not mean we should be accepting of everything and never attempt to make improvements. It does however mean that society should focus on what works, what has a proven track record. Regardless of whether the reduction in crime rates is 3 or 25 percent, we know from multiple sources, if done right, punishment will deter. Better to go with the best trade off than to continue in vain, the gratifying quest for some chimera, especially when people's lives are at stake.

Impact on Community

Alexander argues that the criminal justice system has locked up so many people it now causes more crime than it prevents. She says that incarceration is "ripping apart fragile social networks, destroying families, and creating a permanent class of unemployables."[171] Her first contention is basically that once you lock up so many people, you begin to lock up less and less prolific offenders, and therefore get fewer bangs for your incarceration buck.

But as we have already seen, the clique-approved JFA institute has calculated that only 3 percent of violent and property criminals ever even go to prison.[172] This means that the majority of those getting locked up, especially since clearance rates are much lower than they used to be, must be very prolific offenders.

Her next point, that locking up people destroys families and the communities they live can only be supported partially. Consider D.E. and his brother. Although the horrific circumstances he and his brother grew up in are not the norm even for high-rate offenders, it is beyond argument that having their abusive, ex-con father tell them the cops were the bad guys contributed to their delinquency.

The types of crimes one has to commit to be sent to prison (with a few exceptions) normally demonstrate that these individuals are incapable of being a good father or husband. Having these types of people locked up helps families more than it hurts them. And poor black neighborhoods benefit the most from tough-on-crime policies because such a large proportion of crimes are committed there.

Consider the Gallup/Newsweek poll in 1992, when crime rates were much higher than they are now, showing that 91 percent of black respondents placed crime at the top of their list of problems. A subsequent poll asked, "Which issues [do] you think are important for the Presidential candidates to discuss and debate?" Ninety-two percent of Blacks answered that crime was "very important." This very real and legitimate fear of crime, not only makes many Blacks "afraid all the time"[173] as a woman in Los Angeles put it, it also causes employers to think twice about setting up shop in such high crime areas, decreasing employment opportunities for those who need them most.

Costs Outweigh Benefits

Finally, Alexander claims that the cost of the prison system outweighs its benefits. She says that spending $200 billion a year on incarceration is too much and that in some states more Blacks are going to prison than college. She fails to site her source for the $200 billion price tag. However, in 2008, the New York Times had an article that claimed, "The 50 states last year spent about 44 billion in tax dollars on corrections, up from nearly 11 billion in 1987.[174] I do not know what the federal system costs, but as I have previously mentioned, it only holds 12 percent of the nation's inmates. Therefore, I find it very hard to believe that it could make up the difference between Alexander's $200 billion figure and the one quoted by the clique's paper of record.

A good question to ask when considering whether or not the prison system costs too much is what would it cost the taxpayers if criminals were allowed to roam free? One calculation showed that in America it costs $10,000 a year more than to keep them locked up. A similar estimate for England put the annual cost of their corrections system at $1.9 billion, and the cost of their criminal's yearly crimes at a total of 60 billion Euros.[175]Any hedge fund manager not in prison for a ponzi scheme would sell his soul for those rates of return. Just ask George Soros, Alexander. The fact that more black males have put themselves in Illinois prisons instead of its universities is heartbreaking. But Alexander, who remember, believes we have free will, makes it sound as if the state—it's legislators and citizens— just up and decided to send so many black males to prison and so many to college. She seems to have no idea whatsoever that the type of person who excels academically and can get into college is totally different from a personality standpoint than the high-rate offenders who end up in prison.

Why would anyone assume these very different groups of people and their numbers should be compared? They could not be more dissimilar and unconnected. (The next chapter will delve deeper into the common denominators amongst criminals who end up in prison.) As she does throughout the book, Alexander again makes it sound as if a criminal record is something that just happens to black males somehow. If states could simply choose between sending black males to college or prison, they would certainly choose the former.

Think about how much more income tax revenue the state's politicians could collect if all black males in a state were college graduates. Prison expenses, amongst other budgetary expenses, keep legislators from passing their favorite laws: Pay raises for legislators.

Most people will dismiss the dubious comparison of college students with prison inmates as quickly as they would the comparison of selling crack and drunk driving. And a breakdown in the ability of a lawyer like Alexander to reason coherently would normally, for someone like myself who was screwed over royally by the justice system, be cause for amusement. But this bogus, yet very incendiary claim, has already made its way into at least one rap song by Lil' Wayne, which guarantees a bunch of black kids who also have Lil' affixed in front of their names will say something along the lines of: "yeah my nigga, Lil' Wayne speakin' the truth. Them white folks ain't gon' never letta nigga have nothin'! Might as well hit this lick cause they gon' lock us up anyway."

They then do what clique members tell them is logical when trapped in a white man's racist, unjust world. They go to the local "stop and rob" and demonstrate how these establishments acquired such monikers. Lastly, they pull up to this bar-b-que where I reside, and one of the worst self-fulfilling prophecies ever conceived is fulfilled. Way to go Alexander, Pitts, and the rest of the clique. White supremacists everywhere are tipping their hats to you for a job well done. Your proliferation of the narrative is truly a root cause of crime.

Inheritable Guilt

Like many in the clique, Alexander says that white people do not like talking about race. To buttress this claim, she enlists the following quote from President Obama's book, *The Audacity of Hope*.

> Rightly or wrongly, white guilt has largely exhausted itself in America; even the most fair minded of whites, those who would genuinely like to see racial inequality ended and poverty relieved, tend to push back against racial-victimization—or race specific claims based on the history of race discrimination in this country.[176]

Alexander says further, "We need to talk about race openly and honestly... People must come to understand the racial history and origins of mass incarceration…" and that "finally we must admit out loud, that it was *because* of race that we didn't care much about what happened to 'those people' and imagined the worst possible things about them"[177] (emphasis hers). There are plenty of white people willing to talk about race; Jonah Goldberg, John Stossal, Michael Shermer, just to name a few. The problem is that most of them do not agree with the clique's premises and conclusions, and in turn are summarily dismissed as racists.

I have not read *The Audacity of Hope*, President Obama's second memoir. I have however read his first, *Dreams From My Father*, and I understand most of his views because I held them myself well into my twenties. His statement above is classic. Right out of the gate he tells us that white guilt is no longer what it once was. He qualifies this with "rightly or wrongly" in an attempt, as politicians often do, to make what comes next seem measured and unbiased.

Because I have not read *Audacity of Hope*, I do not know the context of President Obama's statement, however I am certain of why Alexander quoted it. She believes that white guilt is necessary in order to bring about "A radical restructuring of our society,"[178] which is, for her and the rest of the clique, the only way to end the "New Jim Crow." Make white people feel guilty enough, and they will give up even more money to government agencies which will then redistribute it to non-whites; and make sure that all those white CEO's do not make more than some predetermined multiple of their black workers' incomes.

I find this notion, in light of the evidence, bewildering. It is somewhat like me telling Alexander to feel guilty about the fact that 89 percent of interracial crimes are committed by Blacks against whites.[179] Personally, I do not think she should, since she is a lawyer and not a black criminal who committed a crime against a white person. And even if she were, she should only feel guilty about the particular crime she committed, and the injury caused to particular individual she committed it against.

If a white person today keeps a black person from getting a job or a place to live because of their skin color, I hope they feel guilty. No other white person however is on the hook that reprehensible act, just as Alexander and Pitts are not on the hook for something any other black person not named Michele Alexander or Leonard Pitts Jr. has done.

Judging from her endorsement of 'public agencies' and their ability to help poor black people, we can be sure that Alexander has never given much thought to whether or not white guilt is in reality a good thing for black people. Even though it is undoubtedly good for the clique from an emotional standpoint—"we really stuck it to those patriarchal asleep-at-the-wheel white folks"—white guilt was an unmitigated disaster for Blacks from a social policy standpoint. As Berkley Professor John McWhorter, who happens to be black has said, "The expansion of welfare created more black misery than any number of brutal policemen, white thugs yelling nigger, real estate agents turning black applicants away, or white teachers not calling on black boys in school."[180]

Especially puzzling is the way Alexander wants contemporary black criminals to be forgiven and accepted but yet wants contemporary whites to feel guilty about slavery and the real Jim Crow. There is of course, no comparison between enslaving and selling drugs. But the slave owners are no longer with us, and since we are not holding the children of drug dealers responsible for their parent's crimes, we ought not hold the great, great etc. grandchildren of slave owners responsible for slavery either.

The clique will point out that the drug dealer "did his time," while the slave owner went unpunished. And for the most part, this is true. However much of the South was destroyed during the civil war, and as we saw above, according to the JFA Institute, plenty of criminals do not get locked up.

Pitts recommends the book *Been in the Storm So Long*. It recounts several tales of the complete destruction of slave owner's plantations and even situations where some slave masters, male and female, were whipped by former slaves. The author tells us these instances were exceptional and "isolated."[181]

I do not know whether or not that translates to 3 percent, and it is immaterial anyway. You cannot tit-for-tat with totally different flesh and blood human beings over a period of hundreds of years. Nor is the total destruction of black criminals measurable.

Intertemporal Abstractions

President Obama's statement also includes "even the most fair minded whites... tend to push back against racial victimization—or race specific claims based on the history of race discrimination in this country."[182] As usual, it is 'the history' argument dealing with what Dr. Sowell calls Intertemporal abstractions:

> ...in the United States today, where issues of group 'reparations' have been raised—reparations to Blacks for slavery or to the indigenous American Indian population for the dispossession of their ancestors and the collateral damage that went with it. Here again the issue encompasses

what can be called intertemporal group abstractions, rather than simply flesh-and-blood contemporaries...it remains painfully clear that these people who were torn from their homes in Africa in centuries past and forcibly brought across the Atlantic in chains suffered not only horribly but unjustly. Were they and their captors still alive, the reparations and the retribution owed would be staggering, Time and death, however, cheat us of such opportunities for justice, however galling that may be.[183]

Intertemporal abstractions not only facilitate taking sides, such abstractions can also facilitate moral equivalence, such as that between people who committed atrocities against the defenseless and those whose only offense is being born descended from people who committed evil acts in the past.[184]

'Inter' means between or among. 'Temporal' means pertaining to time. 'Abstract' means a thought apart from reality—unspecific and theoretical.

When civil rights leader X says, "We've been oppressed for 400 years!" he is referring to inter-temporal abstractions, and not actual black people. This statement is made in such a manner to induce white guilt—a goal common to most civil rights leaders today. These types of remarks were instrumental in causing bloodshed in countries as different as Sri Lanka and Nigeria, as we learned in the first chapter.[185]

Intertemporal abstractions can breed envy and the belief that "strong group solidarity"[186] is required in order for their chosen side to win. Alexander strongly encourages group solidarity amongst Blacks when she calls for "solidarity with the least among us."[187] The 'least' are black criminals who mostly commit their crimes against other Blacks. And remember, Blacks only become criminals "when work disappears"—which means they are not to blame for their crimes—the white business owners who moved their factories overseas are. Racism is also to blame when Blacks get arrested for drug crimes.

This view creates a significant problem. When you blame 'greed' and racism for crimes you commit instead of yourself, it mitigates strongly against behavioral change. It also keeps others from judging a criminal as harshly as they probably should.

One of the most important actions the impoverished Chinese and Jewish immigrants took when they came to America was their refusal to shelter criminals in their ranks. For example, Chinese immigrant leaders in San Francisco encouraged police officers to not spare the lash when dealing with the Chinese criminals in their midst. Some of these immigrants were so gung-ho about dealing with the crime problem amongst "their own" they took the law into their own hands, "for the gagged bodies of some of these criminals were found floating in San Francisco Bay."[188]

In contrast, Gunner Myrdal said over 50 years ago that American Blacks would "protect any Negro from the whites even when they happen not to like that individual Negro."[189] Solidarity along ethnic lines for ethnicity's sake creates the wrong constraints and incentives for individual behavior within any group seeking advancement. You see this progress-hindering form of solidarity surrounding the domestic abuse case of singer Chris Brown and murder trial of O.J. Simpson. It tells the potential woman batterer, "We don't care if you're wrong. You're black, and the last thing we'll do is agree with the white folks about your behavior." In other words, this extreme form of group solidarity, combined with blaming criminality on white people's greed and racism, lowers the standards for Blacks, while simultaneously worsening the opinions held by other people about Blacks.

Intertemporal abstractions, like many other cogs in the narrative created to induce white guilt, can cause even the educated and successful to indulge in victimhood and grievance transferal—seeing history as a record of events, which require taking sides.

In President Obama's first memoir, *Dreams From My Father*, he wrote about a man named Mr. Foster, a business owner and president of a local chamber of commerce. Mr. Foster says, in regards to why black merchants will not work long hours like other business owners, "I guess we worked so long for nothing, we feel like we shouldn't have to break our backs just to survive."[190] Obviously, Mr. Foster was never a slave, working for free. Nor has any black person living in America today had to do so.

It is troubling that someone successful enough to become president of a chamber of commerce would attempt to ally himself with actual slaves, however, it is no longer surprising. It seems the emotional satisfaction derived from seeing oneself as the ultimate underdog/victim is apparently more rewarding than reality, even when reality reflects successful business ownership.

Later in the same book, Obama tells us it is difficult for black businesses to succeed because of "… the barriers to entry, the lack of finance, the leg up that your competitors possessed after having kept you out of the game for over three hundred years."[191] The barriers to entry, as we saw in Chapter Three, are the regulations and licensing fees—the domain of democrats like Obama. Lack of finance is a problem for most everyone trying to start a business. Established brands make it hard for anyone to 'get a leg up' with any product or service. Nor has any flesh and blood human being been around for 300 years, continually trying to market some product. These problems are not exclusive to black people.

It is interesting to note the actual failed product that had Obama waxing intertemporally: A toothpaste made by Louis Farrakhan's Nation of Islam. No, that is not a joke. The success of Mr. Foster and the education of President Obama are no match for the shot of dopamine their brains give them every time they confirm a belief, even one as half-baked as this involving intertemporal abstraction.

In 2008, Tamara Douglass, a black high school teacher from Springfield Illinois, became distraught upon learning that a racial riot between Blacks and whites had taken place there in 1908. She said, "I was angry. I found it hypocritical that in this town, it's all about Lincoln. We want to embrace him. Then you find... this is who we are. This is Springfield."[192] This is a woman with at least a bachelor's degree. Yet somehow, she manages to connect Abraham Lincoln—who died in 1865—to a race riot in 1908, and herself and other current residents of Springfield in 2008.

Howard Zinn's *A People's History of The United States* is seen as a legitimate history text in many colleges today. This approach to history teaches students to view events in the past as moral Rorschach tests, which all good and virtuous seekers of racial justice must make similar pronouncements upon. No objectivity is allowed. The riot that happened in Springfield was bad. Springfield is where Lincoln is from. Springfield, Lincoln, and Springfield's current residents are therefore all bad because this riot happened.

In this approach, Ms. Douglass cannot look at Springfield as a typical town with a typical history of triumphs and failures. To do so would deny her the opportunity to be allied with 'the good guys.' Unfortunately, by connecting individuals and groups who share only one thing in common— Springfield—she makes the 'bad guys' out to be even more insurmountable opponents than they really are. This makes her all the more praiseworthy for taking them on. If you do not become angry like Ms. Douglass at the 'hypocrisy' that is Springfield, you are taking the wrong side of that historical event.

Pitts gets in on the intertemporal abstractions' fun fairly often in his columns. One particular occasion had him lamenting the fact that in California, over 70 percent of Blacks voted for Proposition 8, which banned gay marriage. In another, he mentioned his disappointment over an incident in Buffalo, New York where several black males assaulted a white male for walking his black girlfriend home. Pitts said he could not understand how a people who had been mistreated for so long could turn around and mistreat others in the same manner.[193]

Pitts looks at the black voters in California and sees the same black people that used to be forced to work in the cotton fields or drink from separate water fountains. That is, he engages in grievance transferal. He expects all Blacks today to see themselves as he sees them: enslaved or segregated like those in the past. But they do not all share his vision, because the average black person alive today has not been oppressed. The black people who voted against Proposition 8 do not see themselves as victims of all atrocities, past, present, and future, inflicted upon Blacks. They therefore do not wish to engage in a fellowship of victimhood with their supposed comrades in oppression, homosexuals.

Malcolm X once said that Blacks should not allow white men to walk around black neighborhoods with black women because white men did not allow the inverse. It's unlikely any of the black assailants in Buffalo were ever told they could not date white women. In fact, according to the Census Bureau, when it comes to interracial marriage, black males today are twice as successful at getting white women to marry them as white men are at getting black women to marry them.

These assailants did not live in Malcolm X's time. They, like the black voters in California, have not been mistreated or discriminated against. Pitts however wants to make the racism other Blacks have faced applicable to them simply because they share the same skin pigment.

Pitts ought to ask himself, from where did these black men get their provocation? They surely did not have a cross burned in their yards by the Klan. Nor do the current statistics suggest they are being kept from dating white women. They beat the white man down because he violated the rules they have established for white people. The reason they have such a set of rules is not white racism on their victim's part. Rather they formed their rules because the narrative told them that any and every failure in their lives can be attributed to the 'white man.'

The Pitts and Michelle Alexanders of the world disseminate this narrative. These same people blame something like the shooting in Tucson that left several people dead and a congresswoman severely wounded on Rush Limbaugh (even though the shooter was a fan of Karl Marx). Yet they fail to see all the Barry Buhol Jrs., beltway snipers, and racist thugs in Buffalo they themselves create with their 'victim' narrative.

Summary: Part 1

Black and brown people are not overrepresented in prison. Inmates 'of color,' like all inmates, are representative of the crimes they get caught committing. The majority of people here in prison are here for violent or property crimes, not drug crimes.

Jim Crow laws were applied to the vast majority of Blacks in the South. In contrast, the criminal justice system applies to everyone. And even amongst the demographics with the highest rates of felony conviction — black males aged 20–29 — only about one-third are under the supervision of the criminal justice system.[194]

Jim Crow affected almost every black in the South. In order to be subjected to Jim Crow, you merely had to be born black in the South — something completely out of anyone's control. To get a criminal record, most of the time you have to get caught committing a crime. The use of self-reports as iron-clad evidence that Blacks commit drug crimes at the same rates as whites is dubious at best.[195] Also, conducting a survey of 'households' misses people who are in state youth correctional facilities and living a transient lifestyle. More importantly, the overall percentage of Blacks in prison has increased little since the war on drugs began.

Judging people to be 'oppressed' or 'privileged' according to their skin color is no different than judging them to be superior or inferior according to their skin color. Colorblindness allows for individuality and thus, more freedom and liberty.

The color conscious standard favored by the clique does just the opposite. It restricts everyone to one of two groups: oppressor or oppressed. Acceptance of such a standard increases polarization along racial and ethnic lines. This leads to a populace with a tribalistic mentality like we have in prison.

The New Jim Crow is a fairly slick attempt at inducing white guilt, and it must be taken seriously because such sophistry has often been the impetus for racial upheaval and tumult. The narrative is a fallacy.

> During the 1960s, one neighborhood in San Francisco had the lowest income, the highest unemployment rate, the highest proportion of families with incomes under $4,000 a year, the least educational attainment, the highest tuberculosis rate, and the highest proportion of substandard housing of any area of the city. That neighborhood was called Chinatown. Yet in 1965, there were only five persons of Chinese ancestry committed to prison in the entire state of California.[196]

PART II — INTER-RACIAL CRIME

John Hope Franklin, a historian Pitts recommends, says that the 1998 murder of James Byrd Jr., a black man in Jasper, Texas, by three white men, was "not all that much of an aberration. We have at least several incidents like that every year."[1]

Another professor, Vivian Gordon says, "Black men are a hunted and endangered species. You kill off the mate and leave the woman vulnerable and without a partner. They [whites] have done everything to devastate us by devastating our men."[2]

Reverend Sharpton, after a black teenager was shot and killed by a white male, said he wanted Americans to see the murder for what it was: "A national epidemic" of whites killing Blacks.[3] And the New York Times ran an editorial by a black male who claimed that he was afraid to visit certain areas of New York because he believed there were "gangs of white people just waiting to kill him."[4]

If the murder in Jasper, and all others in which the victim is black and the killer white, is "not all that much of an aberration," then what are we to call the much more common occurrence of Blacks killing whites, and the even more common occurrence of Blacks killing Blacks? In a normal year according to government statistics, about 4 percent of all murders in America are committed by whites against Blacks. The corresponding number for Blacks killing whites ranges from 13 to 20 percent.[5] This means that over 90 percent of all black murder victims are killed by other Blacks. Most people would not consider 4 percent of white on black an "epidemic" level.

Blacks have been murdering whites at 3 to 5 times the rate whites have murdered Blacks for at least half a century. You would never know this from listening to Professors Franklin and Gordon.

The New York Governor's Advisory Committee for Black Affairs (GACBA) also published misleading information when it reported that "racially motivated or targeted violence may arise in the context of organized hate groups such as the Ku Klux Klan, Neo-Nazis, The Order, the Aryan Nation, or others whose purpose or ideology is premised on racist or supremacist ideologies."[6] In spite of all these white supremacist groups, the vast majority of interracial crimes are committed by Blacks against whites.

Inter-Racial Crime

You could add up all the black lives these white supremacists have taken over the years, and it would not come close to the number of Blacks killed by the average black street gang. The few real white supremacists I have met in prison (who actually belong to some organized group) have often told me that when members gather in the free world it is mostly about drinking beer and wondering why they cannot get more girls to attend these classy shindigs. That is, they are not sitting around plotting how to commit genocide on the black race. It's not as Hollywood portrays it.

The GACBA report also gave the opinion of one Dr. Harvey Brenner, a sociologist who claims that when whites commit hate crimes against Blacks, they do so because of "national and regional economic situations, and especially the rates of unemployment [which] represent [the] dominant influence on violence against Minorities."[7]

Dr. Mary Frances Barry, who chaired the U.S. Civil Rights Commission, blames, not economic downturns, but white supremacy for the supposed epidemic levels of white on black violence.[8] She said, "The primary explanation for racially motivated violence against Blacks has been the need of a segment of the white population to preserve its belief in the inferiority of Blacks, and to maintain the social and political subordination of an historically outcast group by any means, including violence."[9]

Based on what Dr. Harvey and Dr. Barry said, white on black crime should have spiked during the Great Recession of 2007 and in response to America's election of its first black President. In spite of these two cataclysmic events, the percentage of crimes by whites against Blacks, according to the FBI, has remained the same.

We have already seen that Blacks murder whites at 3 to 5 times the rate whites murder Blacks. But what about crimes other than murder? Surely the fact that the white population is six times larger then the black population—and racist to its core—would translate to a stratospheric number of white on black offenses. But for whatever reason, this is not the case. When white criminals offend, they only choose black victims 3 percent of the time.[10]

Compare this with black criminals, who choose white victims 45–54 percent of the time. In particular, when whites commit a robbery, only 8 percent of their victims are Blacks. But when Blacks commit a robbery, 64 percent of their victims are white.[11]

Clique members howl that this 'disparity' is the result of whites having all the wealth worth robbing. But when it comes to assault, a crime that normally does not make the perpetrator better off financially, Blacks and whites assail each other interracially at much different rates. Whites commit roughly 3 percent of their assaults against Blacks, while black assailants commit 52 percent of theirs against whites.[12]

According to the FBI, hate crimes that are "anti-white" account tor 63 percent of all hate crimes in America. And when it comes to racially motivated murders, the Southern Poverty Law Center has reported that Blacks commit almost 50 percent of them.[13]

In general, a black person is 50 times more likely to commit a violent crime against a white person than vice versa. Robberies by Blacks of whites occur at 24 times the rate of whites robbing Blacks.[14] These figures come from government agencies that are staffed with left wing bureaucrats. They were not taken from some white supremacist website.

The clique will cry out that no matter how many crimes Blacks commit against whites today, it pales in comparison to the number of crimes whites have committed against Blacks. They will bring up slavery and claim that 100 million black Africans died in the Atlantic slave trade. The problem with this is that, unfortunately, slavery was an accepted institution amongst every race and society on the planet back then. The lopsided interracial crime rate in America however, is (and has been), occurring in our lifetimes.

In addition to slavery, many in the clique will bring up the crime of lynching. As I have already mentioned, lynch mob justice was not an ad hoc creation for Blacks. Billy the Kid, a white criminal, and William Lloyd Garrison, a white abolitionist, narrowly escaped being lynched. When it came to Blacks being lynched by whites, 1896 was the worst year ever. In total, lynch mobs murdered 161 Blacks that year.[15] Before the Civil War, over 90 percent of all people lynched in the South were white.[16] And from 1862–1968, 3446 Blacks were murdered by lynching.[17] The point here is that when Professor Franklin and Reverend Sharpton say that whites killing Blacks is common or an 'epidemic,' their words do not reflect the facts. This is a shameful evasion of responsibility by a renowned historian and 'civil rights' leader.

The crime of rape is no different. After Tawana Brawley's claims of being gang-raped by white cops and members of the Klu Klux Klan turned out to be a hoax, Reverend Saul Williams said "from a historical standpoint.... I have to believe her... America is a rapist of Blacks."[18]

Stanley Diamond, a white anthropologist argued that it was of no consequence if it was a hoax or not, since the issue was a "model of what actually happens to too many black women."[19] Never to miss out on such an occasion, Civil Rights Attorney William Kunstler added that, "because a lot of black women are treated the way she was treated,"[20] it did not matter whether or not Ms. Brawley was telling the truth. Not to be outdone, Ms. Brawley herself, years after the claim was known to be fraudulent, said, "What happened to me happens to hundreds of thousands of women everyday" in America.[21]

More recently, in 2006 another well-publicized gang rape of a black woman by white men also turned out to be a hoax. A black stripper named Chrystal Mangum claimed that several white lacrosse players at Duke University sexually assaulted her. For good measure, she threw in that while they took turns raping her, they used racially offensive language.[22] So not only were they rapists, they were racist white rapists.

Perfect. They were the personification of the narrative after which the clique so relentlessly seeks—the golden ring all clique members are constantly reaching for. Because of this, as was also the case with the election of President Obama, no one vetted the accusations. Before even a shred of actual evidence became available, nearly 100 members of Duke's faculty took out a full-page ad in the Duke University Newspaper. The headline read, "What does a social disaster sound like?" They avowed universal support for Ms. Mangum, without even the presumption of innocence for the accused. A typical passage read, "This is not a different experience for us here at Duke. We go to class with racist classmates, we go to the gym with people who are racist... It's part of the experience."[23] Another line stated, "...the disaster didn't start on March 13, and won't end with what police say or the court decides."[24] In short, racist white men raping black women is a pervasive, timeless problem.

The problem is so pervasive in fact, that like imperialism (*Avatar*),[25] evil white suburbanites (*American Beauty*),[26] and class warfare (*Gangs of New York*)[27] clique members in Hollywood—which is like saying tall guys in the NBA—decided to make a movie about it. So in 1996, they put out *A Time to Kill*,[28] starring eminent clique members Kevin Spacy and Sandra Bullock. The movie is about a young black girl being raped and hung by two white men. After this horrific crime takes place, the victim's father says that just recently, four other white men raped another black girl and got off 'scot free.' He then decides he must kill these two white men, and even though he is apparently poor, he manages to come up with an AR-15 rifle, that in the 1990s would have cost him $600.00 or more, and achieves his goal.

The use of the AR-15 is calculated to condition white movie goers to hate this type of gun as much as clique members do. Showing its use to kill a white person heightens the emotional response against these types of guns and hopefully increases support for gun control policies the white moviegoer would not have embraced before.

On the small screen, you have ad nauseum re-runs of the television show Cold Case.[29] One particular episode set in the 50s or 60s, shows a black woman being gang raped by several of her white boyfriend's equally white friends. As they do this, the white boyfriend just stands there, too scared to do anything. The woman is screaming, but instead of helping her, the cowardly white boyfriend tries to cover her mouth so he does not have to hear her. Doing this ends up smothering her, and she dies because of his cowardice. So a white man suffocated the woman, while white men gang raped her.

I saw two other Cold Case episodes that featured white men being romantically involved with black women. In one (also set in the 50s or 60s), a white man meets a black waitress who he is attracted to. He is ashamed however to be with her in public, because she is black. The other featured a high school couple in the 1990's. The black girl had a father who abused her so the white boyfriend went and killed him. In other words, white males apparently do not make good boyfriends for black women according to Cold Case.

Are these all cases of art imitating life? Does belief in white supremacy cause white men to view black women as less than human and treat them accordingly? Is Duke University history Professor William Chafe correct when he says, "White slave masters were the initial perpetrators of sexual assault on black women, subsequent generations continued the pattern"?

First, it wasn't racist white men who were the initial perpetrators of sexual assault on black women. The original perpetrators were African and Arabic. Thus to say that "subsequent generations continued the pattern" makes it sound as if black women never knew rape before they encountered white people. Do you really think Zulu or Masai warriors did not rape the women of the tribes they conquered as did the Aztecs, British, Mongolians, etc.? And what is this "pattern?"

During slavery a slave master could rape his slaves with impunity. Today, all a woman has to do is call the police and say she was raped by person X, and person X is likely to be arrested. Just ask the former Duke Lacrosse team. These two very different circumstances strip rape today of any pattern.

So just how much of a problem is white-on-black rape? And how do the numbers compare to black-on-white rape?

Inter-Racial Crime

Considering the clique's claims and depictions, whites must rape Blacks at numbers all out of proportion to their percentage of the population. And certainly since Blacks did not own whites in America's past, they must rarely if ever rape whites. To even get close to reality, we have to turn these notions upside down.

- In 1958 and 1960, two studies reported that only 3.6 percent of all rapes were white on black.
- During the 1970s however, black on white rapes occurred at 10 times the rate of white-on-black rapes.
- In 1974, a Denver, Colorado-based study showed 40 percent of all rapes were Blacks raping whites. That same year, not even one case of white on black rape was reported.
- In 1998, there weren't even 10 cases of whites raping Blacks reported across the entire United States. The number of black on white rapes reported however was 9,400.
- In a report issued a few years later, there were over 20,000 white women raped by black men while white men raped 100 black women.[30]
- In 2007, according to an FBI report, black men raped 14,000 white women, while there were no reported cases of white men raping a single black woman.
- The only "pattern" here is that when crimes cross racial lines, they are much more likely to be committed by Blacks against whites than vice versa.

Unfortunately, even though black rapists choose white victims at a rate (59 percent) that is consistent with the rates at which black robbers and assailants also choose white victims, clique members in particular, and black people in general express tremendous skepticism towards rape statistics.

The skeptics believe that white women strongly desire sexual encounters with black men because they are better endowed than white men and that they cannot have these encounters because their friends and family members are all racists, and would ostracize them if they did. So, they supposedly have to sneak around to have sex with the apparently 'privileged' original man. Once in a while they get caught. When this happens—because these white women are really racists too—they lie and claim they were raped.

America Apart

I do not doubt this happens. Women, just like men, are capable of lying. There are also racist people who would ostracize their children, siblings or friends for being in a relationship with someone of a different race. In the 1990s while I was in high school, several of the black females I dated had parents who would not allow them to date white guys. I would have to pick them up at a friend's house, or they would "sneak out." I even had a male friend, A.W., who whenever I gave him a ride home after we finished playing basketball, would tell me to drop him off at the end of his street—not in front of his house—because his father would not tolerate him hanging out with a white guy.

However, even if we agree only for the sake of argument that fully 50 percent of all white women claiming to have been raped by black men are lying, black on white rapes still not only occur at a much higher rate than white on black rapes, the overall number of actual interracial rapes still is greatest for Blacks raping whites. This fact did not stop Tyler Perry from making a movie based on the theme that when white women are caught having sex with black men by their racist fathers, they cry rape.

In *Daddy's Little Girls*,[31] a white woman whose racist father catches them together falsely accuses a very virtuous, hardworking single black father of rape. The man goes to prison, and it almost ruins his chances to be with a wealthy black women because she will not date convicts.

These types of things happen, yet they are portrayed as the rule instead of the exception to it. This causes even more Blacks to believe that they cannot make it in America and intensifies the hatred so many of them already have for white people. Such portrayals of stereotypes, further widens the gulf that separates the races.

If you are still unconvinced that the crime component of the narrative is destructive, consider the actress Gabrieal Union. She had to endure the unimaginably horrific experience of being beaten and raped. She has spoken openly about this in several interviews.[32] The man who raped her happened to be black, and because she believed there were too many Blacks in prison and did not want to contribute to this 'problem,' she was ambivalent about reporting the rape to the authorities.

Think about this for a moment. Miss Union was so sure that the justice system was racist towards, and oppressive of Blacks she considered not reporting the rape because the rapist was black, and she thought there were already too many Blacks in prison. Before you scoff at Miss Union and write her off as an anomaly, consider this. The narrative's message apparently resonates the most amongst college educated Blacks. A poll in 1990 revealed that 67 percent of Blacks who had been to college believed that it "might be true" or absolutely was "true" that, "the government deliberately makes sure that drugs are easily available in poor black neighborhoods in order to harm black people." Blacks with only a high school diploma were less likely to believe such conspiracy theories, at 42 percent.[33]

Fortunately for other women, Miss Union went to the police, and the man who raped her was taken off the street. This is not always the case however when it comes to Blacks dealing with black criminals. Scores of race-based jury nullifications have resulted in numerous black criminals—most of whom committed their crimes against other Blacks—returning to the streets because their jurors bought into the narrative.

In 1995, a report uncovered that black defendants in Bronx, New York, were found 'not guilty' about 50 percent of the time. This is almost triple the nation's average. Similar rates were found in Washington DC where the juries are majority black as well.[34]

The legal arm of the clique endorses this practice of freeing black criminals, by calling it 'black self-help.' George Washington University Law School professor Paul Butler declares, "It is the moral responsibility of black jurors to **emancipate** some guilty black outlaws." (Emphasis mine.) He hoped doing so would "dismantle the master's house with the master's tools."[35] Again a clique member tries to draw equivalence between Blacks in slavery and black criminals today.

The fact that contemporary whites have never owned slaves, never known anyone who owned slaves, or even been alive when slavery existed in America matters none. You have been cursed, white people. You must pay eternally for the sins of your forefathers: while their slavery and oppression were far from unique, you are required to demonstrate a unique form of ad infinitum guilt. And as long as grievances and injustices are heritable and profitable, you will never be allowed to remove this yoke.

Former U.S. Attorney General Eric Holder seems to be a big believer in the proposition that injustices against contemporary whites are legitimate punishment for past injustices against Blacks. He refused to prosecute one of the clearest cases of voter intimidation ever known. On election day in November of 2008, members of the New Black Panther Party, dressed in uniform, stood outside of a polling station in Philadelphia, waving billy clubs and saying things like "A black man is gonna be elected today." They were recorded on a video that also captured their voices. In spite of this overwhelming evidence, Holder refused to prosecute them.

When George Zimmerman killed Trayvon Martin in self-defense, the New Panthers put out a bounty for Zimmerman, saying it could be collected whether Zimmerman was delivered "dead or alive." Bounties like this are federal crimes, yet Holder didn't even issue a warning. The New Panthers were outspoken and confident that they would not be prosecuted by the feds. And why would they not be? Holder himself said that the reason he did not prosecute the New Panthers in Philadelphia was because he believed the Voting Rights Acts were written exclusively for a group of citizens he referred to as "my people."

It should shock the average person that the nation's highest legal officer does not see his "people" as all Americans, but only those who share his skin pigment. This is the tribal mindset of the average inmate.

I speak plainly and honestly about these sensitive issues because misdiagnosis of the problem has exacerbated it. I have no desire to bash black people. However, even if I were a rabid racist, it would not disprove anything I have said. Going around telling non-whites 1) that all of their problems stem from white supremacy and 2) that the only way to cure their illness is to make whites feel guilty so that they will support tax increases to fund more "Public Agencies"—when all previous agency's attempts at improving the lot of non-whites have been catastrophic failures—will not improve the situation.

You cannot continue to characterize the greatest non-sequitur of our time—the statistical disparities in outcomes for different groups—as evidence of discrimination and proof of perpetual white racism and expect the civil society you live in to remain civil. How many more Barry Buhol Jr.'s must the clique create before they realize this? Blaming crime on poverty or unemployment is just as misguided as blaming it on racism.

As the late scholar James Q. Wilson said, "…crime rose the fastest in this country at a time when the number of persons living in poverty or squalor was declining" and, also "the work force was at an all time high at the same time as were the welfare rolls…" "…while the non-white unemployment rate had fallen to 6.5 percent,"[36] crime was increasing sharply.

Instead of recycling the many bogus "root causes" of crime arguments—poverty, racism, unemployment—why not try and determine what really causes criminals to offend, and why Blacks do so at a higher rate? If the real cause can be determined, measures to improve the situation could be developed.

Inter-Racial Crime

Wilson, a professor of government at Harvard University, made a large contribution toward figuring out the causes of crime before his death. And neuro-scientist David Eagleman, is working on the methods that could combat these causes. We will explore their work in the next chapter.

CHAPTER 6

THE REAL CAUSES OF CRIME
AND THE REAL CORRECTION

We have already seen that poverty, racism, and the unemployment rate have little if anything to do with whether or not someone becomes a criminal. Such pseudo explanations have been disproved so many times even a flaming liberal like columnist Richard Cohen admits they are bogus. They persist because they must, because to deny them is to deny Jean-Jacques Rousseau's claim that "man is born free, and everywhere he is in chains."[1]

These chains are seen everywhere, and it is the clique's goal to 'liberate' everyone from nuclear families, life in the suburbs and racism. Basically, civilization, especially Western civilization, has captured people with its oppressive 'social constructs.' They believe people's brains are for the most part a blank slate. This is why they think giving little girls toy trucks to play with instead of dolls, will make them more masculine. Or that jobs will make criminals take the straight and narrow.

Jon Bon Jovi, encapsulates this perfectly in a song: "…and I blame this world, for making a good man evil, and it's this world, that can drive a good man Mad…well I blame this world for making a good man bad!"[2] Moreover, when a person is born, he or she can be whatever they want so long as society's institutions do not put them in 'chains.' Criminals therefore are made, not born.

WHAT WE KNOW

Most people already know that males between ages 13–39 commit most crimes. Less known, is that in addition to age and gender, body type, personality, and intelligence are also correlative. These components are called 'constitutional factors'[3] because they are "usually present at or soon after birth." This is not to say there is a 'crime gene'[4] which makes a person become a criminal. It simply means that there are certain traits people can inherit that increases the probability of them becoming the type of high rate offenders that end up coming to prison.

We will start with body type. Most physiques fit, albeit not perfectly, into one of three categories: ectomorph (very little muscle or fat—think marathon runners), mesomorph (more muscle than fat—think of hockey players), and endomorph (more fat than muscle—think Homer Simpson). Mesomorphs are usually shorter, like running backs, while ectomorphs are usually taller like basketball players.

Experts on this type of categorizing, called somatyping,[5] say that the average person's body is a composite of all three body types. In prison however, you are much more likely to see inmates with mesomorphic and endomorphic traits than ectomorphic. Inmate's bodies are also more andromorphic which denotes a broad chest flaring towards the shoulders, low waist, relatively large arms, prominent muscle relief, large bones and joints, fat distributed evenly throughout the body.[6] (Think TV wrestler.)

Plenty of studies corroborate these observations. One was conducted using 177 female criminals and 123 coeds from Oxford. The criminals, as expected, weighed more than the students, who were on average, taller than the criminals.[7] Another study, using 500 male, teenage offenders and non-offenders, showed similar results. The offenders were much more likely to be mesomorphic than the non-offenders even though the study controlled for "age, race, ethnic background, and socioeconomic- status." A study of 58 criminal boys in London showed that, when compared to college students, the law breakers were substantially more mesomorphic and endomorphic.[8]

Professor Wilson on the subject:

> The general thrust of the evidence should be apparent. Whenever it has been examined, criminals on the average differ in physique from the population at large. They tend to be more mesomorphic (muscular) and less ectomorphic (linear), with the third component (endomorphy) not clearly deviating from normal. Where it has been assessed, the masculine configuration called andromorphy also characterizes the average criminals. Physique does not cause crime, nor is it an inevitable correlate of it.... The mesomorphic, non-ectomorphic physique often predominates, not just among criminals, but among other occupational groups such as salesmen and politicians. In several studies the mesomorphic component has been

associated with expressive, extroverted, domineering temperaments, given to high levels of activity.[9]

In prison, there are several custody levels which separate inmates. 'Minimum custody' is what most of you in the free world are referring to when you say general population. This is where most inmates do the majority of their time unless they incur a disciplinary infraction (fighting or having some contraband like drugs or cell phones, for example). A severe enough disciplinary case will get you 'rolled' to medium or closed custody, and possibly administrative segregation.

When I started writing this book, I was on medium custody. I had been rolled from minimum custody for some Xanax and a $100.00 bill that belonged to my cellmate. He was up for parole and offered me some money to take the case.

The first thing you notice about medium custody inmates are their younger ages and more mesomorphic builds compared to the minimum custody inmates. Yet even in minimum custody, where guys are going to school and working jobs, the population of inmates exhibiting mesomorphy and andromorphy is higher compared to guys in the free world.

On medium and closed custody that proportion almost triples. The observations about height bear out as well. I am six feet three inches tall. On minimum custody, I am regarded as tall. In the average 48 man section, I am normally the second or third tallest person. On medium custody, which had about 500 inmates on my unit at the time, there were only three guys taller than me. And when it comes to personality, medium and closed custody inmates are much more boisterous and aggressive than those on minimum custody. You see more fights and stabbings, and there is a much greater chance you will get caught up in a riot. In the year I spent on medium custody, two people were killed.

This is all very logical. Yet people in general are apprehensive about attributing criminality to something inheritable like body type. They think (wrongly) that by doing so, they are relegating an offender to a life of incarceration because he cannot change characteristics that are "genetic." But little is further from the truth.

As Wilson points out, phenylketonuria, which is an inheritable enzyme deficiency, will damage a child's brain to the point of "severe mental retardation."[10] However, if it is diagnosed, merely changing the child's diet may remedy the problem. Some diabetics, including those who inherited the Type I form, can at least reduce the amount of insulin they need by eating low-glycemic food that requires little to no insulin to digest.

Again, you have to diagnose the problem correctly if your goal is to treat it effectively.

Various studies involving adopted children and their parents from 1924 to 1947 also shed light on whether or not genetics can predispose people to criminality. One study conducted in Denmark involved 14,427 men and women who had been adopted. The researcher's goal was to determine who was more likely to have been convicted of at least one violent or property offense: adoptees with biological parents who had criminal records, adoptees whose parents had criminal records, or some combination of both. The largest percentage of adoptees with criminal convictions (24.5 percent) turned out to be those with both biological and adoptive parents who had criminal records. Second behind this group (at 20 percent) were adoptees with biological parents who had criminal records but whose adoptive parents did not. Of adoptees whose biological parents had no criminal record but were adopted by parents that did, 14.7 percent became criminals. And lastly, 13.5 percent of adoptees who had neither biological nor adoptive parents with criminal records were convicted of violent or property crime. To sum these findings up: "The criminality of the biological parents is here more important than that of the adoptive parents, suggesting genetic transmission of some factor or factors associated with crime."[11]

The same study also found that boys whose biological parents had multiple offenses on their records were 300 percent more likely to be repeat offenders themselves than boys whose biological parents were not criminals.[12] So apparently, even if adopted, the apple does not fall far from the tree.

Hormone levels are also largely genetic. Risk taking is linked to testosterone[13] levels, as are body size, muscle strength, and a lower percentage of body fat. Castrating "leads to obesity, softer tissues, and a more placid temperament." A study done on young, violent, male inmates in which their testosterone levels were recorded over a two week period demonstrated a correlation between their criminal history and testosterone levels.[14]

The researchers also compared these inmate's testosterone levels with those of prison guards. They found no significant difference between the two groups. I would like to proffer an explanation for why this is so, and why it is misleading. Although I am certainly not an expert when it comes to body typing, I like to think I am at least capable of determining mesomorphy after being around so many mesomorphs for the last 17 years.

Causes of Crime and Correction

When it comes to prison guards, their rates of mesomorphy seem to be almost as high as those of inmates. And we know high levels of testosterone lead a body towards mesomorphy and andromorphy.

Prison guards also exhibit many of the same personality traits inmates do. And judging by the enormity of the underground prison economy of drugs, cellphones, and prostitution, quite a few guards must be highly prolific offenders. In other words, inmates and prison guards probably have in common higher than average testosterone levels. A better comparison would have been, say, 23 year old college graduates with 23 year old offenders.

Intelligence, which is less 'genetic' than hormone levels and body type, also correlated with criminal offending. Inmates have, on average, I.Q. scores that are 6–10 points below that of the national average.[15] Being less intelligent could increase a criminal's chances of being caught, directly affecting conviction rates. Indirectly, being less intelligent makes it more difficult to be successful in school and therefore may cause some youngsters to search for something they can succeed at outside of school. Unfortunately this can be criminal activity. (This is entirely different from saying it is the schools or their Eurocentric curriculum which is at fault.) A study of 9,000 white juvenile delinquents in Tennessee found that I.Q. was a better predictor of criminal behavior than socioeconomic status. In Philadelphia, researchers compared the scores of almost 9,000 males and found that criminals with multiple offenses on their records were more likely to be of lower intelligence than non-criminals. And a study done in London, England, involving 400 male juveniles produced equivalent results. In particular, low levels of verbal intelligence correlate more strongly to criminality than low levels of other types of intelligence.

A study of 500 'seriously delinquent' boys compared their I.Q. scores with those of 500 non-delinquents, controlling for age and socioeconomic status.[16] The researchers found that the delinquents' and non-delinquents' I.Q. scores were only 2 points apart (92 for the former, 94 for the latter). The delinquent's verbal scores were substantially lower than the non-delinquents. Professor Wilson collected the results from 21 different studies involving over 2000 criminals and found that verbal scores were on average 7.9 points below performance scores. Verbal I.Q. is measured by questions involving "information, comprehension, digit span, arithmetic, similarities, and vocabulary." Performance I.Q. on the other hand measures "picture arrangement, picture completion, block design, object assembly, and digit symbol." In all but one of these 21 studies, verbal scores were lower than performance scores.[17]

Lower verbal intelligence normally makes it more difficult for a person to reason in the abstract. This means that when they contemplate the effects of their crimes, they are less likely to reach the same conclusion, from a normal standpoint, as someone with a higher verbal intelligence. As one researcher put it "perhaps it is no coincidence that those with the ability to erect large anonymous hierarchical communities based on abstract relations between strangers, also have the ability to live amicably within them."[18] Low verbal intelligence also reduces one's ability to associate a certain result with a certain behavior. "Without the internal monologue, time horizons shrink: behavior becomes more tied to its immediate consequences."[19]

There also seems to be some correlation between I.Q. and the types of crimes an offender commits. 'White collar' crimes like counterfeiting and securities fraud, are normally committed by offenders whose I.Q.'s are higher than offenders who commit violent crimes.[20] Consequently, the justice system does not have to discriminate against offenders with low I.Q.'s. Their preferences for violent crimes dictates that they will make up a disproportionate percentage of the prison population, "systematic discrimination," not required.[21]

Below average intelligence also seems to predispose people to a mindset that is "unconventional, anti-social, irresponsible, and present-oriented."[22] Being "present oriented," or impulsive, especially in circumstances where the reward for crime is immediate, and the punishment unlikely or in the distant future, obviously makes a person more likely to engage in criminal activity. A study measuring the impulsiveness of a group of seventh graders correctly predicted which of these youngsters would become drop-outs or criminals.[23]

Temperament and disposition, like intelligence, are to an extent, heritable. No more than a casual review of the evidence on this matter is necessary to come to such a conclusion. This does not mean that nature trumps nurture, or that people with naturally muscular bodies, impulsive and aggressive personalities, and above average levels of testosterone are doomed to a life of crime and prison. But "current estimates place the heritability of intelligence between 50 and 80 percent, and the heritability of most common dimensions of personality perhaps 20 percent lower, on the average."[24] Even more troubling for the clique's Rousseuian claims that it is capitalism, racism, poverty, etc., that are to blame for criminality, is that the common denominators amongst criminals—impulsiveness, mesomorphy, low intelligence—are evident in the future delinquents years before they encounter the labor market or racist, capitalist, Klan members like Mitt Romney and all other successful white men.[25] Thus it seems highly probable that criminals have bad experiences with schools and employers—not because of the composition of these institutions—but because criminals possess constitutional factors that predispose them to. And how well one does in the genetics sweepstakes cannot be blamed on society.

Does any of this help explain why Blacks commit crimes at higher rates than whites? Perhaps. Perhaps not. The black population in America is on average younger than the white population. In particular, the average black male is about 7 years younger than the average white male.[26] This means that there is a larger portion of the black male population between ages 13 and 39—which is when most men commit felonies—than there is in the white male population. The problem with this as an explanation however, runs into trouble when you consider that the Hispanic population is just as young as the black population, and also has similar rates of poverty.

When it comes to body type, black males are more likely to be mesomorphic then white males. However, there are studies claiming that mesomorphy does not predispose Blacks to offending as it does whites. (To the best of my knowledge Jeremiah Wright did not conduct any of these.) Specifically, one study reported that even though black inmates were more mesomorphic than white inmates, there was no correlation between their mesomorphy and their crime rate.[27]

Criminals normally have personalities unlike those of non-criminals. Several studies also tell us that black and white males score differently on personality tests like the Minnesota Multiphasic Personality Inventory (MMPI).[28] The MMPI consists of 556 "self-descriptive" statements such as "everything tastes the same," or "I have never been in trouble with the law," to which it's taker is to answer true or false.[29] The higher the score, the less 'normal' their personality is said to be. "On all scales except the one measuring femininity," Blacks score higher than whites. This was still the case after controlling for socioeconomic status.[30] The Jeremiah Wrights, Soledad O'Briens, and Michael Johnsons of the world will cry foul and say that Blacks use a different part of their brain to think and have different, superior genes that make tests like the MMPI invalid for them. But Victor H. Elion and Edwin I. Megargee have already researched that predictable rebuttal:

They found that Blacks in federal prison had significantly higher scores on the PD scale than either whites in prison or black college students (who themselves tended to come from deprived backgrounds); and that among the prisoners, recidivists had higher scores than first offenders; and that among black college students, the PD scale discriminated between those who on a self-report questionnaire showed themselves to have committed the most and the fewest delinquent acts. The authors concluded that the PD scale on the MMPI was "as valid for Blacks as for whites."[31]

The 'PD Scale' refers to the psychopathic deviate scale on the MMPI which has questions designed to measure how likely a person is to have "conflict of authority" and "shallow personal attachment" issues.[32] Offenders, regardless of their color, that had the "most deviant profile" were the most likely to get locked back up and to incur disciplinary problems while incarcerated.[33] If Blacks score higher on all scales including the PD, then it should come as no surprise that they offend at higher rates than whites. Simply teaching impulse control, instead of promoting 'express yourself' at all costs, could lead to a reduction in the black offense rate.

In the foreword to *What is Your Most Dangerous Idea?* Harvard psychologist Steven Pinker mentions that black males have baseline testosterone levels higher than those of white males. Most of the evidence currently before us demonstrates a strong link between testosterone levels and risk taking and aggression. Pinker also points out that this could mean nothing because other variables in the equations of risk taking and aggression could be calibrated upward in accordance with Blacks testosterone levels.[34] However, we cannot know this because no one will do the research for the fear of being called a racist.

Obviously the vast majority of black men are not criminals. But what about the criminal population's margins? What if the most violent offenders of all races have testosterone levels, which if lowered, would make the offenders less aggressive and more risk averse? Because black criminals make up a disproportionate share of that margin, they would benefit the most from such a treatment approach.

About the only thing more taboo and politically incorrect than mentioning the differences in hormone levels between Blacks and whites is mentioning their differences in I.Q. scores. Blacks as a whole, not just black offenders, have I.Q. scores that are 12–15 points lower than those of whites. This does not change when the study controls for socioeconomic factors. Even "among the lowest-status persons...the black white difference is about eleven points."[35] As mentioned above, several studies have shown that regardless of race or socioeconomic conditions, offenders have lower I.Q.'s than non-offenders.

Do these statistics doom Blacks to higher rates of crime? No. When the Jews, Italians, and Poles first arrived in America their I.Q.'s also averaged 15 points below the national average. Today, Jews have some of the highest I.Q. scores and the Poles and Italians often score above the national average.[36] There is no reason whatsoever to believe black's I.Q.'s cannot do the same. In fact, black children adopted by white parents have average I.Q.'s of 106, putting them six points above the national average.[37]

Even if we believe these constitutional factors contributed to black's higher rates of crimes, we would be hard pressed to prove they accounted for all of the vast differences in offense rates, especially considering the fact that West Indian Blacks, who have the same genetic make-up as American Blacks—and are also descendants of slaves—have lower crime rates than American Blacks. Irish immigrants were once locked up at very high rates, and they obviously do not have all the same constitutional factors as American Blacks.

Unfortunately, because clique members control most of the scientific research centers on America's college campuses, questions about the heritability of crime and race will probably never be answered—if anyone is even courageous enough to ask. This consequence of political correctness is potentially robbing many inmates of treatments that could actually help them stop their criminal behavior and become productive members of society. On the other hand, at least nobody has his or her feelings hurt!

So just why do Blacks offend at higher rates?

BLACK BUBBA

As far as anyone can tell, Blacks have been offending at rates much higher than those of whites for quite sometime. During the 1890s in Philadelphia the black murder rate was 300 percent higher than the white murder rate.[38] And from the mid to late 1900s, the black murder rate was 1200 percent higher than the white rate. Why was it higher early on, and why did it explode in the 1960s? The second question has already been answered for the most part: declining clearance rates made murder and all crimes a better bet and changes in the welfare laws did what hundreds of years of slavery and decades of Jim Crow laws could not; destroy the black family. We will focus now on the first question.

America Apart

If you like rap music, proving how tough you are, and having children before you get married, you might be a redneck. Nine-tenths of black Americans, regardless of where they live today, can trace their lineage to the American South.[39] When African slaves were brought to the U.S., with few exceptions, they were dispersed throughout this region. And this region was a world apart from the much more cosmopolitan North. The South's inhabitants and culture could not have contrasted more from their New England counterparts in the North. The immigrants that came to call the South home were known as the "problem children of Ulster" on the other side of the Atlantic. They brought with them a 'warlike culture'[40] that was forged over "centuries of continuous warfare" against the Romans and English.[41]

In addition to fighting these two military superpowers, the Celtic tribes of Scotland, from which the Scots-Irish descended, spent generations fighting each other, refusing to unite. Scotland itself was just as harsh as the people who inhabited it. Like sub-Saharan Africa with few navigable water ways and domestic crops, Scotland was "a land of difficult water barriers, sharp mountains and deep hollows, soggy moors and rough pastures, and of thin, uncultivable soil that lies like a blanket over wide reaches of granite."[42] Because of these geographic impediments, and the Celtic people's ferocity and love of weapons, the Romans and Normanized English would-be conquerors never had much success implementing their top-down forms of government on this bottom-up group of people. And so they remained isolated and primitive, with little to no education.

In *Born Fighting: How the Scots-Irish Shaped America*, U.S. Senator James Webb, himself of Scots-Irish descent, writes that the Scots-Irish enjoyed "games of physical challenge such as racing and wrestling." Despite the very strict rules of Calvinism, they were known for public displays of sexually themed humor and marriage at an early age. In fact many of them said "I do" with a child already on the way. "Much of Calvinism's harsh discipline could be attributed to the attempt by the church leaders to tame this highly spirited people"[43]—most of whom had never been to school or taught a trade. If they happened to be literate, which most were not, the only book they had probably ever read was the Bible.

The Scots-Irish could best be defined by one principle: "If any man, no matter how highly born, should strike or offend them, it was their credo to strike back twice as hard."[44] And the harder one struck, the more praiseworthy they were.

Causes of Crime and Correction

I know this culture personally, because it is the one my family comes from. Reading Webb's book, in which he chronicles his family's history in America, reminded me of my paternal grandmother, a genealogist, and her stories of my family's journey.

There have been book length treatments of the theory that the African slaves and their descendants in the American South adopted the Scots-Irish or "Celtic fringe" culture. Dr. Sowell documents in *Black Rednecks and White Liberals* how much of what is today considered African-American culture actually comes from "the Northern borderlands of England, as well as from the Scottish highlands and from Ulster County." He writes, "Fringe areas were turbulent, if not lawless regions, where none of the contending forces was able to establish full control."[45] Impulsiveness was practically bred into these people. For they lived in a world of "Impotent laws, daily danger, and lives that could be snuffed out at any moment," causing them to jump at anything desirous, regardless of its danger, or the temporary nature of its reward.[46]

Needless to say, the culture these people came equipped with was not conducive to achieving prosperity in a society governed by the rule of law. When they arrived in America, this culture, especially their ability to fight, caused the 'powers that be' to consign them to the mountains where they served as human fences, protecting the English aristocracy from the Indians.[47] They eventually diffused, mostly into the South.

For those who think senseless shootings in black ghettos — "He's staring at me. That's disrespectful!" — are caused by self-hate, poverty, or white oppression, and therefore exclusive to Blacks, Dr. Sowell gives several examples of similar behavior by white Southerners, occurring long before such ghettos existed.

One instance involved two friends falling out over a verbal slight. The man who felt 'disrespected,' as we say in here, 'called out' his friend who made the comment. People gathered around the duel. Each man fired his rifle, and one went down with a bullet in the leg. His former friend dropped his long gun and strode to where the injured man lay. Kneeling down beside him, he pulled out his 'bowie knife and deliberately butchered' the defenseless man. The crowd approved. The victor was never punished and stayed in that same community, where he took a wife. Much like using drugs, and believing in Marxism are resume enhancements for clique members, so was this cold-blooded murder amongst the descendants of the Celtic fringe.[48]

Other examples include a man threatening to kill another because he fired him from a job he neglected to do, and a Louisiana man murdering his young neighbor because he made a verbal pass at his wife.[49] Equally important to this behavior is the reaction of the surrounding community. They practically celebrated these demonstrations of brutality.

Even though Alexander and many other cliquesters like to believe all Blacks in the ghetto ostracize criminals, Reverend Jessie Jackson once told a group of gang members that they were the future leaders of the Civil Rights Movement. Like white rednecks in the past, black rednecks today encourage their peers to "act a fool" and "keep it real."

Another feature of Celtic fringe culture that unfortunately made it to America and was picked up by black folks was improperly spoken English. In America today, saying "I be going to the store" when you should be saying, "I am going to the store" is considered 'talkin' black.' Yet whites around the borders of England were saying "you be," when they meant "you are," and "it don't" when they meant "it doesn't" back in the 1600s before they ever even saw a black person.[50] Dr. Sowell writes that there were other words and even some customs wrongly attributed to a false black identity:

> From these same regions of England came such words as "yaller" for "yellow," "ax" for "ask", "acrost" for "across, "yawl" for "you," "bile" for "boil," "do" for "door," "dis" for "this", and "dat" for "that." Many of these usages have long since died out in England, though the word "chitterlings" for hog entrails continued to be used in some localities in England, even in the twentieth century, as such usage remained common among black Americans. But no such words came from Africa. Nor did the Holiday Kwanza, which originated in Los Angeles. The slave's custom of marking their marriage by jumping over a broomstick... was in fact a pagan custom in Europe in centuries past and survived for a time among Southern whites.[51]

Am I pointing out these facts in yet another attempt to dispossess Blacks of their culture and achievements? No. The point here is not to denigrate Blacks. It is to show that defending ebonics or barbarism is really a defense of redneck culture. And more importantly, a defense of that which is counterproductive for a group of people trying to get ahead.

How many black people would keep up the improper usage of grammar if they knew doing so would mean they were talking like a redneck? What if black kids in the ghetto were taught that 'keepin' it real' by fighting over words or how long someone looked at them was in reality part of cracker culture?

What if Blacks in general, and Professor Chaffe in particular, knew that "rape was prevalent amongst this rough and tumble Celtic fringe long before its men encountered black female slaves?" For instance in Virginia, "the sexual exploitation of white indentured servant girls was common before the slave population had grown large enough for white servant girls to be replaced by black women." Which means any 'pattern' of rape amongst these people had to have started before they lived amongst Blacks. What if Blacks knew the Southern whites' low regard for life,[52] which writer Gunnar Myrdal blamed on racism and slavery in his book *An American Dilemma*, was common amongst the Celts before they ever set foot on American soil, much less encountered African slaves in the South? Is it possible that the narrative's proponents might have a little less firepower? And if that were the case...

Being tough, and eager to prove it are not characteristics restricted to Americans of Scots-Irish and African descent. The Machismo elements of Mexican and Puerto Rican culture have also led to higher than average incarceration rates even though in the case of Puerto Ricans, most of them are white.[53] In prison black and white rednecks and macho Latinos all agree, you must use violence if somebody disrespects you. Changing these culture's norms, unfortunately, is much more difficult than changing the sentencing laws for crack cocaine or shaking down a business because the "disparate impact" standard allows claims of phantom racism. Nor can a politician campaign on "I'm the candidate to vote for because I think you need to change yourself and your culture!" A politician who says, "The reason you are not doing as well as those white folks, is because of those white folks" will undoubtedly garner more support—human ego's being what they are.

Change in attitudes and beliefs cannot take place in the blink of an eye, like a majority vote. And as long as the narrative is around, the particular changes lagging groups need to make in order to get ahead, will not be forthcoming.

In short, the black crime rate has always been higher than the white crime rate because 90 percent of American Blacks lived in the South surrounded by the redneck or cracker culture of the Celtic fringe. This particular culture did not affect whites as a whole, because only 30 percent of whites trace their lineage to the South.

This is identical to what happened with the expansion in welfare benefits. Clique members love to claim that if the Great Society programs were what led to the increase in illegitimacy and declining labor force participation amongst Blacks, these programs should have caused the same results among whites. But the proportion of Blacks on welfare—just like the proportion of Blacks living in the South—was several times that of whites. However, where whites have been on the welfare rolls at the same clip as Blacks were in America in the 1960s, white populations exhibit identical results. You can read further about this in Theodore Dalrymple's book, *Life at the Bottom*.

If 90 percent of any group spent hundreds of years trapped amongst a people known for "an aversion to work, leanings toward violence, neglect of education, sexual promiscuity, improvidence, drunkenness, lack of entrepreneurship, and reckless searches for excitement,"[54] their chances of ending up in prison would be much higher than they would have if they had of spent the same amount of time around a group such as the Quakers.

Any attempt to use this theory to buttress the argument that black criminals offend at higher rates than whites because they are trapped in the ghettos—where the white man forced them—ignores the facts. Even if Blacks are 'products of their environment' like everyone else other racial minorities in America have lived in similar circumstances and have displayed an entirely different outcome:

> The low rates of crime among Asians living in the United States were once a frequent topic of social science investigation. The theme of many of the reports that emerged was that crime rates were low not in spite of ghetto life but because of it. Though Orientals were the object of racist opinion and legislation, they were thought to have low crime rates because they lived in cohesive, isolated communities. The Chinese were for many years denied access to the public schools of California, not allowed to testify against whites in trials, and made the object of discriminatory taxation... what is striking is that the argument used by social scientists to explain low crime rates among Orientals—namely, being separate from the larger society—has been the same argument used to explain high rates among Blacks.[55]

The redneck culture helped produce William Wallace, President Andrew Jackson, General George Patton, and many other great leaders. It gave America its distinctly populist version of democracy.[56] And it was never as evil and racist as Hollywood made it out to be. Most of the Scots-Irish have managed to discard the more unproductive elements of the culture their ancestors brought from Ulster and the border regions.

My paternal grandfather, who only had a sixth-grade education, walked halfway across Texas to find employment with Exxon as a teenager. He kept this same employer for over 40 years and would have given you the fight of your life if you insulted the oil giant. In the meantime, he fought in World War II, as one of the heroes that stormed Omaha Beach in Normandy, France. He was awarded the bronze star and a purple heart. The latter because his back was broken by a grenade. When the U.S. declared war, he did not wait on a draft card but enlisted, even though he was well into his thirties.

When America went to war in Vietnam, my dad was in ROTC, a practical pipeline to the bush. A doctor restricted him from going because of a skin condition my dad never brought up. The kind of thing those who fled to Russia to protest the war dreamed of, my dad saw as a curse. My mother once told me not being allowed to fight like his father and friends devastated him, because fighting is what you do when these are the people you come from, and there is a war to be fought.

Yet my grandfather and father both waited until they married to procreate. They never had any problems with alcohol or improvidence. And whenever one of my black friends needed a place to stay because their own parents would not take them, my dad would open the door to his very modest home, and never charge them a dime of rent.

People, and even cultures, can change. Doing so however, especially when it comes to the latter, is a daunting task. The Oprah Winfreys of the world only make it more difficult for Blacks when they rob them of feedback by promoting a non-judgmental society.

I love and revere my grandfather and what he stood for. But I am glad he left parts of our culture behind. He and his father were known for saying "I don't need no damn union to keep my job." My father related this to me often. But he also corrected me quickly whenever I spoke a double negative and would have tanned my hide if I had said the word damn.

My father is the quintessential redneck. He has more fishing poles than a rich woman has shoes. He is proud to be "one of them old boys raised on shotguns." But he knew how to conduct himself in a job interview and therefore was never out of work for very long when he did get laid off. This might not have been the case had he or my grandfather been worried about "preserving" the way we often round off words like government into 'gubment,' lest we become 'sellouts.'

America Apart

These men held onto the love of weapons, especially guns, because those weapons serve important purposes. Gun safety and maintenance teach responsibility. Learning to shoot accurately allows you to defend your family, some endangered third party, or your country. And as good as the deer and hog taste, the best part of those hunting trips are the bonds you forge, and the memories you make. That cultural weeding-out process that my ancestors had to go through would have never begun had there been ready-made excuses dispatched for their unproductive behavior. This has not been the case for black Americans.

If you doubt the connection between Blacks in the ghetto and rednecks from Europe, try listening to your local hip-hop station for an hour and then doing the same with the local country music station as well. The women singers/rappers are often sensual and provocative, while at the same time professing a strong belief in Jesus (think Beyonce or Carrie Underwood dancing half-naked or destroying a car in a song, yet praying before they perform).

The male performers on the other hand will kill you if you insult them, but cry like a baby when someone kills one of their friends. Their "mama's tried," but they were too hard headed. They are all, male and female, heartbroken over someone of the opposite sex.

At night, the country station plays their slow jams on a program called something like "cryin', lovin', and leavin'." The D. J. goes out of her way to make her voice sound like it is "real" country. The Hip-Hop station plays their slow jams on a show called something like "The Quiet Storm" or "The Love Hour." The male D.J. sounds like he is doing his best impersonation of the late Barry White.

When it comes to the actual songs, several have been recorded by both country and rhythm and blues artists. When I was a teenager "Nobody Knows" by the Tony Rich Project also had a country version, and most remember the late Whitney Houston's version of Dolly Parton's song "I Will Always Love You," better than the original.

In prison, white rednecks from rural areas and black rednecks from the inner city enjoy each other's company more often than you would think. They may have different tastes in clothes and automobiles, but their temperaments and love of sports are often identical. Even though they come from different worlds, they have some common ground.

Senator Webb says that Americans of African and Scots-Irish descent have more in common than any other two ethnic groups in America. And that if they could learn to come together at the bargaining table, they could force politicians to pay attention to issues they heretofore have not.

There has been no shortage of reasons the relationship between Blacks and whites in general has been as strained as it has been. The clique's fallacious racial narrative increases the strain by convincing Blacks white racism is the cause of any and all of the problems they have. You can blame whites for the redneck culture. Doing so will do about as much good as enacting more government programs to get at the 'root causes' of crime in hopes that doing so will lower the black crime rate. That will require individual change, which is difficult because so many in the clique believe they must preserve what is wrongly thought to be black culture.

Fortunately at the time of this writing, no lobbyist group is trying to protect impulsiveness. And the technology to improve upon this "hallmark" of criminality, could well be on its way. In his book *Incognito: The Secret Lives of the Brain*, neuroscientist David Eagleman claims that exercising the brain's pre-frontal cortex could lead to better decision making for criminals by making them less impulsive.

> Poor impulse control is a hallmark characteristic of the majority of criminals in the prison system. They generally know the difference between right and wrong actions, and they understand the seriousness of punishment, but they are hamstrung by an inability to control their impulses. They see a woman with an expensive purse walking alone in an alley, and they cannot think but to take advantage of the opportunity. The temptation overrides the concern for their future.[57]

Exercising the right part of the brain makes the circuits dealing with future consequences stronger than the short-term circuits. It conditions a criminal's brain to be less present oriented, causing the distant pain of a prison sentence to outweigh the immediate pleasure from the purse snatching. Eagleman gives an example of someone needing help turning down chocolate cake.

> In this experiment, you look at pictures of chocolate cake during brain scanning—and the experimenters determine the regions of your brain involved in the craving. Then the activity in those networks is represented by a vertical bar on a computer screen. Your job is a make the bar go down. The bar acts as a thermometer for your craving: If your craving networks are revving high, the bar is high; if you're suppressing your craving, the bar is low. You stare at the bar and try to make it go down. Perhaps you have insight into what you're doing to resist the cake; perhaps it is inaccessible. In any case, you try different mental avenues until the bar begins to slowly sink. When it goes down, it means you've successfully

recruited frontal circuitry to squelch the activity in the networks involved in impulsive craving. The long term has won over the short term. Still looking at pictures of chocolate cake you practice making the bar go down over and over until you've strengthened those frontal circuits. By this method, you're able to utilize the activity in the parts of your brain that need modulation. And you can witness the effects of different mental approaches you might take.[58]

Raise your hand if you think you have made better decisions as an adult than you did as a teenager. Your hand is up because the decision making part of your brain does not finish forming until you are well into your twenties. This is why car insurance costs much less once you reach 25. The insurance companies know from statistical analysis of car crash data that you are much more likely to get into a wreck as a teenager and charge accordingly. The objective here is to give the individual a more mature brain. You cannot stop someone from wanting chocolate cake or money. The hope is that a much more developed frontal lobe will allow them to resist acting upon their "impulsive thoughts."[59]

On the politics of such a treatment, Eagleman says:

The goal is to…inhibit impulsivity. To encourage reflection. If a citizen thinks about long-term consequences and still decides to move forward with an illegal act, then we'll deal with those consequences accordingly. This approach has ethical importance and liberal appeal. Unlike a lobotomy, which sometimes leaves the patient with only an infantile mentality, this approach opens an opportunity for the willing person to help himself. Instead of the government mandating a psychosurgery, here a government can offer a helping hand to better self reflection and socialization.[60]

Eagleman also says that this treatment should increase the effectiveness of deterrence by making that potential long prison sentence seem like more of a reality for a would-be offender.[61]

The current rehabilitation programs, at least in the Texas prison system, are a waste of time and taxpayer money. It is basically a self-help book converted into classroom instruction with a bull session mixed in. The instructor tells the class how to make better decisions, saying that they should ask themselves before they make a decision "Will this help meet my needs over time?" The problem with this of course is that it does nothing to address the weakness in the pre-frontal cortex where decision-making takes place.

The impulsiveness of high rate offenders usually shows up no later than elementary school. It is not a choice. If Alexander and Pitts really want to get at the "root cause" of crime, they should be advocating Eagleman's treatment and not crusading against white supremacy, whiteness, white privilege, and Glen Beck.

In 2012, at a cultural proficiency workshop for Minnesota educators, an Asian teacher asked one of the workshop's black facilitators, "How do I help the [black] student who blurts out answers and disrupts the class?" To which came the reply, "That's what black culture is."[62] No, it is not, and it is a shame that a black person leading a conference on 'cultural proficiency' thinks it is. Speaking out of turn and being disruptive are remnants of redneck culture.

A black teacher at this workshop, Aaron Brenner, heard the exchange. "I should of said: How many of you spoke out in college? They're trying to pull one over on us. Black Folks are drinking the Kool-Aid: This let them clown philosophy could of been devised by the KKK."[63]

CHAPTER 7

ORIGINS AND ABETTORS

Sherlock Holmes himself would have trouble pinpointing exactly when and where the clique's narrative began. As we saw in Chapter One, evolution has tailored our brains to release a torrent of feel-good chemicals when we are able to perceive ourselves as heroes or heroines of the downtrodden. This is not always a good thing. While we cannot be certain who came up with the idea of using victimhood to extort preference for favored groups, a good deal of the blame should be placed upon Herbert Marcuse.

Marcuse began his career in academia in the early 1930s at the Institute of Social Research (ISR) in Weimar, Germany.[1] In addition to contributing significantly to the development of the field of victimology, Marcuse made a large contribution to the related field of oral artistry in which people expand the definitions of words or change their meanings entirely. In the U.S., Marcuse would eventually teach at Harvard, Yale, Brandeis, and Columbia before settling at the University of California at San Diego in 1965.[2]

In 1937, while still at the ISR, one of Marcuse's colleagues, Max Horkheimer, penned an essay titled "Traditional and Critical Theory." A theory is a hypothesis that has been tested over and over again and never disproven. Critical theory, by this definition, is not a theory. However, like many social scientists and academics, the scholars at the ISR used the word theory to wrap their opinions in the mantle of science, conferring validity upon them.

The *New Jim Crow* offers a good example of critical theory. In it Alexander is 'critical' of the U.S. Justice system while offering few ways to improve upon its problems. If you tell a critical theoretician that, say, the U.S. is a free country, they will likely respond by saying, "How can it be free if I can't afford a house?" or "If it's free, why do I have to show up for work even when I don't want to?" In short, critical theory criticizes things the clique does not like, yet offers no solutions whatsoever so its practitioners cannot be criticized in return.[3]

Marcuse sidestepped criticism of his beliefs by saying, "...we are still confronted with the demand to state the concrete alternative. The demand is meaningless if it asks for a blueprint of the specific institutions and relationships which would be those of the New Society."[4] In other words, your society is trash, you must rebuild it because I say so, but do not bother me for the 'blueprint' to create this better society.

The scholars at the ISR took Horkheimer's critical theory and added a pinch of Marxism, and a dash of Freudian psychoanalysis, before turning their dish loose on Western society—and only Western society. They determined that the West's problems were capitalism, the nuclear family, patriotism and religion. All of these things had to be destroyed to make the West 'right.' But instead of making victims out of the worker, as traditional Marxism does, their newfangled cultural Marxism replaced the proletariat with non-whites, homosexuals, and women as the victims[5]—all of whom were to be viewed as having been born with inherited grievances against white men.

During the eleven years Marcuse spent at Brandies University, he completed his two most celebrated books, *Eros and Civilization* and *One Dimensional Man*. *Eros and Civilization* claims that capitalism requires a person to spend too much time working. Because of this, people cannot satisfy all of their sexual urges—which Marcuse viewed as a travesty. He believed "the length of the working day is itself one of the principle repressive factors imposed upon the pleasure principle by the reality principle."[6] So in order to have 'freedom,' the workday would have to be reduced severely. This expansion of the definition of 'freedom' is very common in Marcuse's work and endemic amongst the clique today.

In *One Dimensional Man*, Marcuse proclaims, "Fiction calls the facts by their name and their reign collapses; fiction subverts everyday experience and shows it to be mutilated and false."[7] This means, amongst other things, that communism failing, or conquest and subjugation occurring in places other than the West are false—because to acknowledge those facts would subvert Marcuse's vision. To him, a one-dimensional man could only understand the actual physical environment in which he lived.[8] But the learned, two-dimensional man could understand and visualize the utopia Marcuse desired.

Origins and Abettors

In other words, the ability to live in la-la land is praised, while being grounded in reality is disparaged. It brings to mind the never-say-die attitudes of the Reverends Sharpton and Jackson when it comes to something like the Tawana Brawley hoax. Eventually, they had to know it was a hoax. Yet, they kept it going, which suggests they believed that shaming white people into even more guilt would make things better for Blacks. They, and the rest of the clique, believe that if they pretend there is more white racism in society than there is — thumbing their noses at reality — they will be able to procure more wealth transfers for government agencies to remedy problems like inequality.

Ignore the reality that non-whites are better off in America today than they are anywhere else in the world. Indulge and proliferate the fantasy that non-whites today are under constant attack from racist white men — despite the fact that 89 percent of interracial crimes are black on white. It is a means to a noble end — giving Whitey his comeuppance via reparations (AKA fair taxation). The truth does not advance the agenda so it is discarded in favor of a fiction that does.

Marcuse also detested logic and the scientific method. He believed the two-dimensional man should liberate himself from "the senses" and science because they allow for an "evermore effective domination of man by man **through** nature"[9] (emphasis his). This domination empowered militaries and polluted the environment. The parallels between Marcuse and today's clique members is glaring.

Like many in the clique Marcuse reached his conclusions by using inter-temporal abstractions. In reference to groups like the Black Panthers, Marcuse wrote, "If they use violence, they do not start a new chain of violence but try to break an established one."[10] That is, white men committed violent acts when they were colonizing the world, therefore non-whites are more than justified in any violent acts they now commit against white men — regardless of whether or not the white male victim of this righteous violence ever committed any crimes himself. They are only trying to settle the score. So Bull Conner may not be alive today, but someone with his same skin pigment is just as good.

The ISR's critical theory is taught today at most institutions of higher learning. Schools like the University of North Carolina, Brown, Harvard, and scores of others all have courses in victim studies that would make Marcuse proud. They apply critical theory to race, gender, and sexuality and determine, through pseudo-analysis, that non-whites, women, and gays, are all oppressed at every turn in the Western world.[11]

These classes are taught by some of the nation's most highly recognized educators. It is said that Angela J. Davis, a professor in the University of California system, was taught and guided by Marcuse personally.[12] The late Harvard Law School professor Dereck Bell wrote extensively on "critical race theory" which does nothing but degrade America and white people. Bell is admired greatly by plenty of influential people including President Obama and Al-Jazeera anchor Soledad O'Brien.

Andrea Mitchel of NBC News said that Dereck Bell was a "distinguished professor" and "not a radical firebrand." Soledad O'Brien described him as a "renowned Harvard Law School Professor" and recommended his book *Ethical Ambition*. President Obama, during his days as a law school lecturer, required his students to read Bell's *Race, Racism, and American Law*.[13] This is a book that asserts all of the laws in the U.S. are bogus because they come from the 'white power structure.' In his best seller, *Faces At The Bottom Of The Well*, Bell argues that most whites are incorrigibly malicious and wish they could mount a "black holocaust or some other all-out attack on America's historic scapegoats."[14] Bell arrived at these conclusions based on a faulty premise—whites are exclusively wicked because they owned slaves. Bell writes, "Slavery is, as an example of what white America has done, a constant reminder of what white America might do."[15] Apparently the facts are of no consequence—that every race on the planet has owned slaves and that only after Western whites used force to do so was slavery eradicated.

Dr. Thomas Sowell, who was at Stanford University when Bell was teaching law there, gives a plausible reason for why Bell wanted to perpetuate an alternative reality where whites were always on the cusp of initiating a "final solution to the black problem."

> Bell's options were to be a nobody, living in the shadow of more accomplished legal scholars, or to appeal to a radical constituency on campus and beyond. His writings show clearly he chose the latter path. Bell even said that he took it as his mission to say things to annoy white people. Perhaps he thought that was better than being insignificant in his academic setting. But it was in fact far worse, because the real damage was to impressionable young Blacks who took him seriously, including one who went on to become President of the United States.[16]

In addition to critical theory, Marcuse also popularized the use of double standards. Oral artistry aided this double standard—the changing of a word's original definition such as we discussed in Chapter 5 with the word justice. For example, in order to achieve 'liberating tolerance,' Marcuse proposed that "the cancellation of the liberal creed of free and equal discussion" was necessary, because real tolerance consisted of "intolerance against movements from the right, and toleration of movements from the left."[17] Everyone likes tolerance. However, what definition do we use to define it?

Marcuse may not be sole creator of this phenomenon, but his influence shows up in most of the victim studies classes in universities and colleges all over the world. One journalist even said, "If a museum of double standards is ever built, we should name it for Marcuse and put a huge statue of him on the roof."[18]

Whether it was tolerance, violence, or anything in between, Marcuse had one standard for his beliefs, and another for anyone who opposed them.

ABETTORS & DOUBLE STANDARDS

The clique has used double standards, embellishments, and what I call the exclusivity delusion, in abetting the narrative for decades. Most readers are familiar with at least some of the double standards, such as the mainstream media's and civil rights leader's portrayals of interracial crimes. Most are also aware of the way clique members embellish even the most tragic events like the Trayvon Martin case in which NBC News employees edited George Zimmerman's 911 call to make it sound as if Zimmerman said Martin looked suspicious only because he was black. Less familiar is the exclusivity delusion. When clique members depict a certain type of evil as only happening to or being perpetrated by a particular group, they are employing their exclusivity delusion.

In October of 2008, the Houston Chronicle published an op-ed by Starita Smith criticizing churches for "endorsing candidates or engaging in activity that is biased for or against candidates."[19] The editorial only mentioned right-wing, pro-life, McCain–Palin supporting churches as being a problem. Not a word appeared about Jeremiah Wright at Trinity United endorsing then candidate Obama.

Wright told his congregation Obama knew what it felt like to be "A black man living amongst rich white people." And, that one of Obama's opponents for the Democratic Presidential Nomination was apparently inferior to him because, "Hillary ain't never been called Nigger!" These and other pronouncements, too numerous to list, were de facto endorsements of Obama and were well known at the time Smith's op-ed ran in the Chronicle.

America Apart

Louis Farrakhan's Nation of Islam sells T-shirts that read "WELFARE = FAREWELL," meaning do not get on welfare because it will make you dependent on government. Rush Limbaugh says the same thing. Yet when Farrakhan says welfare is a bad thing, he is said to be "that strong brother, speaking the truth." When Limbaugh says it, he is called a racist. I asked a friend of mine here, D.B., who has a portrait of Elijah Muhammad tattooed on his chest, about this double standard. He acknowledged it, then shook his head, and then shrugged. Farrakhan also considered Muammar Gadhafi a righteous leader of the Libyan people. We also know he disliked all American Presidents—until Barack Obama was elected—because America has so many Blacks in prison and supposedly "brutalizes" them there. Yet even after Gadhafi murdered 1200 inmates in the Abu Salim prison in Tripoli, Farrakhan's support for the dictator never wavered.

On March 5, 2012, the Houston Chronicle ran an article on its front page. The article told the story of a black mother named Toni Carter who wanted to move to the suburbs. Carter wanted a bigger house for herself and her children but was worried about "raising her children in what would be an all-white enclave." She said, "I didn't know much about the suburbs. I expected it to be white-bread land."[20] My Random House *Webster's Dictionary* defines 'white-bread' as "Disparaging of or characteristic of the white middle class." Nowhere did the Chronicle writer say Carter's term was insensitive or disrespectful.

Years before this article, John Lopez, a sports columnist for the Chronicle, referred to the Houston Astros front office as 'lily white.' Lilies are flowers and therefore soft. Lopez's comment continues the stereotype, very prevalent amongst non-whites, that white men are soft and weak.

Can you imagine if one of the Chronicle's white sports writers went to a country that was 70 percent Native American or Mestizo and said that their soccer team's front office was bean-brown? What about calling the NBA Players Association boot-black? Any white writer doing so would be fired immediately.

In taxpayer-subsidized colleges and universities all across America, classes with titles like 'whiteness studies' invariably criticize white people. Black, Chicano, Asian, or women's studies however, invariably exalts Blacks, Chicanos, Asians, and women while also criticizing white men. Cesar Chavez was against illegal immigration, yet is held up as a hero by Americans of Mexican descent. Yet, any white against illegal immigration is a racist.

Origins and Abettors

The National Football League's T.J. Houshmandzadeh, while playing for the Cincinnati Bengals, was criticized by the host of a local sports talk radio show for skipping out on an interview with him. When told of the criticism, which had nothing to do with Houshmandzadeh's race, he called the talk show host a "punk ass white boy," even though this host was well into adulthood. The host called Houshmandzadeh a racist in response. He was promptly fired for doing so.

Why would a black man call an adult white male a 'boy?' The answer calls for a little inside baseball.

Many Blacks believe white men are inferior, especially that they are not as manly as black men. I first became aware of this when I was in junior high. At the local mall on the north side of Houston, Greenspoint, I often saw T-shirts worn only by black people with a parody of the NFL's Oakland Raiders' saying, "Real Men Wear Black." The shirts looked identical to those worn by Raiders fans with one slight variation. Instead of "Real Men Wear Black," they read "Real Men Are Black."

Normally, I was with a black friend of mine and, like any other white kid indoctrinated — err, educated in public schools, I had been taught that anytime a white person criticizes a black person, they do so because they are racist. So I never said much.

Over the years, I learned the specifics of why so many Blacks believe white men are a lesser breed. Conversations overheard between Blacks after they thought I was out of ear-shot, and hearing rapper after rapper assert the same, are very informative. Many have heard, "White men can't jump" (after all, some white men made a movie with that title). I personally proved that one wrong. I could dunk once I was a six foot tall junior in high school. But did you know white men also cannot fight, dance, sing, play musical instruments, or invent anything unless they first stole it from the black Egyptians? Oh, and I almost forgot white men cannot satisfy women as well as "real men" can, either.

Actor/Comedian Damon Wayans said on "The View," in reference to Don Imus' comments about Rutgers University's womens' basketball team, "It let me know where he stood."[21] Then, in jest, Wayans said that once he saw the girls himself, he "stood with" Imus in his characterization of the ladies as "nappy headed hoes" and "gangsta bitches." Oprah Winfrey never held a two-part show about Wayan's joke like she did Imus' joke. Imus was fired; Wayans was never even reprimanded (as well he should not have been).

America Apart

The white rapper Eminem once made a song in which he claimed black women were "dumb," and only wanted men for their money. Although this song was never released for public consumption, Eminem felt compelled to issue a written apology, saying he wrote the song after a black girlfriend of his had broken his heart.

In stark contrast to this, one of my favorite black rappers as a kid, Ice Cube, once made a song called "Cave Bitch," disparaging not just gold digging or treacherous white women, but all white women. *Lethal Injection* was released on Priority, a major record label. It was sold in all the large chain music retail stores nationwide. The title of the song refers to the Afrocentric belief that because white people were living in caves at one point, they are inferior to, and less civilized than, Blacks. The song itself has stereotype after stereotype about white women's bodies and choice lines like "cause ya can't tame me, wit' no bitch named Amy." An unaccredited voice, whose tone and cadence are very similar to Louis Farrakhan's, assists Ice Cube on his ballad. The song ends with this same person referring to white women as "subject to the itch, mutan-caucazoid cavebitch[s]."[22] To the best of my knowledge, Ice Cube has never issued an apology of any sort.

Those in the clique, of which Ice Cube is definitely a member, defend this—and other anti-white songs like it—by saying rappers are just "strong black brotha's" fighting the "White Power Structure." In the case of "Cave Bitch" in particular, they will say that Ice Cube is simply letting white women know he prefers black women. After all if Black men run off with white women, the black community will be destroyed. So, when Ice Cube says he cannot be "tamed" by a "bitch" named Amy, he is merely saying, "I will not let the slave master's wife turn me into an uncle Tom and conquer my people"—and that sentiment is always commendable amongst the clique.

The clique also says that white people do not understand black speech and that there is a tradition of Blacks engaging in bombastic word play that is not meant to be taken seriously. All this is pure rubbish. Rationalization elevated to an art form.

If you tell a clique member that a white rapper could never get away with releasing a similar song about black women, they would scream that it is an invalid comparison. They say that the historical context—particularly that Blacks have not been in control of America's institutions since its founding—changes the rules and calls for them to be applied differently to whites and Blacks. Many also claim that the 'black community' is facing extinction, and this alone entitles Blacks to be held to a different, lower standard than whites are. This is rationalization of current injustice (in this case of a double-standard) because of injustice in the past.

Ice Cube can diatribe against white women with impunity because Blacks—before he was born—were slaves and second class citizens. The facts that he was raised by both his parents, moved to a wealthy neighborhood as a teenager, and went on to become the most successful member of the hyper-talented group N.W.A. (the rap world's Beatles), made mainstream movies, sold millions of albums and created his own television show apparently do not matter. Nor does the fact that some Blacks are descended from 'free Blacks.'

If Ice Cube wanted to tell white women that he believes dating them will hasten the destruction of the black community, he could do so without calling them cave bitches. As for the belief that black men marrying or dating white women hinders the black population, facts don't support it. Black women have always had higher birth rates than white women. The current demographic trends show that Blacks are increasing their percentage of the American population, while the percentage of whites is decreasing. And as mentioned earlier, only about 7 percent of all marriages are black males marrying white females. In short, Ice Cube can relax. No need to worry about those "straight up and down," "no frills no thrills," cave bitches trying to conquer him and the other strong brothas in order to commit genocide upon black people.

I doubt Ice Cube is actually a racist. If memory serves, I believed he helped the white pop/rock/rap/country singer Kid Rock get into the music business. I have also heard him on the Jim Rome show whose host is white. However on every album he has ever put out, there are numerous references to white people as 'devils.' This is the word used by Nation of Islam members when referring to whites—whom they believe are a mutant race created by a two-brained scientist named Yaccub. Yaccub was supposedly angry about something and so he created whites for the sole purpose of inflicting harm upon black people.

Despite the inclusion of racist lyrics in all his albums, major movie studios continue to cast Ice Cube—even in family movies like *Are We There Yet?* Even Coors Beer Company has given him a lucrative endorsement contract. This sends a strong message to other Blacks. There are no consequences for saying racist things about white people.

It also widens the gulf between these two groups, because whites see Blacks getting away with things they know they cannot. It encourages whites to develop resentment towards Blacks not unlike the resentment Blacks had towards whites when they were treated as second class citizens.

Filmmaker Spike Lee, award-winning rhythm and blues singer Jill Scott, and the rapper Common (another former favorite) have all said publicly that they disapprove of interracial relationships. Spike Lee has been quoted saying that when he sees interracial couples he stares "daggers" into them. Yet ESPN still tries to include him in every 30 for 30 film they ever make. Scott said that when she found out a black friend of hers was married to a white person it "hurt [her] spirit." But no one at MTV or any of the nation's radio stations has ever refused to play Scott's or Common's work. Could you imagine what would happen if a white musician came out against interracial dating?

Not only has no one even been critical of Scott or Common, the latter was invited to the White House by First Lady Michelle Obama to read some of his poetry. I wonder if it ever dawned on Mrs. Obama that her husband would not exist if his father and mother had shared Common's views on interracial relationships...

Consider the double standard in political circles. During the nomination of Sonia Sotomayor to the Supreme Court, pundits on the right got ahold of a statement Sotomayor once made. She had said she hoped "a wise Latina, with the richness of her experiences" would reach a better conclusion than a white male justice, when dealing with a legal matter. They correctly pointed out that if a white man had said white males reach better decisions than Latinas, his career would have ended the moment he uttered it.

Clique pundit and Washington Post columnist Eugene Robinson quickly deployed the "Historical Context" argument. He said that Latinos had not "run the world for the last millennium."[23] Such statements argue that white people reached a higher level of achievement in the past, so for equality's sake, we should give special treatment to Latinos today—hence, they are to be given a pass when they make comments like the one Justice Sotomayor made. Robinson, like clique members often do, is confusing intertemporal abstractions—whites and Latinos of the past—with flesh and blood humans of the present.

When Sotomayor was going to college, very much in the affirmative action era for America's Universities, she was privileged because of her ethnicity, not discriminated against. Sotomayor's historical context is not a millennium of oppression. Therefore, she should not be given a pass, for the same reason giving passes to Ice Cube or anyone else is unacceptable.

As for the actual comment, clique columnist Richard Cohen rationalized that it was a "comment about the innate astuteness of a wise Latina."[24] Others tried to spin it as Sotomayor simply suggesting that as a Justice, she would draw from her cultural heritage.

As someone who has been unlawfully kept in prison for 17 years, unable to raise my daughter, because some Justices issued an opinion on my appeal not rooted in Texas or U.S. law, I can say with certainty, we do not need Justice Sotomayor to bring her perceived superior cultural experiences with her when she goes to work. From what I have seen, Judges and Justices have enough trouble ruling on matters of law and fact correctly without dragging their cultural heritage into the equation.

Regardless of how the clique's spin masters explain the comment, the bottom line is Sotomayor meant what she said. She really believes Latina's experiences make them better legal decision makers than white males. She is the personification of identity politics. Whites oppress Latina's. Oppression makes Latina's stronger, wiser, and more understanding than those dumb, asleep-at-the-wheel, trust-fund-baby white Justices. Even if all Latina's were the victims of discrimination, there is no proof that the oppressed make better legal decisions than the non-oppressed.

For instance, Houston-based Federal District Judge Vanessa Gilmore, a black woman, has had more of her opinions overruled by the higher 5th Circuit Court than practically any other judge at that level. While I am no expert, it seems black women are higher on the totem pole of oppressed victims than Latinas like Sotomayor.

In 2006, Steve Cohen was elected to the U.S. House of Representatives as the only white congressman representing a majority black district. After arriving in Washington, Cohen applied for membership in the Congressional Black Caucus (CBC), which holds its meetings, and functions in taxpayer-funded offices on taxpayer-funded land. Cohen, like Peter Stark and every other white person who ever applied for membership, was denied because he is white. Caucus member William Clay Sr. claims that it is critical that the CBC stays "exclusively African-American." About Cohen in particular, Representative William Lacy Clay Jr. said, "Mr. Cohen asked for admission, and he got his answer… It's time to move on. It's an unwritten rule. It's understood. It's clear."[25]

If double standards like this persist, it is going to become more difficult to tell those rocket scientists who claim we need "White History Month" or a "United Cracker College Fund," to shut up. They will realize that two can play at this lucrative game of grievance politics, and before long 'oppressed whites' could become as common a phrase as 'wise Latina.'

In August of 2012, presumptive GOP Presidential nominee Mitt Romney gave a speech in Israel. Amongst other things, he suggested that it was possible Israel's and Palestine's vastly different rates of economic growth could be attributed to their vastly different cultures. Reporters and a spokesperson for the Palestinian Authority quickly issued their obligatory charges of racism. The mainstream media in the U.S. of course followed suit. But what Romney said was no different than what appeared in a recent U.N. report. This report stated plainly, "Culture and values are the soul of development," and that "traditional Arab culture and values" are among the main hindrances to economic prosperity for Arabs. Specifically, the report blames the "rampant corruption, repressive governance and lack of women's rights as major contributors to backwardness in the Arab world."[26] Romney merely suggested that culture might make a difference. The report stated unequivocally that culture not only made a difference, but that it was the main problem when it came to progress in the Arab world. Romney was called a bigot, while those who produced the report are held up as heroes. Is that what you call privilege?

Do you remember the media circus surrounding the alleged rape of a black stripper by white lacrosse players at Duke University in 2006? The allegations turned out to be false, and clique members like ESPN's Jamelle Hill were forced to resort to defensive oral artistry. Hill in particular claimed her premature determinations of guilt were really just comments on the 'racial climate' at Duke.

Do you remember the wall-to-wall media coverage of the 15-year old white girl who was kidnapped from a bus stop in New York and then raped by multiple black males? Clique members might say that the Duke case had racial undertones, when in reality it did not. The lacrosse players had actually requested a white and Asian stripper. In contrast, Clique members might suggest the case in New York was just a random act of violence. However, when the 15-year old girl, who actually was raped (unlike the stripper), asked her attackers why they had chosen her, they replied, "Because you are white and perfect."[27]

A few years ago, three black men and one black woman kidnapped a young white couple in Knoxville Tennessee.[28] The black kidnappers raped and tortured the white man first before killing him, forcing his girlfriend to watch the entire ordeal. They then raped and mutilated her before taking her life as well. In an attempt to wipe out DNA evidence, the kidnappers poured "bleach and some other cleaning agent" down her throat and over her genitalia before dumping her body. This case of course received little to no national media attention.

Editors at the Chicago Tribune, The New York Times, and Los Angeles times have "admitted to deliberately censoring" the details and motivations of black-on-white crimes in order to "guard against subjecting an entire group of people to suspicion."[29] Apparently they have no such qualms about subjecting white people to "suspicion" of across-the-race racism when a white-on-black crime occurs.

Another obvious case of black-on-white crime, motivated by black racism at least partially caused by the narrative, happened in North Carolina. Melissa McLaughlin, a white woman, was kidnapped and raped by seven black males. After each of them had raped her numerous times they threw her into a tub of bleach.[30] McLaughlin was then shot 5 times, killing her. Surely this was just another case of random violence, right? No racial motivation whatsoever, right? After being arrested, one of the kidnappers asserted that "400 years of white oppression" was what drove him and his friends to commit their crime against McLaughlin.[603]

In December of 1984, Bernhard Goetz was riding a subway train in N.Y. when four teenagers attempted to rob him. All four would turn out to have criminal records. Goetz pulled out a pistol and managed to shoot all four of the would-be robbers. While they all survived, one of the teens did become paralyzed for life. They were all black. Goetz was white. Unwisely, Goetz fled the scene and went underground. Ten days later, after a large-scale manhunt was well under way, Goetz turned himself in and was charged with several offenses including attempted murder. But after weighing the evidence before them, the grand jury only indicted Goetz for possession of an unlicensed weapon, an offense for which he would have to serve 8 months in prison.[32]

That was not the end of Mr. Goetz's troubles. The teenager paralyzed in the attempted robbery sued and won a $43 million dollar judgment against Goetz. The teen's attorney, clique member Ronald Kuby, celebrated his client's dubious victory, saying it sent "a real clear message to all the bigots out there, all the racists with guns, all the people who consider the lives of young black men to be worthless. These lives are worth a lot and so you better keep those guns in their holster." The media assisted Kuby in re-branding the case by rarely mentioning that these teens all had criminal records and were attempting to rob Goetz.[33] After all their heavily biased coverage, four common criminals were turned into Civil Rights heroes and a man, who simply defended himself, into a Nazi.

America Apart

Bernhard Goetz became a household name. Austin Weekes however, does not ring a bell for most. Four years prior to the Goetz incident, while also riding a subway train, two white teens approached Weekes, spit on him and asked, "What are you looking at Nigger?" Weekes then retrieved a pistol from his bag (for which, like Goetz, he did not have a license) and fired it at one of the teens. The young man died, and Weekes fled the scene, just like Goetz.

Unlike Goetz, Weekes refused to turn himself in. He was not apprehended until six years after the incident occurred. He was charged with second degree murder. Weekes cried while being questioned by the police and told them he was only carrying the gun to prevent himself from being mugged again. The Brooklyn grand jury before which his case was heard decided against indicting Weekes. He walked, scot-free.[34] He did not serve 8 months time for the unlicensed pistol. He was not called a racist. The media did not vilify him. He was black and his attackers were white.

When whites commit crimes against Blacks, or merely defend themselves against Blacks, as was the case with Bernhard Goetz, the media deems the race of all involved, relevant. When the shoe is on the other foot, that is, when a black person commits a crime against a white person, mentioning the race of the perpetrators and victims is unadvised because, at least at the Los Angeles Times, The New York Times, and the Chicago Tribune, they must "guard against subjecting an entire group of people to suspicion."

These aren't isolated cases. In March of 1994, 12 elderly women were beaten and robbed by five adolescents in Brooklyn New York. The most severe of those assaults was endured by a seventy-year old who had her skull and hip fractured by the thugs. As you may have guessed by now, the New York Times and New York's other dailies failed to mention that all five of these robbers were black, and all twelve of their victims were white.

It is difficult to understand how the newspapers came to the conclusion that the race of those involved in this case was not worth mentioning. Especially considering that one of the robbers said he and his co-conspirators had a pre-crime agreement that they "would only take white women."[35] If these hoodlums had been white, and it became known that they exclusively targeted elderly black women, the paper of record would have deemed their race newsworthy.

Also in the Big Apple, back in 1997, a member of an Afrocentric spinoff of the Nation of Islam brutally attacked a white woman named Luara Zirinsky. Her assailant kicked her in the head so hard that only emergency brain surgery kept her alive.[36] When the assailant committed the crime, he actually had a journal on his person overflowing with racist writings about whites and calls for a race war. But as was the case with the Beltway sniper's racist, anti-white drawings, very few in the media had the stones to mention the journal and it's contents. Apparently, when racism is the motive, the press only finds it noteworthy if someone white commits the crime.

Motive was also barely reported on in the case of Christopher Peterson, a black male in Indiana. Peterson used a shotgun to slaughter seven people, all of whom were white. He was unambiguous when he explained why he murdered these people. He freely admitted he was motivated by "a deep-rooted hatred of white people."[37]

Hulon Mitchell was the leader of the Afrocentric, black supremacist religious movement, Nation of Yahweh, in Miami, Florida. From the mid 1980's into the early 1990's, he taught a 'killing class' in which he instructed his followers to kill 'white devils.' By the time Mitchell was arrested, his group was known to be responsible for a minimum of seven murders.[38] All of the victims were white, and according to one of his followers, Mitchell himself was responsible for killing at least three white people. Body parts such as fingers and ears were cut off victims and given to Mitchell by his followers as if they were memorabilia. Like the aforementioned black criminals, Mitchell made no secret of why his victims were white.

He said, "One day Yahweh is going to kill the white devil off the planet." And, "we are going to catch him and… kill him wherever we find him. All over America, white heads are going to roll."[39] But at the time of Mitchell's trial, when the media should have been reporting on this, they had the country captivated by another criminal trial with racial overtones: the LAPD officers charged with beating Rodney King.

Think about that for a moment. Think about the difference in media coverage between these two racially charged cases. In Miami, a hate group is responsible for at least seven human beings losing their lives. In Los Angeles, the cops beat a felon after driving in excess of 120 mph, while drunk and endangering the lives of all the innocent people on the freeway that night. And where was the media's attention focused?

We were all told directly and indirectly that the cops beating King after he had thrown punches at them was one of the most hideous, yet common examples of racism: white men in positions of power abusing the preeminent victim for all times, a black man. But during Rodney King's lifetime, Blacks have assaulted, robbed, raped, and murdered many more whites then whites have victimized Blacks. Remember, interracial crimes do not occur that often, but when they do, 89 percent of the time they are black-on-white. And when it comes to 'hate crimes' in general, the FBI states that 63 percent of them can be labeled as 'anti-white.' As for murders in particular, 50 percent of those in which race is identified as the motivating factor are committed by Blacks who only make up 12 percent of the population.[40]

The old media saw goes something like this: Dog bites man, no story. Man bites dog, story. In other words, they want sensational. Why is it not more sensational that seven people were murdered because they were white than that some cops overreacted to a drunk ex-con driving recklessly and taking a few swings at them?

The media rationalizes this obvious double standard via the historical context argument. Because it was once legal for whites to beat Blacks, they point to current occurrences as proof history is just repeating itself. Because of this belief, they reason that preferential policies and reparations are due for all non-whites.

This double standard could not exist without journalists holding non-whites to a lower standard. In their world, you cannot hold Blacks to the same standards you do whites because they are victims of white oppression. It is not too much of a leap from there to say that when Blacks murder and mutilate seven white people, it is only revenge—not racism—for they are the eternal victims of the blue-eyed devils.

Many in the clique will call the above black-on-white crimes isolated incidents. And in the grand scheme of crimes, they are actually right. However, because they have bought hook, line, and sinker, the historical context argument—an intertemporal abstraction fallacy if ever there was one—they refuse to acknowledge that cases like that of Trayvon Martin are even more isolated. Yet just as it was with the Tawana Brawley and Duke Lacrosse players' cases, the Reverends rode into Samford, Florida, and called the tragedy an epidemic.

My Random House *Webster's Dictionary* defines an epidemic as 1) affecting many individuals at the same time, 2) prevalent; widespread. Mestizo men who are classified as white Hispanics, or just plain white, killing 17-year-old black kids is not epidemic in society. Over 90 percent of all black murder victims are murdered by Blacks, not whites, not white Hispanics, and certainly not half white, part Peruvian Indian, part black (by way of his maternal grandfather) Mestizos—which is George Zimmerman's actual heritage.

Origins and Abettors

While the Martin case was receiving a tremendous amount of media attention, approximately 40 black people were shot over a single weekend in Chicago. Many of them including a six-year-old girl, died. I never saw this mentioned on CNN, NBC, ABC, or CBS. Nor did I hear either one of the Reverends call that weekend of carnage 'epidemic,' even though that type of black-on-black violence is much more prevalent than half-white, half-mestizo, part black-on-black violence.

When it comes to racism in general, clique members like to believe that non-whites cannot be racist because they lack 'institutional power.'[41] In response to this claim, Dr. Sowell points out that this would mean that Adolf Hitler "could not of been considered a racist when he was an isolated street corner rabble-rouser, but only after he became Chancellor of Germany."[42] And in America there are scores of black litigators, cops, police chiefs, Mayors and even a half-black President. But Whitney Young, a member of the National urban League claims that black "anti-white feelings" are not to be compared with racism from whites because doing so would "equate the bitterness of the victim with the evil that oppresses him."[43] This expansion of the definition of racism is really just a way for clique members to rationalize and excuse the racism of non-whites. They truly believe white men created so many injustices in the past that it's okay to press new injustices upon whites today in order to even the score.

The wide ranging approval of Nathan McCall's book *Makes Me Wanna Holler* by the clique's literary critics is one of the better examples of how accepted black racism is. Their favorable reviews helped propel the book to the bestseller list. When I entered the Texas Department of Criminal Justice in the late 1990s, I became friends with a black inmate, who happened to be reading it. We will call him D.G.

Like myself, he was locked up for capital murder. Before a friend of his convinced D.G. to go along with him in a robbery attempt of some Columbian drug dealers, D.G. had a good job working for a gas company. His mother, who was a schoolteacher, and his father, who was a Federal Marshall, raised him in Acres Homes on the north side of Houston.

We got to know each other even though black and white inmates did not talk to each other much, because the apartment complex I lived in when I was arrested was close to where D.G. had once lived. We found we knew some of the same people. He was ten years older and reminded me of one of my roommates who was at times like a big brother to me. They were both Christians, liked playing basketball, and neither seemed to feel like it cramped their style when we were around other Blacks to have a younger, too-cocky-when-he-played-ball white kid with them.

When I was moved to D.G.'s wing, I had just gotten back from having my broken hand set at the hospital in Galveston.

It all began in the dayroom. Several Mexicans (their preference because they say, "A Hispanic is a black," and apparently that is bad) from various gangs (called families) and I disagreed over what to watch on the dayroom T.V. When I tried to leave it alone and walk away, one of the Mexicans approached me and said that they always watched the Spanish channel at that time. "So what's up!"

In here when there is a chance to "get whitey" or "get the gringo," non-white gangs, who normally fight each other, often join up to share in the fun. I took the "what's up" as a challenge, and yelled at every Mexican in the dayroom. "I told you motherfuckers I don't care about that TV. Now, y'all get your bitch ass in the shower!" The shower is where we go to fight because guards cannot see into it when they are sitting down (which, they normally are). The whole incident almost started a riot and left me with a broken hand.

I explain all of this because it speaks to the friendship D.G. and I had. When I was assigned to his section, some tension still existed between the whites and the Mexicans. There were only two other whites in that section, and unlike me, they were not peckerwoods—whites who will fight. I had a cast on my hand and was awaiting surgery. If any of the Mexicans had chosen to retaliate, I would have been in trouble. So D.G. sat with me every day when I was in the dayroom. He was not going to fight for me. That is what you do for a 'ho,' who is paying commissary or sexual favors for protection. But he was going to fight **with** me, or at least make sure I only had to fight with one at a time.

The threat of retaliation was very real. Yet D.G. and his 20-year old 'little brother' sat next to each other on the same bench every day, until I had the surgery, and later got the cast removed. In short, I had a ton of respect for D.G. He was a real friend.

Every day, D.G. either brought a Bible, (which I criticized to no end Richard Dawkin's style), the USA Today sports page, or some other reading material to the dayroom. One day he brought the Nathan McCall book. I recognized the title as that of a Marvin Gaye song and figured it was about a guy going through some things, and trying to make something of himself. At the time, I could have counted on one hand how many books I had read in my entire life. Looking at the cover photo, I assumed McCall was really smart. He was wearing the type of hat a lot of the "conscious" rappers of my youth wore and, well, he had a published book. I asked D.G. if it was any good. He said, "Yeah, you wanna check it out?"

The first page was a little disheartening, especially for someone like me who has a child with a black woman and needs this experiment in diversity known as 21st century America to work. McCall's best-selling autobiography begins with him telling the reader how good it felt to kick an innocent white kid in "his balls" after he and his friends pulled the kid off his bike.[44] McCall makes it sound as if there is no more enjoyable activity for him and his friends than "fucking up white boys." He says further that he and his friends liked the Black Panthers because they "hated white folks." Not because of "all that political stuff." McCall also says that he bragged to his friends about how he "fucked up some white folks" after shooting a shotgun into a white family's living room and how doing so made him feel "proud."[45]

As I read all of this, I just knew McCall was going to have some sort of epiphany that would cause him to change his racist views. After all, D.G. said it was a good book. Good thing I was not holding my breath. McCall eventually goes to prison for armed robbery. At which point, I gave up all hope for a happy ending. I knew exactly what a trip to prison would do. Sure enough McCall became even more radicalized in his views of white people.

While locked up, McCall learned about "the white man's evil ways" and came to believe that "white men are the most lying creatures on the face of the earth." And, that they "oppressed people of color whenever they encountered them."[46] This last notion was reinforced after McCall got out of prison and attended a historically black college where he was taught that whites "place a premium on conquering people and developing objects."[47] There is of course no perspective whatsoever in these indictments of white people. Nothing about the Zulu and other tribes in Africa conquering and enslaving people or the Aztecs, Mayans, and Incas doing the same in the Americas. Nor is there any mention of the fact that before they had boats, whites conquered and enslaved other whites.

The Pitts of the world will say that it was not the Zulus or Aztecs who oppressed McCall and that is why he does not mention them. This would be a relevant point were it not for the fact that, as best I can tell from his book, McCall, was never discriminated against. The clique however believes that McCall's' ancestors being discriminated against is good enough.

After graduating from college, McCall works for a couple of newspapers before landing a coveted gig at the Washington Post. Now comes the "ah-ha" moment where he has a revelation that hard work, determination, and sacrifice in America can lead to even a convicted felon working at one of the nation's most respected newspapers, right? Not quite.

Instead we get this gem: "The dumbest thing a black person can do is trust a white man."[48] So after white people hire McCall, and he becomes successful, he still finds it more to his liking to see them as immutable and perpetual enemies. Success is rewarding, but apparently not more so than seeing yourself as a rebel fighter behind enemy lines, as President Obama saw himself when he was working in the private sector. The hard truth that keeps coming around like a gravity-defying boomerang is that human beings are going to do what feels good. If it is more emotionally satisfying to see yourself as a victim/underdog because it makes an accomplishment like working for the Washington Post more gratifying, we are all in trouble. If Nathan McCall of all people cannot admit that black's success in America, at least in the present day, is controlled by what they choose in life, he is in denial. And he is certainly not alone.

I ended up going back to the hospital to have my cast removed before I finished reading *Makes Me Wanna Holler*. When I did finish it, I was on a different wing, and reading someone else's copy of it. It is very popular here. D.G. was shipped to another unit to go to college before we got a chance to discuss the book. Nine years passed before I saw him again, when I was shipped to the same unit to also go to college. We got to talk a few times in the hallway, but I always forgot to tell him I finished reading the book.

We were always so busy bragging to one another about our daughters or commiserating over the Rockets, Texans, and Astros. I like to think that if someone like D.G. can think *Makes Me Wanna Holler* is a good book, and still be friends with a white guy like me, in prison of all places, maybe the future is not so bleak.

However, numerous incidents keep me pessimistic. For example in the spring of 2014, the National Basketball Association banned the owner of the Los Angeles Clippers, Donald Sterling, for life because he told his half-black, half-Latina girlfriend not to take pictures with black people or bring them to games. NBA Commissioner Adam Silver decided Sterling was not fit to own the team and ordered him to sell it.

The media coverage for this incident is actually what discourages me about the future. ESPN gave wall-to-wall coverage on two of its networks, ESPN and ESPN 2. ABC, NBC, CBS, and all of the cable news channels ran multiple stories on the racist, soon to be former owner of the Clippers. They told the public Sterling had a history of racism, including an incident in which Sterling expressed a desire to not rent any of the apartments he owned to Hispanics.

So it was an open and shut case. Sterling was a serial offender against the public's racism laws, and he was to be punished. The facts that Sterling gave up draft picks in order to obtain a black coach, Doc Rivers and paid him a salary higher than any other coach in the league mattered none. Nor did the fact that Sterling's team had more black players than the average NBA team, and these players were paid the sixth highest payroll in the NBA. In other words, there was no evidence Sterling discriminated against 'them,' (i.e. Blacks) in his capacity as the owner of the Los Angeles Clippers.

Donald Sterling apparently believes there is something intrinsic to black people that makes their company undesirable. He was banned from team ownership for life for saying that he didn't want his girlfriend taking pictures or attending Clippers games with black people.

How is this different from believing all white people are 'wicked and weak?' This belief is a tenant of the Nation of Islam and it's spinoff, Five Percent Nation. A couple of weeks before the Sterling conversation was made public, the rapper Jay-Z, who owned part of the NBA's Brooklyn Nets and a sports management agency that represents players in the NBA and other pro leagues, was shown on national television — at a Nets game — wearing a large gold medallion of the Five Percent's symbol.

One of the daily newspapers in New York City reported on Jay-Z's choice of jewelry and asked him if he shared the beliefs of the Five Percenters. Jay-Z replied, "Something like that." The reporter called the Five Percenter headquarters in New York and asked them if Jay-Z was a member. They said, "Not to our knowledge."

Tom Jackson, Lisa Salters, or any other clique members working at ESPN, never mentioned Jay-Z's endorsement of the black supremacist group. Neither has the rapper Nelly's rumored membership in The Five Percent Nation, while owning the Charlotte Bobcats with Michael Jordan made ESPN news. Magic Johnson did not call for a boycott of the Nets like he did the Clippers. Nelly and Jay-Z are guilty of the same thing Donald Sterling is — not actual discrimination, but aligning themselves with organizations which promote the belief other races are inferior to their own. ESPN, like the rest of the clique, apparently only see racism from whites as being newsworthy.

The obligatory rebuttal by the Pitts of the world continues along the lines of, "The Five Percenter guys help keep brotha's out of prison and off drugs. They don't run around oppressing white people." But their beliefs, that "black man is God" or that all white people are 'wicked and weak,' are not necessary elements of a strategy to keep black men on the straight and narrow. And all you really have to do is ask yourself, would a white NBA team owner, or a white sports agent like David Faulk, be able to get away with wearing a medallion of some white supremacist group in public? Would ESPN avoid even running a single story on such an incident, as they did when Jay-Z made such a public statement of what he believes?

The next rebuttal will of course be that Sterling has a 'history' of racism. However, during the otherwise great song *Regrets*, from his debut album, Jay-Z refers to a person with 'eyes like a Korean' as a 'chink.' This is a blatant slur of Asian people, and if Jay-Z were white, it would qualify him as having a history of racism.

Jim Crow laws were struck down because they were double standards. McCall's book was successful largely because there is a double standard for black racism. Jay-Z and Nelly are still involved with the NBA because of this double standard. Today allowing such hypocrisy to stand nourishes the narrative and pushes the races further apart, just as surely as separate water fountains did in the past. The Pitts of the world think that they are helping non-whites by letting them get away with things that they would never let whites get away with. They think that just because black's ancestors were enslaved and discriminated against in the past, their descendants are not at fault for their racism. However, they fail to realize that in order for a society to function, it must have the same set of rules for everyone. If not, the races become polarized like they did in Sri Lanka and many other places.

EMBELLISHMENT

The clique also likes to embellish and flat-out lie about racial incidents in hopes of inducing more guilt in whites, enabling them to further their agenda. Take a look at clique-controlled Hollywood. In 2008, they released a movie about Ernie Davis, the first black college football player to win the Heisman Trophy, called *The Express*. In one scene, they show Davis' Syracuse team playing on the road against the West Virginia Mountaineers. All of the Mountaineer fans hurl bottles or racial insults at Davis because he is black. However, in reality that particular game between Syracuse and West Virginia was played in Syracuse sans the airborne bottles and racial slurs. Another scene shows the Syracuse football team riding a bus to a game in Texas because the black players were supposedly barred from flying in the same plane with their white teammates. Pure fiction. The entire team made the trip together on the same airplane. Black players are shown being forced to sleep on threadbare cots in unkempt rooms when on the road at away games. In real life however, these players slept in hotel suites. Another fiction in this based-on-a-true story movie is the entire team refused to go to an after-game banquet because the black players are not allowed to go. What really happened? All the players were welcomed and attended the banquet together—until the black players chose to leave early so they could attend a black-only banquet put on for them by the NAACP.[49]

Black athletes were discriminated against. Jackie Robinson and others in the past even received death threats. As late as the early 1990s, I can remember hearing Warren Moon, the quarterback for my then beloved Oilers, saying that fans, even at home games, called out racist slurs. Yet, we must ask, "What purpose does making a despicable situation worse than it was serve?" Is it to make white people feel guilty so that they 'spread' the wealth around?

Another deplorable racial incident the clique has embellished and distorted wildly to their advantage is the Tuskegee experiment. Most people today believe a bunch of racist white doctors in Alabama secretly injected black males with syphilis and then watched them die. In reality, a group of black and white doctors recruited Blacks who already had syphilis and monitored them to learn about the disease. Scholars disagree over whether or not these men could have been cured at the time, but there is no disputing Klan-member doctors did not inject them with the disease.[50] This misunderstanding is why today, Jeremiah Wright and Louis Farrakhan can tell Blacks their higher rates of HIV infection are due to racist scientists putting the virus in soda cans in vending machines located in black neighborhoods. This of course hurts Blacks by keeping them from identifying the real causes of their higher infection rates.

The history of America, or anywhere else for that matter, should be taught in its entirety—as it actually happened. Not as historians or Hollywood producers wish it had happened. For instance, portraying University of Kentucky basketball coach Adolph Rupp as a rabid racist in the Disney movie about a West Texas team that was the first to have five black starters—when there is no evidence of Rupp being a racist—is not only a disservice to a human being unable to defend himself because he is no longer with us; but it is also harmful to those more-important-than-everyone-else 'youths of color.' How? The same way it is harmful to tell 'youths of color' the justice system is rigged against them: it makes them believe the odds are so stacked against them that they might as well not even try. They see and hear it all their lives in movies like *Daddy's Little Girls*, songs like "White Man's World" by Tupac, and at rallies where spiritual leaders are claiming that whites killing and raping Blacks is 'epidemic.' In everyday life, racial embellishments lead to more kids in the ghetto giving up and going with the flow around them.

All of us should be angered by injustice. America's history—like every country's history—has its share of injustices. But playing up the racism in movies such as *The Blind Side*, or treating *Roots* as fact, when Alex Haley himself called it a myth,[51] leads to more beltway snipers and Yahweh cults. Clique members express little concern about these extreme cases. As you read their commentary, it appears these incidents are nothing more than the chickens coming home to roost. Time for those white folks to pay the piper. They should keep in mind however that there is a reason the fable "The Boy Who Cried Wolf" has been around for so long.

EXCLUSIVITY

The narrative is also abetted by what I call the exclusivity delusion. Clique members love to portray conquest and subjugation as if they are exclusive to America. An excellent example of this appeared in the Houston Chronicle in March of 2012. A Houston-based writer named Beverly McPhail in a piece titled "We Must Acknowledge the Existence of Racism in America," asserted, matter-of-factly, "… our great country was built on racism and discrimination, from enslaving Africans for forced labor and later enforcing a Jim Crow system of apartheid, to the near annihilation of indigenous peoples while stealing their land, to forcing Japanese Americans into training camps during World War II and excluding Chinese through the Chinese Exclusion Act, and profiting from cheap labor of Latinos while simultaneously punishing them through hostile immigration policies."[52]

The problem with this statement is that every evil she lists has occurred on every continent, at the hands of every race. Yet she makes it sound as if conquest and subjugation, racism and discrimination, are unique to America. If she said all of these things are tragically a part of the human condition, and not exclusive to America, her article would be much more accurate. She also recommends *Silent Racism: How Well Meaning White People Perpetuate the Racial Divide*, a suggestion which reinforces the left wing belief that only America and its white population have ever done these types of things.

When you hear that America is built on racism, you assume that the U.S. and racism are analogous to a house and its foundation. That is, if you removed the racism and slavery from America's past, it would crumble like a house without a foundation. We will explore this hypothesis briefly before demonstrating that America's past injustices are not exclusive to the land within her borders.

In 1790, black slaves constituted 18 percent of the U.S. population. From a proportional standpoint, this represented the apex for the black population in America. In order for Ms. McPhail's claim to be true, that America was built on the supposedly racist practice of slave labor, it would have to be proven that a group of people who never made up more than one-fifth of the country was responsible for creating the majority of the country's wealth. Every piece of verifiable evidence available says otherwise.[53]

In the early 1780s, Pennsylvania enacted a law to free its slaves with Connecticut and Rhode Island doing the same a few years after the Quaker State. New York followed suit in 1799. Soon after their emancipations, these state's economies began to expand rapidly due to increases in production, trade, and the growing financial institutions in the cities of Philadelphia and Manhattan. None of this was fueled by slave labor. It was the same story in the Midwest where the Northwest Ordinance outlawed slavery in 1787.[54]

The story in the South however, where slavery remained legal, was entirely different. "In terms of bank capital, the North topped the South by more than four to one, while the value of the North's manufactured goods exceeded Southern production by a staggering ten to one." When it came to the amount of railroad tracks laid, the North outpaced the South by 300 percent. While "commercial shipping" played a large role in the North's economy, it was "virtually nonexistent in the South."[55]

The American South was not an exception to the ostensible rule of slavery making people rich. "Brazil, which imported several times as many slaves as the United States, and perhaps consumed more slaves than any other nation in history, was nevertheless still a relatively underdeveloped country when slavery ended there in 1888, and its subsequent economic development was largely the work of immigrants from Europe and Japan."[56] And just as it was with the U.S., when slavery ended, the poorest regions of Brazil were those that had slavery. Nor was this result limited to slave owners in the new world:

America Apart

The slave societies of North Africa and the Middle East, which absorbed even more millions of slaves than the western hemisphere, lagged conspicuously behind the technological and economic level of the West, both during and after the end of slavery until oil, not slaves, raised their standards of living in the modern era. In Europe it was the nations in the Western region of the continent, where slavery was abolished first, that led the continent and the world into the modern industrial age.[57]

Black slaves did contribute to America's greatness. However, the official numbers from the census show that by 1860 only about 25 percent of the population in the American South owned slaves. And only a scant 0.7 percent of slave owners presided over plantations with 50 or more slaves.[58] In other words, as one researcher puts it: "The typical Southern slaveholder was more likely to be working in the field beside his slaves than sitting on the verandah sipping a mint Julep."[59]

There is no cause and effect relationship between racism and slavery, and American prosperity, as Ms. McPhail claims. Capitalism, demographics, and a constitution that allowed people to profit from their abilities, without the fear of having the King commandeer all they had worked for were the most prominent ingredients in the foundation America rests upon.

Ms. McPhail also says that America is built on the "near annihilation of indigenous peoples while stealing their land." Because of the perspective-lacking scrutiny of America's founding, many have come to believe that conquest and subjugation are exclusive to those from the west, that is, white men. Jesse Jackson once chanted, "Ho, ho, ho western civ has to go" while protesting the curriculum at Stanford University. The other famous reverend, Al Sharpton, said while speaking to black students at Kean College in New Jersey, "White folks was in the caves while we was building empires... we built pyramids before Donald Trump even knew what architecture was... we taught philosophy and astrology and mathematics before Socrates and them Greek homos were born,"[60] belittling the achievements of the West.

Pointing out that racism, slavery, and conquest occurred in all other societies is not an argument against the fact that those things happened in America. It is merely an attempt to tell the entire story. When trying to educate people as McPhail's column was supposed to do, writers should aim for the most informative rendering, not the account which fits an agenda. Human beings are emotional creatures prone to interpreting things in whatever light is most beneficial to them.

Origins and Abettors

Could non-whites increase their victim status in America if they were the only ones to ever have had their ancestors conquered and subjugated and themselves discriminated against? This delusion would buttress the claims that America is irredeemably evil and therefore in need of "fundamental" change via spreading more of the wealth around.

When it comes to "near annihilation of indigenous peoples," commentators as varied in their occupations and opinions as evolutionary biologist Jared Diamond and economist Dr. Thomas Sowell, have both pointed out that 95 percent of the Native Americans who died after European contact did so because of germs, not governmental policies of genocide and annihilation. These germs were passed before anyone had even proffered the germ theory of disease. Europeans and their livestock brought germs into the western hemisphere its natives unfortunately had no natural immunity to. As P.J. O'Rourke puts it, the "horrors that beset ancient Americans following 1492 would have happened if the Nina, the Pinta, and Santa Maria had been manned by Jimmy Carter, the Dalai Lama, and Bono."

We're told white people should never have come at all. Before the Europeans arrived, Native Americans were living in harmony with one another and the environment. Which is why it is so terrible that whites brought their evil ways of private property and slavery to these otherwise blameless people who had never known such treachery. This fairy tale line of thinking is actually very common amongst the clique.

Before the Europeans arrived, in what for them was a New World, Native American tribes and empires conquered and subjugated their weaker peers constantly. In Central America, the Mayans were a blood thirsty people, notorious for their barbaric methods of torture. They prosecuted full-fledged war against other groups of natives for the sole purpose of acquiring slaves who would then be dismembered in any one of their many sadistic rituals requiring human sacrifice. Slaves were also bought and sold amongst the Mayans. If a Mayan committed a crime punishable by death, it normally meant a life of slavery for his/her remaining family members. And to recognize something as mundane as a new leader coming into power, the Mayans mutilated and sacrificed numerous innocent people in ritualized massacres.[61]

The Aztecs were equally oppressive. They also built their expansive empire by subjugating vulnerable neighboring tribes through warfare, raping, pillaging, and murdering all they conquered. The Aztecs routinely slaughtered the prisoners they took from defeated tribes whose skin and hair color were identical to theirs. This means that they did not see themselves united as one nation of "Bronze People." Some of those captured prisoners were kept alive and murdered in rituals that called for their hearts to be ripped out of their chest cavities while they were still alive. In fact the Aztecs kept the slave population in the tens of thousands so they would have plenty of human stock for their various ceremonies that required the dismemberment of human beings. The hatred of the Aztecs brutal tyranny by the surrounding natives was so intense that when Cortes and the other Spaniards arrived, many native tribes joined forces with these white men in order to vanquish the Aztecs.[62]

During the 1400s, the Inca's ruled a vast area that encompassed modern day Peru, Ecuador, Bolivia, Columbia, and Argentina. They numbered in the millions and were ruled by a king and byzantine bureaucracy of some 40,000 aristocrats. Incan rituals required the murders of thousands of innocent people in the name of some god or pleasing those in power. The amount of carnage involved in these rituals was so staggering that some "Inca Priests actually collapsed with exhaustion from stabbing so many victims."[63]

In short, these were not groups of people living in harmony with each other as they were portrayed in Kevin Costner's "Dances With Wolves."

...long before the first Europeans arrived in the New World, an elaborate slave trading network developed among the Indians of the Northwest American coast, where slaves constituted as much as 10 to 15 percent of some tribes' populations... Indian slavery in this region was of nearly as much importance to its practitioners as was the plantation slavery of the antebellum South. Possessing no human rights whatsoever, slaves of the Northwest coast were considered property in every sense and were subject to sale or disposal at any time. Many were killed ceremoniously, as in the ritual of the Kwakiutl cannibals, who sacrificed and then ate their slaves. Other tribal chiefs routinely killed slaves in potlatch festivities—solely to demonstrate that they were wealthy enough to waste large quantities of their own human property. Slave raiding was also common among the Natchez of lower Mississippi, the Cherokees of the Appalachian highland, and the native tribes living along the Atlantic coast, from Florida to Virginia. When the transatlantic slave trade brought Africans to the New World, some Indian tribes—among them the Cherokees, Choctaws, Seminoles, Chickasaws, and Creeks—took black slaves as well. Though most Indian slave masters owned just a few slaves, others owned dozens and treated them terribly. The Cherokees, for instance, were notorious for their cruelty to slaves. Over time black slavery became an integral part of life for many Indians—as evidenced by the fact that some tribes continued to keep slaves until 1866, a full year after the civil war's end. At that point, under pressure from the American government, they reluctantly agreed to end the practice.[64]

Examples of native and European brutality are abundant in George Franklin Feldman's book, *Cannibalism, Headhunting, and Human Sacrifice in North America: A History Forgotten*. Feldman's treatment of the subject is evenhanded. Instead of trying to please the clique by overstating the savagery of the Europeans and the serenity of the natives, he gives detailed accounts of the events as the evidence suggests they actually happened. For example, he points out that the Spanish explorers were mostly interested in gold, and like the English who were interested in the land, showed "no mercy" to the indigenous people they encountered. The French however, seemed more concerned with finding trading partners and according to the "Indians own accounts, were reasonably kind and tolerant."[65]

The thought that different groups of white people could conduct themselves differently is inconceivable to most in the clique and illustrates why they believe in white privilege, even though there is ample evidence of Irish, Scots-Irish, and Italian immigrants being discriminated against. According to the clique, all white people are English aristocrats who had everything dumped in their laps.

Feldman's research uncovered numerous cases of savagery by natives and Europeans alike. Several tribes along the Gulf Coast, including the Taensa, were known to sacrifice their own children in order to please a deity. One episode witnessed by an explorer involved five toddlers being thrown into a fire that had started when lightning struck a place of worship. Thinking someone above was angry with them, they sacrificed the infants to "appease the sun god." Another Gulf Coast tribe, the Natchez, had a caste system (before they ever encountered whites mind you) in which those from the lower ranks could only rise by "wring[ing] the neck of the infant" who they would then "throw at the feet" of a deceased chief to honor him. At the end of the day, they would "receive the compliments of all the warriors and honored men" whose ranks they would now join.[66] Ritualistic sacrifice and cannibalism were very common amongst the Gulf Coast tribes. The Cuddoans, a group of tribes, had a detailed description of these practices recorded:

> When one nation makes war with another, the one that conquers puts all of the old men and old women to the knife and carries off the little children for food to eat on the way; the other children are sold; the

vagabonds and grown women and young girls are carried off to serve them with the exception of some whom they reserve to sacrifice in the dance before their god and saints. This is done in the following manner: they set a nailed stake in the ground in place where they are to dance the Mitote, they light a big fire, tying the victim who is to be danced about or sacrificed to the stake.... They approach the victim and cut a piece of flesh off of his body, going to the fire and half roasting it in sight of the victim, they eat it with great relish, and so they go on cutting off pieces and quartering him until they take off all the flesh and he dies.

They do the same thing with priests and Spaniards if they catch any. Others they hang up by the feet and put a fire underneath them... roasting them and eat them up. For others they do not use a knife to cut them to pieces but tear them to pieces with their teeth and eat them raw.[67]

Slavery and slaughter were not the only evils Native Americans shared with Europeans. Although the late Howard Zinn and many others in the clique like to believe that 'private property' and wars over land were exclusive to, or at least caused by, white men, they could hardly be more wrong. The Comanche's, for example, attacked whites because they were moving into Comanche territory.[68] This same territory was land the Comanche's had taken by force from the Apaches, Caddos, and other 'bronze' people long before the blue-eyed devils sailed the ocean blue. When it comes to stolen land, as was the case with many other subjects, Mark Twain said it best:

There isn't a foot of land in the world which doesn't represent the ousting and re-ousting of a long line of successive "owners" who each in turn, as "patriots" with proud swelling hearts defend it against the next gang of "robbers" who came to steal it and did—and became swelling-hearted patriots in their turn.[69]

McPhail claims the U.S. has immigration policies that are hostile to Latinos. How a set of policies that are rarely enforced and much more relaxed than those of Mexico, Japan, Switzerland and many other countries could be considered "hostile," we are not told. McPhail, and anyone who shares this belief with her, should rejoice the U.S. does not have the same immigration policies the Comanche's did. They could be summed up as "You can live here until we decide you're getting too big, at which point we will plunder and murder you and rape your women." The U.S. policy on the other hand is "you are here illegally but we're not really going to do anything about it. You can plunder, murder, and rape our citizens, and we will wring our hands over even building a fence to secure our own border because the Democrats want Hispanic votes, our business

Origins and Abettors

owners want your labor, and just enough of our population is so petrified of being called racists, they put their fingers in their ears and sing, "La, la, la, diversity is our strength," every time someone even questions America's immigration policies. America lets in more immigrants now than it or any other country ever has! We have a President that makes sure of it by telling law enforcement not to deport illegal aliens.

McPhail's main contention is that America is not "acknowledging" racism today or in its past. But every textbook I have ever come across from kindergarten to college has done much more than just "acknowledge" racism. And Americans themselves voted for the politicians who passed the Civil Rights Acts, documents which materialized because white Americans believed racism was a problem. The War on Poverty and Great Society programs would not exist if voters hadn't acknowledged discrimination. There have been multitudes of movies made, books written, and diversity training programs held, all in the name of acknowledging racism, as McPhail implores Americans to do. Will it ever be enough?

In order to shrink the gulf between the races, how about trying a new list of 'acknowledgements?' How about acknowledging that nothing white men in particular or Americans in general have done in the way of conquest and subjugation is exclusive to them? When it comes to enslavement of Blacks, how about an acknowledgment that the slaves who were marched across the Sahara desert by Arab slave traders had higher mortality rates "than among those subjected to the horrors and dangers of the Atlantic crossing." To "explain slavery as being a consequence of certain European ideas leading to bondage for Africans is to ignore the glaring fact that slavery extended in time and space far beyond Europeans and Africans, and far beyond those shared particular European ideas."[70] How about when Nas raps "long before we came to this country, we were kings and queens, never porch Monkeys," McPhail writes a column "acknowledging" that Blacks were enslaved by other Blacks and Arab Muslims—who probably thought they were lower than monkeys—porch or otherwise—long before whites bought Blacks from black and Arab slave traders? These Arabs mind you, had names like Raheem, Rhashid, and Jamal—'black' names.

How about an acknowledgment that when it comes to life expectancy and per-capita income, Blacks in America do better than Blacks anywhere else in the world? Or that the Irish under British rule had shorter life expectancies than African slaves in the American South?[71] What about the life expectancy of black slaves in Brazil only being 20 years of age because they were literally worked to death? (This is why Brazil had to import several times as many slaves as the U.S.) What about acknowledging that the income gap between eastern and western Europeans is greater than that of black and white Americans?

And since McPhail actually admits that Chinese and Japanese immigrants were discriminated against, how about an "acknowledgment" that these two group's descendants are more likely to 1) be approved for loans, 2) graduate from college, and 3) earn higher incomes than 'privileged' whites? Moreover, there should be an acknowledgment that as a causal factor, racism and discrimination simply cannot explain all of a given society's disparities amongst its different ethnicities.

Cliquesters like to say that pointing out the universal nature of human evil is akin to a child saying "but teacher, everybody else was doing it" after getting caught shooting a spit wad at school. However, this is another failing "George Bush and Saddam Hussein are the same person" analogy. When a kid has been told specifically not to do something by an authority figure, it is entirely different from the programming of evolution (or the depravity taught by Christianity), which naturally leads humans of all colors to engage in conquest and subjugation.

This is why the Ashanti and Yao tribes in Africa preyed upon the weaker tribes and enslaved them—not because they were white supremacists. The fact that human nature does not vary from race to race conveniently escapes the clique. Acknowledging such an obvious fact would keep them from assigning everyone a role as either an angel or a demon in one of their melodramas. They are loathe to relinquish such an emotionally gratifying method, not because they are uniquely evil, but because they are human and therefore controlled by brains that are the product of evolution by natural selection, processes with little guide other than reproductive success.

There are two reasons for emphasizing the fact that every race of people has at one time or another conquered and enslaved other groups of people. First, in order to address those very real "disparities" in many of society's outcomes, 'youth of color' cannot think whites are the only ones that engaged in such behavior. Why? Because getting good grades and behaving in school are classified as 'acting white.' If they grow up believing white people are exclusively and irredeemably evil, they are more than justified in behaving in a way that is antithetical to however they perceive whites to behave. Thus poor grades and rebellious behavior in school becomes the goal of ethnic groups who buy into the "anti-white" rhetoric.

Secondly, a lot of the animosity between the different races in America is predicated upon the erroneous belief that whites are the sole practitioners of conquest and enslavement. This encourages the "us" against "them" mentality with its score settling and tribalism—like we see here in prison.

The Reverends Sharpton and Jackson like to disparage Western civilization. Since we are on the subject of things that need to be acknowledged in order for us to all 'get along' better, these self-anointed leaders would do well to acknowledge that if not for Western civilization, slavery would still be the universal institution today it was hundreds of years ago, probably exploiting the Reverends themselves. "Slavery did not die out quietly of its own accord. It went down fighting to the bitter end, and it lost only because Europeans had gunpowder and weapons first."[72] And it should be duly noted that prior to the 1700s, there is no record of any society anywhere on the planet mounting a substantial fight to end slavery.

In the late 1700s, Great Britain was leading the world in the trading of human beings for profit. At the time, no sane person would have predicted that within a hundred years, a universal institution like slavery, thousands of years old, would be outlawed by legislation, much less ended in actual practice. It was the Quakers who got the abolitionist ball rolling. They were a group of hyper-religious white Christians that publicly condemned slavery, and dictated that no Quaker could own slaves. They turned out to be the prototype for the evangelical elements in the Church of England that would sow the seeds for an eventual war on slavery.[73] The prominent leader of this group, William Wilberforce, would today be labeled a Bible thumping, Jesus freak. This is why Glen Beck and other right wing Christians often say 'conservatives' started the anti-slavery movement.

Another prominent leader in this movement was a man by the name of Henry Thornton. He was an evil capitalist banker and also a member of the Clapham sect that spear-headed the war against slavery.[74] It should be no wonder then why the clique has such a hard time acknowledging how slavery was ended: the parties responsible included a Bible-clinging white man and white male banker.

Though they were denied time and again, Wilberforce and Thornton continued trying to get a bill passed in Parliament to outlaw slavery. Finally, after 20 years of being shutout, on February 27, 1807, the House of Commons passed a bill that outlawed the enslavement of human beings. During a time when there was no social media or even television, this momentous event came to pass because the public felt so strongly about it. During a single month, Parliament was inundated with over 800 petitions boasting the signatures of over 700,000 white people who wanted slavery to end.[75]

There was no equivalent fervor amongst the people of Africa and Asia. The Sultan of the Ottoman Empire met the British Ambassador with 'extreme astonishment' and a 'smile' when he broached the subject of abolition. The Arab leader finding it hard to believe his guest was serious.[76]

In New Zealand, the Maoris were confused as to why anyone would object to them enslaving the Polynesians, claiming:

> We took possession in accordance with our customs, and we caught all the people. Not one escaped. Some ran away from us, these were killed, and others we killed. But what of that? It was in accordance with our customs.[77]

Luckily for the Reverends and many others, the Brits were not multiculturalists beholden to the belief that all cultures and customs are to be respected. Even though there were no slaves within Britain's borders, the anti-slavery movement became so popular that British politicians began announcing their personal stance on the issue, as it had become imperative they declare themselves against slavery in order to get elected.[78]

The abolition of slavery in the British colonies was largely accomplished with the stroke of a pen. Ending this institution in America and the Islamic world however would require much more than a majority vote. Although most people are aware of the enormous costs of the American Civil War, very few have been apprised of the staggering amount of money and time white Brits spent on ending slavery in the Islamic world. The British began by patrolling the coasts of Africa, the Persian Gulf, Red Sea, and the Indian Ocean.

They were very committed. Not even the tumultuous wars with Napoleon kept the Brits from patrolling the coast of Africa for the slave raiders. On Zanzibar, an island off the East coast of Africa, a slave-trading outpost was forced to end its operation because two British Warships "threatened to blockade the island." In Brazil, the British Navy "seized and destroyed slave ships within Brazil's own waters" because they would not stop the anything but peculiar practice. More formidable opponents from a military stand point like Portugal and Spain were bribed to discontinue the slave trade and eventually aided Britain by policing international waters for slavers and finding places for the newly freed slaves to settle.[79]

From 1870–1890 an estimated "four million Sterling" was spent on servicing the British Naval fleet stationed off the coast of east Africa.

209

Between 1875 and 1885, this out- fit lost "282 officers and men" with many more sent home for an early retirement because of "fever, sunstroke, and dysentery."[80]

In spite of this effort, slave trading continued. Arab dhows—sleeker, faster, slave vessels could elude the British Royal Navy's less nimble ships. These smaller watercraft could travel closer to the shore where the water was too shallow for the Royal Navy's larger vessels.[81] One estimate claims the Brits were only able to seize one out of every eight dhows. Still, from 1866 to 1869, 3,380 slaves were freed from 129 ships.

When they became certain they would be caught, many Arab slavers would attempt to dispose of their inculpatory evidence:

> The worst that could befall the slaves was when the slaver was overhauled by a British cruiser, and they might then be flung overboard to dispose of all evidence. Deveraux mentions a case where Arabs, when pursued by the English cruiser, cut the throats of 24 slaves and threw them overboard. Colom also states that Arabs would not hesitate to knock slaves on the head and throw them overboard to avoid capture.[82]

To counter the elusiveness of the dhows, the British deployed smaller vessels of their own. These boats were often attacked by the slave traders because the larger ships from which they launched were "too far away to reach the scene in time to join the battle." When the British did have the advantage, the Arabs often fled without concern for their Blacks slaves.

One such incident, common in nature, occurred on April 20, 1866. A British ship called the Penguin, fired a couple of warning shots at a dhow to let its crew know they wanted to inspect it. The ship was full of slaves so the Arabs steered it to a rocky area in rough surf that they knew would sink their ship and any other that followed it. The Brits got as close as they could and then several sailors "recklessly dived in and swam through the surf to the dhow. The sailors managed to bring 28 of the slaves back to the boat." Unfortunately, the Arabs had around 200 slaves on this particular dhow and most of them, despite the heroic efforts of the British sailors, drowned.[83] Eventually the tide began to turn. After turning against slavery themselves, France and the U.S., also committed warships to policing the Atlantic.

Clique members like to claim that slaves in the Islamic world were treated more humanely than those in the American South. The evidence says, quite emphatically, otherwise.

> When the Daphne's Cutter captured a dhow with 156 slaves on board, many were found to be in the final stages of starvation and dysentery.

One woman was brought out of the dhow with a month old infant in her arms. The baby's forehead was crushed and when she was asked how the injury had happened she explained to the ships interpreter that as the [British Navy's] boat came alongside the baby began to cry. One of the dhowmen, fearing that the sailors would hear the cries, picked up a stone and crushed the child's head.[84]

African slaves bound for the Islamic world were forced to walk the Sahara desert. The majority of those that perished on this exhausting journey were women and girls. In addition to the horrors of this death march, black male slaves had to deal with the probability of castration. Eunuchs were prized possessions in the Muslim world because so many women there were kept in harems. This put overseers who could not impregnate them at a premium. Even though Islamic law outlawed castration, it still happened frequently. In order to avoid punishment for this heinous act, the slave traders would perform it in rural areas with primitive methods, often resulting in the slave's death.[85]

The British General in Sudan, C.G. Gordon, began giving the death penalty to anyone convicted of castrating slaves. Muhammad Ahmad, the religious leader of the Samaniyya order, responded by putting together an army for the sole purpose of defeating Gordon to continue slavery. In Khartoum, in 1885, Gordon's army was defeated, and the General himself was killed. The slave trade began again with a vengeance. Finally, in 1898, Lord Kitchener and an army including a soldier named Winston Churchill, regained control of the region with a resounding victory on the battlefield.[86]

Therefore when Osama Bin Laden said black Americans should become Muslims because Islam fights oppression, he could not have been more wrong. Islam, like Christianity, has more than its fair share of conquests and slavery. The difference between these two, at least when it comes to slavery, is that Christianity had a large part in the war to end slavery, while Islam had an equivalent part in trying to sustain it.

In prison, as is the case in the free world, very few people are aware of the fact that slavery was not an exclusively white on black crime. Those that do know typically believe that all slaves held outside the antebellum South were treated like members of the family they were serving. Most Blacks in prison I have talked to about this truly believe that whites invented slavery when they first laid eyes upon black people. Imagine what this does to the psyche of the average black person. I will tell you what it did to at least one black male here in prison—my friend I will call B.B.

Origins and Abettors

One day I was sitting in the dayroom reading *Super Normal Stimuli* by Deirdre Barret. B.B. asked me if he could read it. B.B. is, like many Blacks in prison, a convert to Islam. As per his religion, he seeks knowledge from cradle to grave. We had spoken before while lifting weights on the rec yard and were both from Houston, so we shared a little common ground.

B.B. read straight through the entire book in less than twenty-four hours and gave it back to me. At the time, we were on medium custody, so we spent almost 20 hours locked in our cells. During our time outside the cell, we discussed the book. I said I thought Barret leaned too far to the left politically and that it influenced some of her claims. B.B. recounted actual bits of data he found interesting, demonstrating a level of comprehension I quickly became jealous of.

B.B. asked me if I had any more books like that one, and I told him, "No." I asked if he cared about history or current events, and he said, "Yes." The next time the doors rolled, I grabbed *Black Rednecks and White Liberals* by Dr. Thomas Sowell. I told B.B. that it was a collection of essays, so he could read them in any order without it taking away from the book's essence. He scanned the table of contents and decided to read the chapter titled "The Real History of Slavery," first. In it, Dr. Sowell explains how slavery was practiced for thousands of years before whites ever encountered Blacks, that every race participated in it, and that Europeans are mostly responsible for ending it.

The next morning, B.B. came up to me with a smile on his face, nodding his head. He immediately started talking about what he read the night before. He had read the entire 50 page essay and thought about it deeply. He spoke rapidly about how he had never known slavery was universally practiced, that Arabs and Blacks were the original enslavers of black Africans, etc., etc. At one point he closed his eyes and balled up his fists for a second before saying, "Man, if I'd of read that—when I was in the world—I probably would've never come to prison."

The hairs on the back of my neck bristled. I had an idea of what he meant, but I asked him to elaborate anyway. B.B. said that all his life he had felt like he needed to prove to whites that he was not scared of them. He thought whites walked around thinking that Blacks were weak because their ancestors were slaves. Committing crimes was a way of showing how tough and unafraid of whites he was. He thought he had to demonstrate that he could not be enslaved, and that no one had better try otherwise.

B.B. and other Blacks see their crimes as preemptive acts of self-defense against the larger white population because of the way the clique distorts 'disparities' and incidents like the Trayvon Martin tragedy. When it's convenient to do so, they are willing to ignore some of the facts — as they did with Zimmerman (a Mestizo whom they called a white Hispanic) — to continue strengthening the angst between Blacks and whites. They hype up the stories of white men killing black teenagers, and white racism in general, as such overwhelming problems, as proof Blacks must remain eternally vigilant or else be snuffed out. When you combine this with the belief that all Blacks were kings and queens in Africa who were turned into 'porch monkeys,' how could B.B. and other Blacks not be filled with rage? How could they not see committing crimes as a way to settle the score with this group of people, who in their minds committed a uniquely vicious form of oppression against their ancestors?

K.W., another black inmate I talked to about slavery, told me that over 100 million Blacks lost their lives in the Atlantic Ocean while travelling in slave ships. He said that the waters they traveled through are to this very day filled with the most aggressive, blood-thirsty sharks in the world as a result of so many slaves being thrown overboard. He had no idea that in all, approximately 11 million slaves were shipped to the New World and that only 600,000 came to the U.S. The fact that whites were ever slaves — let alone still enslaved in Egypt and Turkey after Blacks had been freed in America[87] was completely lost on him — like it is on most people.

It is not hard to imagine the fatherless, highly mesomorphic B.B.'s and K.W.'s of the world living within the anonymity of a large city becoming enraged. As they walk down the street and see a white person in a new car, they remember one of their teachers (the one with the 'African' print) telling them they were once on top of the world as death-defying members of the Original Man First Airborne in the Egyptian philosopher king's Air Force — until the white man shot them down, stole their culture and enslaved them. Some became so angry over these lies they ended up in prison because of them.

For the sake of truth itself, and keeping other Blacks from going down the same path B.B. did, I formally demand an "acknowledgment" and an apology from Ms. McPhail, the Reverends, and the rest of the clique for making it seem as though whites exclusively perpetrated conquest and enslavement against Blacks. These acknowledgments and apologies should be engraved in stone and presented to black criminals and their victims.

CHAPTER 8

WHAT THEY WANT

The white race is the cancer of human history.[1]

~Susan Sontag

From existentialism to deconstructionism, all of modern thought can be reduced to a mechanical denunciation of the west.... Our past crimes command us to keep our mouths closed. Our only right is to remain silent.[2]

~Pascal Bruckner

In May of 2011, Pitts wrote a column with the heading "Looking Back Can Help Us Navigate Road to the Future." In this piece, he tells us about his commemorative trip aboard the 2011 "Student Freedom Riders" bus. While heading to their destination in Augusta, Georgia, Pitts and his companions watched the PBS Documentary *The Murder of Emmett Till*. It is the story of a young black boy being lynched in the "nothing town" of Money, Mississippi. Pitts says the movie shows "white person after white person spew[ing] the grotesque bigotry that was so common to white people in that time and place." When the movie ended, someone on the bus asked a 20-year old college student named Ryan Price, "How do you feel as a white guy watching a film like this?"

Later on, in a private conversation with Pitts, Price said, "It was a good question,"[3] and that watching the movie as a white person made it difficult "not to be embarrassed.... You get to the point where you almost want to change your skin color so you can show how much you care about issues of race, how much you care about the overt hatred and vitriolic discrimination of the past and today. Of course, you can't change your skin color, but you can be an ally to those who are marginalized in society, and that's something it really spurs me to do."[4]

Pitts calls this a "good, brave answer," and says "such bravery often eludes people two and three times the age of Price." He says the answer older people often give to a question like the one posed to Price is, "Don't look back." "Let sleeping dogs lie." To which Pitts replies, "...no one encounters this dismissal of the past when one commemorates say, the Kennedy inauguration or the Holocaust." Pitts also says that car windshields are just as big in the back as they are in the front, offering a metaphor for his stance. And, that "declaring this one strain of history off limits is to commit an act of plain moral cowardice."[5]

Former U.S. Attorney General Eric Holder concurs with this notion, saying that when it comes to discussing race, America is "a nation of cowards." Along with the narrative in general, these particular notions help con the Susan Sontags and Ryan Prices of the world into ethnomasochism.

We will begin with Ryan Price's response to the question of how watching *The Murder of Emmett Till* made him feel 'embarrassed' as a 'white guy.' Pitt's article makes it clear this is exactly how Pitts and the rest of the clique want white people—especially white men—to feel when white-on-black injustices are brought up. They want whites to lie prone before them, in utter humility, ashamed of their skin color and historical incidents over which they have no control. To the clique, this prostration would be the beginning of a long overdue admission of guilt by a group of people uniquely blameworthy. It is a stance that, until they relinquish it, will halt any meaningful progress in American race relations.

When Price demonstrates his whole-cloth embarrassment, he relegates himself to a form of voluntary slavery in the interest of fairness, equality, and justice—the very concepts that slavery restricts. He also fails to realize that no matter the sincerity of his empathy or the depth of his cowering posture, he cannot satisfy the clique's desire for white men to verbally self-immolate. For they are seeking justice for victims and victimizers who are no longer with us, and therefore the former are unable to say when their desired level of revenge has been reached. Price of course means well. He thinks his figurative prostration shows that he is one of the 'good white folks.'[6] However, saying you are embarrassed over something you had nothing to do with is just like apologizing for some wrong you did not commit. You are signaling guilt to some aggrieved party.

In the context of American race relations, this misplaced guilt does not have the healing effect it is supposed to. Instead of promoting convalescence, it causes those who believe they are victims to become even more emboldened and hostile, weakening the already fragile bonds holding us together. It is the natural course of deductive reasoning: I did X and got Y. Y is good, therefore I should keep doing X. (X equals successful attempts at making white people feel guilty for sins they did not personally commit, and Y is the dopamine marinade they experience as they watch a white man like Ryan Price engage in ethnomasochism.)

Price is young and ignorant. Pitts is not. If improving race relations and the economic levels of non-whites is the goal, Price's answer could not possibly be more discouraging.

Non-whites have had politicians who share Price's embarrassment and then some passing laws for half a century now in State and Federal Legislatures. Look at California. They have everything the clique wants: A majority non-white population speaking different languages, State legislatures controlled by clique members, and higher than average taxes so they can spread the wealth around to its "rightful owners." And yet California has people leaving it in droves. Between July 2007 and July 2008, 144,000, more Californians left than came in for the fourth consecutive year, a larger loss than that of any State.[7]

According to New York Times columnist David Brooks, "eighty-two percent of Californian's say they believe their State is heading in the wrong direction. State growth has lagged behind National growth. Unemployment is at 12.4 percent statewide and at catastrophic levels in the Central Valley. More people are leaving California for Oklahoma and Texas than came here during the Dust Bowl days of the 1930s. Tom Joad is giving up."[8]

When it comes to race relations amongst Americans, things have certainly improved. Yet as the Trayvon Martin tragedy and Ferguson, Mississippi police shooting shows, the clique and their media wing can still take an incident in which race likely played no role, and convince people race held the leading role. Pitts tries to compare the election of JFK and the Holocaust with the lynching of Emmett Till and others, saying if we commemorate the first two historical events why not the third. Apparently, having several movies and scores of books depicting white-on-black lynchings, and an entire month devoted to 'Black History,' and a national holiday for Dr. Martin Luther King Jr. does not qualify as commemoration.

Comparing slavery in the American South and the Holocaust is not exactly on point.

- Approximately six million Jews were killed in concentration camps in a few years' time. Six hundred thousand African slaves were brought to the United States over several generations.

- Before the Civil War, whites counted for 90 percent of all the people who were lynched in the South.[9] Often, they were suspected of being abolitionists.
- Between 1882 and 1968, lynch mobs killed 3,446 Blacks.[10] During the same time span, 1,297 whites were lynched—often for helping Blacks, but also for opposing lynching.[11]
- Since government agencies began recording reliable crime statistics 50 years ago, black-on-white murders in America have accounted for between 13 and 20 percent of all murders, while white-on-black murders are only 4 to 6 percent.

There is another reason for not bringing up lynchings like those of Emmett Till. Mentioning the events of the Holocaust is unlikely to increase tension amongst present day Jews and Germans. Why? Because these retellings focus on remembering the horror so it is never repeated. Commemorating a President's inauguration ceremony does not create tension. The way white-on-black crimes are brought up, even though 89 percent of interracial crimes are black-on-white, often breeds hostility, because clique members demagogue the issue. Mentioning the Holocaust or JFK has few costs. Referring to white-on-black crimes in the manner the clique does, to induce white guilt, can create a Yahweh Cult, or worse, race riots.

I am glad Ryan Price was on that bus. I really hope he was not the only white person on it. When I was 16 or 17, I would have probably given a similar answer; I too only knew what they taught me in school. But a more informed answer, by a more seasoned individual, is definitely in order. Allow me:

> That is an awful question, and you owe me an apology. My being a "white guy" has no bearing on how a crime I did not commit makes me feel. You should have asked me how did I feel as James Long watching a film like this. Had you done so, I would have told you that the crime committed against Emmett Till made me feel the same way I do when a black inmate targets a white inmate (much smaller than himself) to beat into submission, when no other whites are around, so he can rape him—before passing him around to his 'homeboys' so they can all rape him—which is to say I feel angry—but not embarrassed.
>
> As for the racist comments made by whites during the movie, I feel the same way about them as I do about the racist things I have heard Blacks like Khalid Abdul Mohammed and the New Black Panthers— who are protected by the U.S. Attorney General—say about whites. I get

a similar feeling when Hispanics on taxpayer-funded National Public Radio refer to whites as gringos with heavily accented Spanish appearing only for that derogatory word.

I have all the empathy in the world for Emmett Till and his family and friends. But just as Pitts has never shot and killed white people for being white (like Colin Ferguson and Lee Malvo amongst many others did), and therefore is not responsible for those crimes, I am not responsible for Emmett Till's murder.

I have no desire to change my skin color as Ryan Price does, even though doing so would make it easier for me to get into college and also have the Civil Rights Act apply to me since Attorney General Holder says he will only apply it to those whom he calls "my people," not whites.

I will never bow my head in an attempt to curry favor with Blacks by expressing guilt for the accomplishments or even the sins of my ancestors. Doing so would only encourage black people to keep wasting their time inventing new ways to induce such guilt because it gives them illegitimate power over the Ryan Prices and Michael Moores of the world.

Lastly, Mr. Pitts, the reason some people tell you to "look ahead and move on" is because lynchings, like the one that happened to Emmett Till, are not nearly as grave a threat to black people today as black-on-black homicides or HIV/AIDS. What happened in Jasper, Texas and even Samford, Florida are anomalies compared to the number of whites killed every year by Blacks. There is only so much time and brain capacity available to us. We need black kids worrying about their grades in math and science as much as you worry about white-on-black crime.

The road to a successful future for black youngsters is no longer blocked by Bull Conner, but by "White America, U.S. of KKK," and similar nonsense. Convincing black kids the worst thing they can do is "act like those white folks" (because only white people were evil enough to engage in conquest and subjugation) is destroying the people you claim you're trying to help.

Yes, Mr. Pitts, you are right, a car's back windshield is just as big as the front. But when you are driving the car, which do you spend most of your time looking through?

When the clique says they want to have a conversation on race, they really mean they want to have a conversation between black people who think like Pitts and Michelle Alexander, and white people who think like Ryan Price and Susan Sontag. If you are white and do not think like Price or Sontag, you are one of those lowly souls who "just does not get it."

Pitts was kind enough to bless us with a reading list sure to make even the most "not getting it" amongst us wring our hands and cower in shame. The three books I chose from the list were *The New Jim Crow* (which I already covered in Chapter 5), *Been in the Storm so Long* and *Mirror to America*.

A REFLECTION LACKING PERSPECTIVE

Mirror to America is the autobiography of one of America's most highly regarded historians, Professor John Hope Franklin. Amongst many other distinctions, Mr. Franklin was tabbed by President Clinton to chair an advisory board designed to "promote a national dialogue on controversial issues surrounding race."[12] This board was predictably made up of clique members who believe the road to progress for Blacks can only be paved with the guilt of white people. Franklin writes, "We were criticized because every board member presumably believed in affirmative action, though, so far as I know, that was never a prerequisite for appointment to the board."[13] Whether or not it was a prerequisite has no bearing whatsoever on the critic's contentions. The point was that everyone on the board believed in affirmative action and leaned to the left politically. A dialogue requires two parties. The board Franklin chaired was an echo chamber of one party, the clique.

Mirror to America is a good read, even if you strongly disagree with Franklin's leftist pronouncements like I did. Biographies of people who defied the odds often are. And the odds were certainly stacked against him. Like Dr. Sowell, Franklin earned his degree before affirmative action and before it was 'fashionable' for white people to like black people. Because of this, Franklin's scholarship is second to none. However, I find the conclusions he draws from his experiences and research dubious. Because of this, *Mirror to America* failed to turn me into a Sontag or even a Price.

One of the things that jumped out at me while reading *Mirror* was how spectacularly Franklin succeeded in life despite having numerous episodes of blatant racism directed at him. I could not help but think, "Here is a guy who rose to the top of his profession and also published best-selling books, even though he was called a nigger to his face and had his life threatened by a group of whites that could have turned into a lynch mob."[14] Blacks today rarely experience such torment at the hands of whites. It is much more accepted for Blacks to denigrate whites like Jeremiah Wright and so many black celebrities do than if a white person like Don Imus does the same. In spite of Franklin's phenomenal success, the clique wants us to believe that non-whites cannot make a decent living in America due to racism from whites. So unfortunately for Pitts, Franklin's story is actually proof that one of his most sacred beliefs—white racism being an impenetrable barrier to black success—is untrue.

Franklin, like First Lady Michelle Obama, complains that when he attended a predominately white college he was made very aware of his race.[15] There is nothing intrinsically wrong with pointing this out. But as is so often the case when clique members bring up something they perceive to be a racial slight, they act as if it only happens to non-whites.

When I was a teenager, my friends and I watched movies at the Greens Crossing Theatre in Greenspoint, or the one at Northline Mall, both on the north side of Houston. In the nineties, these movie theatres had mostly Black patrons, and I was often the only white person there. No big deal. Been there, done that. On one particular occasion, two of my friends and I (both of whom happened to be black) went to Northline to see a movie. After we found some seats, a group of five or six Blacks started to sit down in the row directly behind us. Someone in the group said, "I don't wanna sit by no oreo niggas!"

They had problems with us because I was white, pure and simple. My pistol was in my car, and they had us outnumbered. I exchanged a couple of hard stares with two of the guys who were laughing and managed to stifle my anger. One of my friends was about to leave for Illinois State University on a full-ride basketball scholarship, and the last thing I was going to do was get him into trouble, especially considering his older brother was already locked up down here. So I sat there forcing myself to be calm, all the while being very aware of my race, Mr. Franklin and Mrs. First Lady.

Franklin also engages in some moral inequivalence drawing when he compares America's "endemic racism" with Nazi Germany and Imperial Japan. During the 1940's, racism was no doubt a problem in America. Franklin claims that the U.S. was "holding Germany and Japan to higher standards than it set for itself."[16] This incorrectly implies that we declared war on these axis countries because their leaders were racist, which, because America had some racist leaders, would of course be the height of hypocrisy. But America did not declare war on these countries to stomp out racism. These countries were trying to take over the world, and the U.S. set out to stop their aggression, not their racism. As bad as things were for American Blacks in the 1940s, they are a mere candle flame to a bonfire when compared to the atrocities going on in Auschwitz and wherever the army of the rising sun went.

On the subject of the judiciary branch of the government, Franklin sees the Supreme Court as an institution that should "make decisions favorable to the improvement of race relations."[17] That is, the Court should make decisions based on whether or not the ruling will further causes or assist individuals. This is the results-oriented approach to law. Franklin specifically mentions the Warren Court—which President Obama also liked (though he felt the Court did not go far enough into wealth redistribution)—as a model for future judiciaries.

There is a problem with deciding cases based upon how you feel about the parties, instead of upon the law itself. You open the door for the future justices—who may be diametrically opposed to the ends you were seeking—to rule with this expanded power (also based upon their own preferences), because you set the precedent. If the Court rules in favor of defendant X because he is a member of a preferred group, even though the facts clearly state that his contentions are bogus, the decision allows another Court to also ignore the law and rule in favor of one of its favored groups.

I found it ironic that Franklin mentioned the Dred Scot case, whose results-oriented decision did not bode well for black Americans. It appears a results-oriented Supreme Court of Ryan Prices and Thurgood Marshalls would be to Franklin's liking. However, once those justices are replaced, as all Justices eventually are, their seats could be filled with magistrates who seek results Franklin would detest, creating problems even a Warren-styled Court could not remedy. As Dr. Sowell points out, "Judicial activism is a blank check for going in any direction, on any issue depending on the predilections of particular judges."[18]

> While Chief Justice Earl Warren used expansive interpretations of the law to outlaw racial segregation in public schools in 1954, almost exactly a century earlier Chief Justice Roger Taney had used expansive interpretations of the law to say in the Dred Scott case that a black man "had no rights which the white man was bound to respect." It was the dissenters in that case who insisted on following the laws as written and the legal precedents, showing that free Blacks had exercised legally recognized rights in parts of the country even before the constitution was adopted as well as after.[19]

Perhaps the John Franklins of the world are aware of America's changing demographics, and therefore are of the opinion that Judicial activism is preferable because they will eventually have an entire Court of clique members. But eventually the black and Hispanic populations will be large enough that they might no longer unite under the banner of the Democratic Party. The Court and the country will be made up of Sonia

What They Want

Sotomayors and Thurgood Marshalls, all arguing that their particular group is the most aggrieved:

> "We were slaves!"
> "We had our land stolen by the gringos!"
> "We were stolen from our land!"

Back and forth, on and on. For Blacks, like Mr. Franklin, the birth rates are not in their favor. Black and Hispanic women both have higher rates of birth than white women, so no problem there; if whites are appointed, they will be of the ethnomasochist variety, and willing to put social justice above the law in all situations. But because of the high murder and HIV infection rates among Blacks, Hispanics will out populate them, as they already have in most of the Southwest. The MALDEF's and LaRaza's will demand that their grievances entitle them to first dibs on the treasury. Blacks will disagree. The whites who can afford it will flee to some place like New Zealand, and Asians will be doing a mix of both.

Judicial activism, or legislating from the bench as it is called, is something I have unfortunately had personal experience with. The State of Texas has a law that keeps inmates like myself from profiting by telling the story of their crime. So I cannot go into detail about my case, because I wrote this book to make money for my daughter's support, and they would certainly sue me. I can however point out that on my direct appeal, there was a vigorous dissenting opinion written on one point of error longer than the entire majority's opinion on eleven points—saying my case should have been overturned and that a majority (2 out of 3 Justices) created requirements for the 'rule of optional completeness' that came from 'whole cloth.'[20]

Pitts and the rest of the clique may rejoice at this and shout, "Now you know how it feels to be black!" However, this decision was not a total victory. Yes, an evil, right-leaning, privileged white man is still unlawfully incarcerated. However, my daughter—who only has 23 evil chromosomes—has had to grow up without a father and at times even live out of a car because her mother had to deal with an abusive husband who could not hold a job.

Had my case been overturned, and I had been given a fair trial, none of that would have happened. So at least in my case, judicial activism produced a mixed bag. A white man had his chickens come home to roost, but a black woman and half-black child suffered greatly. Also, the whole-cloth proposal for how to interpret the rule of optional completeness is now a precedent, and consequently can also be used to keep virtuous left-leaning people of color locked up unlawfully.

Another area of the law where an originalist interpretation would benefit the little guy, as opposed to a results-oriented interpretation, is that of government-bought-and-paid-for testimony. The U.S. Government Code specifically states testimony cannot be paid for.

Nowhere in the U.S. Government Code does it provide a loophole for the prosecution to pay for testimony. But because pro-prosecution/pro-government Justices have long allowed the government to do just that, there is precedent for it. Let a defense lawyer try to pay a witness by reducing his sentence in exchange for testimony, and he will lose his ability to practice law. This gives the prosecution a tremendous advantage against defendants of all colors.

Until this same "precedent equals legislation" nonsense was abandoned, slavery could not be eliminated. Had precedent continued, William Wilberforce and the British Navy might have had to fight the Revolutionary War all over again.

Even John Hope Franklin had the narrative come a little too close to home when black students at his alma mater, Fisk University, revolted in the 1960s. A mentor and close friend of Franklin's, a white history professor, had his car set on fire and was given an ultimatum: Leave Fisk by sun-down or else, because there is no place "for a white man at a black university."[21] This professor was the main reason Franklin went into history and became a professor himself.

I was astonished at the way this incident never seemed to give Franklin even the slightest pause about his brand of blame-the-white-man history. Surely he had to wonder if a dose of perspective might have kept these students from doing what they did, or at least burning, say, Bull Conner's car instead, to which they would have been justified. Setting fire to the car of one of their own teachers was the kind of thing people do in a rage, without thinking. They were in such a rage, at least partly, because of the one-sided, agenda-driven narrative that Franklin is responsible for. Telling the clique's version of the institution of slavery gets even white clique member's cars burned.

Mirror to America also lets us in on a few epiphanies Franklin experienced throughout his life. For instance, while at a conference on race, Franklin had "three significant revelations:

1) In Japan, the Japanese made clear distinctions among themselves based on skin color,
2) On the Indian subcontinent, Northern Indians had a vague prejudice against Southern Indians because of their dark skin color.
3) In Brazil, the lighter the skin, the better ones chances for rising on the social and economic ladder."[22]

This is another one of those instances that makes me scratch my head because throughout his book Franklin states that discrimination is a problem exclusive to white men in America. Yet at this conference, he clearly saw discrimination was a universal problem.

Indeed, when mentioning the hurtful treatment he and his family received after buying a home in a white neighborhood, Franklin fails to mention that whites from the South were also discriminated against in this manner, or that in the late 1800s in Detroit and other cities, Blacks and whites lived side by side and attended the same schools in some areas. Northern whites did not start rejecting Blacks entirely until after so many Blacks migrated from the South and brought their undesirable redneck culture with them.[23]

> During the early years of mass migration of Blacks out of the South, many Northern-born Blacks condemned the Southern newcomers. They saw in them the danger that the white population would put up new barriers against all Blacks—which is in fact what happened. After the massive inflow of Southern Blacks into Northern cities, which had once allowed its small black populations to live scattered in predominantly white neighborhoods, these cities now began preventing Blacks from living in white neighborhoods by methods ranging from legal prohibitions and restrictive covenants to outright violence. All this happened within a very few years of the mass migrations of Southern Blacks to Northern cities.
>
> If these were mere prejudices, perceptions or stereotypes in the minds of white people...why did the very same views appear among Northern-born Blacks at the same time?[24]

Been In the Storm So Long (BITSSL) is a thorough, authoritative account of the American South during the aftermath of the Civil War. It is a scholarly work, derived from interviews with actual slaves and the journals of slave masters, describing the wretched conditions in which slavery left many Blacks. One particularly gut wrenching example of these conditions, from a mental standpoint, is that of an elderly black woman explaining to a Quaker missionary why she refers to herself as a "nigger." She says, "we are niggers… we always was niggers and we shall be; nigger here, and nigger there, nigger do this, and nigger do that." And even more disheartening, "We've got no souls; we are animals. We are black and so is the Evil One."[25]

I hope that every non-sociopath who reads this is disturbed by it. It requires a tremendous amount of wickedness on the part of the slave master to instill such beliefs in another human being.

Pitts hopes that instances like this one in BITSSL will make white people finally "get it," like Ryan Price and Susan Sontag have. However, as a causal explanation for today's Blacks lagging in education and employment outcomes, or making up an outsized portion of the prison population, it fails. In the seventeen years I have been in prison, I have seen very few Blacks who think like the woman above. In fact, most Blacks I know not only do not believe that they have no souls like the 'Evil One,' but that they are the Israelites, God's chosen people—the real Jews. And while the black crime rate was always higher than average due to the redneck culture, it did not explode until a century after slavery. The same is seen with the problem of illegitimate childbirth. If slavery caused these things, they would have been much more prevalent the closer to slavery Blacks were. Instead, just the opposite is true.

Getting whites to read books detailing the horrors of slavery will not improve the current conditions of Blacks, even if it makes whites feel guilty and therefore open to more wealth transfers. We have already seen the failure of such policies in the form of the Great Society programs. If reparations are a moral issue instead of a financial one, then maybe the words of Frantz Fanon, certainly no Uncle Tom, will help:

> I don't have a right, as a man of color, to wish for the development in the white man of a culpability with regard to the past of my race. I have neither the right nor the duty to demand reparation for my domestic ancestors. There is no negro mission: there is no white man's burden. Am I going to ask the white man of today to assume responsibility for the slave traders of the seventeenth century?…I am not a slave of the slavery that dehumanized my ancestors.[26]

For the sake of argument, Pitts, let us say that you and the clique manage to turn enough white people into Ryan Prices and Susan Sontags. Let us say further, that you get clique politicians like Barack Obama in the White House, and a majority of Sotomayor-like social-justice advocating Supreme Court justices and Congressmen. All the ethnocentric lobbies come out, and propose, "The Equality Tax," complete with a catchy slogan like "It's time."

It passes like Obama care did—strictly along party lines with the clique's only complaint being it does not go far enough. Your dream has come true: Reparations.

What will this look like?

If the book *World on Fire: How Exporting Free Market Democracy Breeds Ethnic Hatred and Global Instability* is any indication, things could very well get just as ugly as they did in Sri Lanka, Nigeria, India, or anywhere else competing ethnic groups have been pitted against each other by demagogic politicians. Amy Chua, the author of *World of Fire* (and not a privileged white male), knows all too well what ethnic polarization can lead too. Her aunt, a Chinese national, was murdered by her own chauffer, a Filipino jealous of the woman and her ethnic group's success.

It works like this: free market economics allow those with the most ability to earn significantly more money than those with less ability. In multi-ethnic nations, this often results in some ethnic groups outperforming others. Democracy allows whoever has the majority to make the laws. If an ethnic majority in a democratic country decides it is not happy with its level of economic achievement, it can simply vote itself some of the wealth earned by one of the more successful ethnic minorities.

Chua explains how this process unfolded in Indonesia where democratic elections ousted a leader who had been protecting the very wealthy Chinese:

> Indonesians were euphoric. After the words "free and fair elections" hit the U.S. headlines, Americans were euphoric. Democratic elections, it was thought, would finally bring Indonesia the kind of peace and legitimacy perfect for sustaining free markets...
>
> That's not what happened in Indonesia. The fall of Suharto's autocracy was accompanied by an eruption of ferocious anti-Chinese violence in which delirious, mass-supported Muslim mobs burned, looted and killed anything Chinese, ultimately leaving two thousand people dead.[27]

Chua also points out that third world countries are not turning over private property to 'the people,' but instead transferring it to the ethnic group with the most clout:

> In Uganda... the politically dominant groups of the North have repeatedly subjected the economically powerful Baganda of the South to bloody

purges. In Nigeria in 1960, tens of thousands of Ibo were slaughtered indiscriminately by furious mobs. In Ethiopia, the relatively prosperous Eritreans were recently expelled en masse.... [I]n Rwanda, the genocidal massacre of the Tutsi minority is inextricably connected with their historic economic dominance.[28]

Chua also mentions Venezuela, and how Hugo Chavez "generated mass support by attacking Venezuela's 'rotten' white elites."

Chavez swept to his landslide victory on a wave of explicit ethnic-based populism. Demanding "a social revolution," Chavez aroused to impassioned political consciousness Venezuela's brown-skinned pardos, who make up 80 percent of the population, who are largely destitute, and, who, like "The Indian from Barinas"—as Chavez refers to himself—have "thick mouths" and "chinese-looking eyes." "He is one of us," wept cheering, growth-stunted washer women, maids, and peasants. "We've never had another president like that before."[29]

Chua summarizes her thesis:

In those circumstances, the pursuit of free-market democracy becomes an engine of potentially catastrophic ethnonationalism, pitting a frustrated "indigenous" majority, easily aroused by opportunistic vote-seeking politicians, against a resented a wealthy ethnic minority. This confrontation is playing out in country after country, from Indonesia to Sierra Lone, from Zimbabwe to Venezuela, from Russia to the Middle East.[30]

This confrontation is destined to come to America if the narrative and the clique prevail. At best, the "Equality tax," or whatever euphemism the clique comes up with for reparations, will turn America into California. I am not a financial expert, but when that happens, I do not think China will want to buy our bonds anymore. In fact they will probably be more concerned with trying to recoup some of the money they have already loaned us.

Just as cities in California were declaring Bankruptcy in 2012, so will cities nationwide. The first responders will not be able to pick up a paycheck, and will have to find something else to do. It will not be the end of the world, but it will be the end of America as a first world nation. That is your best case scenario.

Now for the worst. White Americans, alienated by racial polarization and grievance-mongering politicians, will see the Equality Tax coming down the pike. They will hasten their withdrawal to the Inland Northwest—Montana, Wyoming, Idaho, Utah.

Governors and legislators sympathetic to Mexico run the Southwest. The Southeast is full of black Americans and the whites who could not afford to move on to the Northwest. The Northeast is full of the clique members who in the face of this balkanization are still preaching, "Diversity is our strength," while their kids go to ivy league schools where they have separate graduations, dorms, study halls, etc., for Blacks, whites, Hispanics, and Asians.

The government in Washington D.C. knows it has to raise tax revenues to stay afloat, but intelligence sources report that the Northwest will attempt to secede. They ram the Equality Tax through and freeze all bank accounts over $250,000 belonging to white males, using treason as a pretext. For the time being, civil war is averted.

A decade later the government has run through all the money they unlawfully confiscated and the Southwest declares its intentions to return to Mexico, its rightful home. The Federal government in D.C. wants to stop this, but with most of its military manpower from the Southwest deserting, since Mexico is promising not to extradite its own sons and daughters, it doesn't have the manpower to win the civil wars such action would precipitate.

Mexico now includes Texas and California and all the Border States in between. It sets its sights on the Northwest and whatever money and property the mostly white population has left. Their military moves in, the U.S. government orders them to retreat. Mexico's president tells the U.S., they will not be denied "justice." The white people in the Northwest, particularly "them old boys raised on shotguns," put up a fight. Unfortunately, they are mostly elderly and lack the artillery the Mexican drug lords provide the Mexican Army.

With it now firmly established that the U.S. government will not protect its citizens, chaos ensues in the Southeast. The Hatfields and McCoys are at war with the Jacksons and the Williams. The elites in the Northeast look down their noses and shake their heads.

The President, Jose Williams, who was supposed to be a uniter with his Mestizo mother and black father gives a speech in which he says, "America's chickens have come home to roost."

Just like here in prison, the fighting never really stops. The different sides just take breathers from time to time.

An Open Letter to Ryan Price

Congratulations young man, your heart is in the right place, and with a little education your mind can be too. Wanting to help the less fortunate is a noble sentiment indeed. And the fact that you were on that bus, instead of trying to re-invent the beer bong is encouraging. However, you are going to have to educate yourself if you really want to help those who have been, as you put it, "marginalized."

Start with *Conquest and Culture*, and *Black Rednecks and White Liberals* by Dr. Thomas Sowell. I warn you ahead of time, he is in his eighties and does not do political correctness. He values the unvarnished truth quite a bit, so this will be a departure from what you are used to with the late Howard Zinn, Derrick Bell, and all the other authors your teachers and Soledad O'Brien have recommended to you.

I have been around black people all my life. They put their pants on one leg at a time and bleed red blood, just like you. They value respect, in themselves as well as others. And if you want to help black people, then you are going to have to earn their respect. This is where you have a problem. You see, Ryan, nobody respects a man who does not respect himself. When you tell black people, or any people group for that matter, that you almost wish you could "change your skin color" because of some incident you had nothing to do with, like the murder of Emmett Till, you give the appearance of being weak, and easy to manipulate—unworthy of respect.

The reason you feel this way Ryan, is because people who think like your buddy Leonard Pitts Jr., have written most of the textbooks, made most of the movies, and reported most of the news you have been fed all your life. You probably have no idea that "the number of Blacks lynched in the entire history of the United States would be a fraction of the Armenians slaughtered by Turkish mobs in one year in the Ottoman Empire, the Ibos slaughtered by Hausa-Fulani mobs in one year in Nigeria, [and] the number of Jews slaughtered by mobs in one year in a number of countries."[31] This does not mean Emmett Till's murder, and the many like it, are not to be detested and mourned. It does however mean, that your race is not uniquely evil and blameworthy, Ryan.

Your misplaced guilt also hurts black people by leading them to believe in "the idea of a collective sin that is supposed to be handed down from generation to generation... to permanently stain a people or a community.[32] Remember, Ryan, "Contrition is not a policy. There is no more a hereditary transmission of the status of victim than there is a transmission of the status of tormentor. Unless we create a crime of affiliation, the 'duty to remember' does not imply the automatic purity or corruption of the great-grandchildren."[33]

Think back to 2006, when the Duke Lacrosse players were accused of raping a black stripper. At the historical black college NCCU, also in Durham, a 20-year old classmate of the stripper named Candace Shaw said, "This is a race issue. The people at Duke have a lot of money on their side." Another student, Chan Hall, said that the white lacrosse players ought to be prosecuted "whether it happened or not. It would be justice for things that happened in the past."[34] Ryan, these college students think like this, at least partly because of white people wringing their hands while navel-gazing over racial incidents they had nothing to do with. Ahem.

They are advocating turning incidents that, at least initially, had nothing to do with race into racial incidents, and worst of all, imputing the crimes of one person to another because they are simply the same color. This compares to making your buddy Mr. Pitts Jr. guilty of some unsolved crime witnesses say was committed by a black male. Surely you would not go for that.

The best way to help people is to be a genuine friend. This is where respect matters. You cannot have a true friendship with someone if they do not respect you. Because of discrimination in the past—mainly by unions and the government with its minimum wage laws—black unemployment is much higher than white unemployment. A lot of people find jobs through people they are friends with. This is where you come in Ryan. You are more likely to have friends that go on to work at companies, or maybe even start their own businesses, than the average black person in the ghetto. These places of employment will need workers. If you have black friends, you could direct them to these opportunities.

In closing, I leave you with some words from Pascal Bruckner. He is a French writer who leans to the left politically, a supporter of President Obama. Hopefully his words will help you understand why you must treat black people as equals—not victims—in order to establish real friendships.

> A policy of friendship cannot be founded on the false principle: We take the opprobrium, you take the forgiveness. Once we have recognized any faults we may have, then the prosecution must turn against the accusers and subject them to constant criticism as well. Let us cease to confuse the necessary evaluation of ourselves with moralizing masochism. There comes a time when remorse becomes a second offense that adds to the

America Apart

first without canceling it. Let us inject in others a poison that has long gnawed away at us: shame.[35]

To what must we remain loyal?…To the long Litany of massacres or to the effort made to emerge from servitude and inequality? In the confrontation of the diverse heritages that constitute us, it is better to praise the triumphs than the mourning, for the triumph is mourning plus its transcendence; it is suffering endured and overcome, a collective effort to defy misfortune. Our selective hyper-amnesia recalls only the calamities, never the high points. Why should we take responsibility for the dark periods alone and erase the light that followed them?[36]

EPILOGUE

When I was a kid my best friend was the son of a Mestizo mother and black father. C.B., as we will call him, and his family were from New York where his dad had at one time been a member of the Black Panther Party. They moved into our neighborhood when C.B. and I were in the third grade. From then on, we were joined at the hip. Every day after school, we either played basketball or football. We must have been pretty good together because one day in sixth grade at recess, when as usual one of us was a team captain and had picked the other, a kid protested. He said it was unfair for his team because C.B. and I were 'unstoppable.' C.B. and I looked at each other and smiled knowingly, before agreeing to give up several of the other players we had picked. Our team won anyway.

On the weekends, if I was not spending the night at his house, he was spending the night at mine. I often angled for the former because he had an older sister who was drop-dead gorgeous. (Picture Rae Dawn Chong.) I usually wore a high-top fade back then and she liked to bounce her hand off the top of it. (Unlike President Obama, when girls of another race wanted to touch my hair, it did not induce a severe bout of navel-gazing.) Best of all, she dated a white guy! So I always thought I had a chance even though she was like seventeen when I was ten.

C.B.'s family took me with them to play softball. I once struck out the side with underhanded knuckle balls—honest. C.B. came with me and my dad to shoot guns and fish.

C.B. was especially fond of filling an empty soda can with water, and then shooting it with a shotgun. The can would explode but remain in one piece. We considered it a work of art. Along with sports and artwork, we were really good at going places we were specifically told not to. Unfortunately we were not very good at fooling our parents about these excursions. In short, we were as good friends as two kids could be.

One day, I think I was 12, I was watching T.V. and saw some people wearing white robes with what looked like pillow cases on their heads, standing around a burning cross. I turned to my dad and asked, "What's wrong with them?" He was reading a book about training dogs for hunting, so he only glanced at the TV and mumbled, "They don't like Blacks."

America Apart

I always thought of my friend as C.B., not a black person, so it took me a minute to snap. When I did, I was horrified. C.B. was black, or half black, and several of my other friends were too. I blurted out, "Why don't they like C.B.?"

My dad must have realized the gravity of the situation because he actually put his book down to answer me. He said, "Son, your mother and I watched C.B when he first came over here years ago. When he got done drinking his Kool-Aid, he put his cup in the sink." My dad then promptly picked his book back up and continued reading. I had no idea what he was talking about at that moment, but later my mom told me, "You judge people by what they do, not what color they are."

Sometime later, I asked my dad if anyone in our family had ever been in the Ku Klux Klan. He told me that his grandfather had gone to a Klan meeting to see what they were about and returned with a saying pretty much everybody in my family eventually learned: "A man who's gotta do his business behind a sheet mustn't be doing that good a business."

C.B got his learners permit first. His dad had a Buick with Pioneer six-by-nines and a strong amp pushing them. One day he decided to let C.B. drive it to Greenspoint Mall and let me ride in the front, while he leaned sideways in the back, so it looked like C.B. and me were the only ones in the car. When C.B., with both hands firmly grasping the steering wheel and a few beads of sweat on his forehead—even though the A/C was set on arctic freeze—pulled into the parking lot, I spotted three or four pretty women (who happened to be black) walking the opposite direction C.B. had chosen to turn. C.B.'s dad had apparently seen them too because when I said to C.B., "You may be goin' the wrong way," his dad laughed and said, "That's what I'm saying." He did not say, "Those aren't runaway slaves for you to lynch, white boy."

And that brings us to my point. The son of a Mestizo mother of Cuban descent, and a black father of African descent, a former Black Panther by way of New York City no less, was best friends with the son of a cedar-chopping, hill country mother of Irish descent, and Johnny Reb father from South Texas, of Scots-Irish descent. This was only possible because of two things.

1. My parents never told me C.B. was a victim, and his parents never told him to look at me as privileged. We were equals, not abstractions born with inherited guilt or grievances automatically placing us on different planes.

2. We had an enormous amount of common ground we could build upon.

    a. We had parents who were more or less Christian. Which meant we celebrated most of the same holidays.

    b. We revered the same historical figures: General Patton, Martin Luther King Jr., and Jackie Robinson, amongst others.

    c. We liked the same music. In fact we used to perform Run D.M.C. songs in the back of the school bus. "It's Tricky," complete with the hand motions they used in the video, was our favorite.

    d. We watched the Cosby Show, Tour of Duty, and Martin.

    e. On the silver screen, we watched *Red Dawn*. It confirmed what the popular bumper sticker in those days so eloquently reminded us of: Namely, that "Russia sucks," and that if any pinko-commie ruskie ever set foot in our neighborhood, it would be our duty to break out our pellet guns and send them to perdition. That is, we had the same enemies. In today's America, they had trouble even getting sponsorship for an updated version of *Red Dawn* because it has been deemed offensive.

Friendships like ours will be much more difficult in the years to come as America balkanizes into color-coded regions like those we have in prison. We were two races (or maybe three since C.B. was bi-racial) but one nation. We knew America was not perfect; far from it. Even though our history textbooks led us to believe only people who looked like me had ever done anything wrong, we never doubted that we were both one the same.

The clique in American society is constantly loosening these "bonds of affection," as Lincoln called them, and driving America apart. One day, all that will remain will be ethnicity, culture, and tribe.

PARTING SHOTS

Michelle Alexander closes her award-winning book *The New Jim Crow* with a passage from James Baldwin's *The Fire Next Time*, which she says is "One of the most extraordinary books ever written." In it Baldwin claims that Blacks in his day were doing wrong because white people did not care about them. I believe a rebuttal to this "most extraordinary" book by a most extraordinary scholar, Dr. Thomas Sowell, is appropriate.

> Celebrated black writer James Baldwin claimed that Blacks took the building of a subsidized housing project in Harlem as "additional proof of how thoroughly the white world despised them" because "people in Harlem know they are living there because white people do not think they are good enough to live anywhere else." Therefore "they had scarcely moved in" to the new housing project, before "naturally" they "began smashing windows, defacing walls, urinating in the elevators, and fornicating in the playgrounds."
>
> From this perspective, anything negative that Blacks do is the fault of the whites. But however much Baldwin's picture might fit the prevailing vision of the 1960s, anyone who is serious about whether it also fits the facts would have to ask such questions as: 1) Was there a time before the 1960s when it was common for Blacks to urinate in public areas of buildings where they lived? And 2) If not, was that because they felt that whites had higher regard for them in earlier times?
>
> To ask such questions is to answer them, and the answer in both cases is clearly no! But few ask such questions, which remain outside the sealed bubble of the prevailing vision. What was different about the 1960s was the proliferation of people like James Baldwin, promoting resentment and polarization…[1]

That resentment and polarization is alive and well today in the form of the narrative. Unless it is put to rest, America will not survive in its present state. As H.G. Wells put it:

> It is extraordinarily inconvenient to administer together the affairs of peoples speaking different languages and also reading different literature and having different general ideas, especially if those differences are exacerbated by religious disputes. Only some strong mutual interest, such as the common defensive needs of the Swiss Mountaineers, can justify a close linking of peoples of different languages and faiths.[2]

Before World War One, no one could convince the Marxist intellectuals of Europe that the working class people of each nation would make war upon one another. They were members of the "proletariat," united as "workers," and therefore unwilling to fight a capitalist's war. However, "the call of socialist solidarity was drowned out by the call of tribe and blood."[3] Four years and nine million dead soldiers later, it became apparent ethnonationalism was responsible for the bloodiest war in history, and Marxist ideology could not tame it.

Epilogue

Why then, does anyone think the 'American Creed' or 'American Values' will tame that primal urge of people to be ruled by "their own" in the United States? A nation full of people of different skin colors could work. The same cannot be said of a nation full of different nations. Americans must see themselves as Americans. Not African-Americans, Mexican-Americans, or Asian-Americans. National identity must trump pie-in-the-sky notions like seeing oneself as a 'citizen of the world.'

The former Dean of philosophy at Catholic University wrote in his essay titled "National Identity:"

> One cannot be a citizen of the world. Identity is local; it is characteristic of a people who have inhabited a land over a period of time, who have developed certain collective habits, evident in their manners, their dress, the feasts they collectively enjoy, their religious bonds, the premium they put on education.[4]

I've seen how this works in prison. At least on the two units I have done my 17 years, there are severe staff shortages. The problem became so bad they started bussing guards in from the Houston area some 200 miles away. Many of these guards-on-loan happened to be Nigerian immigrants with impossibly thick accents. The unit I was on when this began was staffed almost exclusively with mestizo Hispanics from South Texas, though they normally refer to themselves as "Mexicans." Many of them also speak a heavily accented English that is difficult to understand. (I once had to have an inmate translate my English to a guard because the guard could not understand me when I said I needed to be let off the wing to get to the law library.)

One day C.J., the black barber who cuts my hair, came back to our wing visibly frustrated. I asked him what was up. He launched into a tirade about "that African nigga and that messcan" keeping him stuck in the barber shop after he had already worked longer than his required time. He said they could not understand that he had to leave the shop to turn in the clippers. At one point, he shook his head and said, "Then they went to trying to talk to each other. But can't neither one of them speak English so they just mumble some shit to each other, then smile and laugh—like they actually knew what they was talkin' about!"

In July of 2012, two officers from the Houston Police Department shot Rufino Lara to death. He was unarmed. The officers involved claimed they told Lara to place his hands on the wall in English and Spanish. Lara did not speak English and a witness claimed the cops only gave their order in

English. Lara took his hands off the wall and turned around 'suddenly,' at which point he was shot. The officers claimed Lara had his hand under his shirt and appeared to be reaching for a weapon. Witnesses disputed this and claimed Lara had his hands in the air.[5]

The clique will tell us this incident is proof-positive that HPD must increase its 'diversity,' and train all of its officers to speak Spanish. But where will that end? There are over 60 different languages spoken in Houston according to the Houston Chronicle. Do clique members really believe the average cop has the time and money to purchase 60 Rosetta Stones and learn 60 languages? Of course not. They know that eventually police forces will balkanize like everything else: Vietnamese cops for little Vietnam, Hispanic cops for the Barrio, Arab cops for Houstonstan, and so on.

"The Diversity!" they may scream from their undiverse high rises and gated communities with their underpaid security guards. But Lara's blood will still be on their hands. Allowing people to immigrate to America without learning the language is part of your platform is it not?

If problems like these two with language barriers are all the clique's vision and narrative ever produce, let's consider ourselves lucky. However, I would not count on it. America truly is exceptional, but it does not exist in an alternative universe. It is made up of flesh-and-blood human beings just like Sri Lanka, Nigeria, and India.

Sadaam Hussein, and numerous Soviet dictators kept their nations within nations together by ruling with an iron fist. In prison, we are kept from killing each other by guards with machine guns and tear gas. My demographic present is your demographic future.

As I was finishing up this book, I was reading *My Infamous Life*, the autobiography of Albert Johnson. He is one-half of the multi-platinum rap group, Mobb Deep (another of my favorites as a kid), and goes by the name Prodigy. *My Infamous Life* chronicles the ups and downs of being a thug and a star in the rap world. Prodigy eventually sees so many of his friends get murdered that he starts asking himself some serious questions about his life. He finds the answers from the "Five Percent Nation of Gods on Earth." The same group Jay-Z and Nelly have ties to. "They believe that the black man is God and that we shouldn't be praying or waiting for Jesus to save us."[6] Prodigy says he did not want to become a member of this group, but he did want to "acquire their knowledge."

Here is some of the "knowledge" he acquired:

Epilogue

When we were in Africa living in peace with the universe, we didn't have Bibles or corrupt corporations. We were spiritual people with our own way of life.

We didn't need for anything because it was all there for us naturally in infinite abundance… Don 't believe the lie when they say Caucasians came to Africa and found black people living in destitution as unruly cannibalistic bush babies and they had to save us from our evil, savage ways, clean us up, civilize and transform us into wholesome, upstanding Christians. This is all propaganda created by the Caucasian pirates to conceal their true agenda of the largest land, natural resources, knowledge, and population heist in history, not to mention the largest mass genocide. We thrived independently for millions of years before they invaded our lives with their wickedness and lifestyle of the beast.

When we were enslaved and shipped to America, the Europeans forced us to follow fairy-tale religions so that they could control our minds. They forced their banking system on us to control our lives with money. If we don't agree with their system and refuse to believe in their religions, then we get killed, sent to jail, or locked in a mental institution.[7]

Prodigy says he is only concerned with the facts. In spite of these 'facts,' Prodigy says he is not into 'race-hating.' However, if all of the above were true, we should all hate white people.

A partial truth can often be a lie. At least one generation has been taught these lies. I hope that *America Apart* will get the facts to him and everyone else who has been misled by the clique.

Good luck America, you are certainly going to need it. As a wise man once said, "Civilization really is a thin crust over a volcano."[8]

NOTES

CHAPTER 1

1   Daniels, Anthony. "The Brute and the Terrorist." *National Review*, March 7, 2011.
2   http://www.dailymail.co.uk/news/article-2085500/Incompetent-foreign-doctors-speak-English-putting-NHS-patients-risk.html
3   Pinker, Steven. *How the Mind Works*. New York: Norton, 1997. 42.
4   Ibid., 12.
5   Ibid., 126.
6   Ibid., 49.
7   Ibid., 39.
8   Ibid., 365.
9   "Concealing Black Hate Crimes." *Investor's Business Daily*, August 15, 2011.
10 Ibid.
11 Williams, Walter. "Killings only get attention if they fit the mold." *Scripps News Service*.
12 Ibid.
13 Diamond, Jared. *The Third Chimpanzee: The Evolution and Future of the Human Animal*. Reissued. ed. New York: Harper Perennial, 2006. 300.
14 Pinker. *How the Mind Works*. 513.
15 Ibid.
16 Ibid.
17 Buchanan, Patrick J. and Schlesinger, Arthur. "The Disuniting of America." In *State of Emergency: The Third World Invasion and Conquest of America*, 10. New York: Thomas Dunne Books/St. Martin's Press, 2006.
18 Ibid.
19 Sowell, Thomas. *Ethnic America*. New York: Basic Books, 1981. 219.
20 Ibid.
21 Williams, Walter. *Race and Economics*. Stanford, California: Hoover Institution Press, 2011.
22 Ibid.
23 Buchanan. *State of Emergency*. 110.
24 Ibid.
25 Ibid.
26 Ibid.
27 Ibid.
28 Ibid.

[29] 3Buchanan, Patrick J., Thernstrom, Stephan, and Thernstrom, Abigail M. "*America in Black and White.*" In *State of Emergency: The Third World Invasion and Conquest of America*, 128. New York: Thomas Dunne Books/St. Martin's Press, 2006.

[30] Buchanan. *State of Emergency.* 128.

[31] Ibid.

[32] Ibid., 129.

[33] Ibid., 82.

[34] Ibid., 127.

[35] Ibid., 128.

[36] Ibid.

[37] Perazzo, John. *The Myths That Divide Us: How Lies Have Poisoned American Race Relations.* 2nd ed. Briarcliff Manor, N.Y.: World Studies Books, 1999.

[38] Sowell, Thomas. *Black Rednecks and White Liberals.* New York: Encounter Books, 2005.

[39] D'souza, D'nesh. *The End of Racism: Finding Values in an Age of Technoaffluence.* New York, NY: Simon and Schuster, 1995. 14.

[40] Perazzo. *The Myths that Divide Us.* 24.

[41] Thernstrom, Stephan, and Abigail M. Thernstrom. *America in Black and White*: One Nation, Indivisible. New York, NY: Simon & Schuster, 1997. 243.

[42] Census Bureau.

[43] Thernstrom. *America in Black and White.* 196.

[44] Ibid.

[45] Ibid., 391.

[46] Ibid.

[47] Ibid.

[48] Ibid. 392.

[49] Ibid.

[50] Ibid., 393.

[51] Perazzo. *The Myths That Divide Us.* 211.

[52] Sowell, Thomas. *Intellectuals and Society.* New York: Basic Books, 2009. 261.

[53] Perazzo. *The Myths That Divide Us.* 247.

[54] Ibid., 293.

[55] Ibid., 294.

[56] Ibid.

[57] Ibid.

[58] Ibid.

[59] Sowell, Thomas. Race and Culture. New York: Basic Books, 1994. 252.

[60] Sowell, Thomas. *The Quest for Cosmic Justice.* New York: Basic Books, 1999. 10.

[61] Perazzo. *The Myths That Divide Us.* 295.

[62] Ibid.

[63] Ibid., 291–296.

[64] Ibid.

[65] Ibid.

[66] Ibid.

[67] Ibid.

[68] Ibid.

69 Sowell. Race and Culture. 126–128.
70 Ibid.
71 Ibid.
72 Buchanan. *State of Emergency*. 82
73 Ibid., 184.
74 Ibid.
75 Ibid.
76 Eliot, T. S. The Cocktail Party, a Comedy. New York: Harcourt, Brace, 1950.

CHAPTER 2

1 Alexandre, Michelle. "Special Report: Mixed Race America." *Ebony Magazine*, May 1, 2011.
2 NAS I Know I Can.
3 Houston Chronicle. 2010.
4 Buchanan. *State of Emergency*.
5 Ibid.
6 Souza, Dinesh. *The End of Racism*. 70.
7 Perazzo. *The Myths That Divide Us*. 585, note 172.
8 Ibid., 532, note 141.
9 Ibid., 415.
10 Shermer, Michael. *The Believing Brain: From Ghosts and Gods to Politics and Conspiracies--how We Construct Beliefs and Reinforce Them as Truths*. New York: Times Books, 2011.
11 Perazzo. *The Myths That Divide Us*. 36.
12 Ibid., 532.
13 Horowitz, David, and Jacob Laksin. One-party Classroom: How Radical Professors at America's Top Colleges Indoctrinate Students and Undermine Our Democracy. New York: Crown Forum, 2009.
14 Perazzo. *The Myths That Divide Us*. 415.
15 Horowitz and Laksin. *One-party Classroom*. 292.
16 Perazzo. *The Myths That Divide Us*. 415.
17 Ibid., 416.
18 Ibid.
19 Ibid.
20 Sowell. *Intellectuals and Society*. 296.
21 Ibid., 80.

CHAPTER 3

1 Pitts, Leonard. "Comparing 'our Blacks' to 'their Blacks'" *Houston Chronicle*, November 4, 2011. Accessed January 19, 2015. http://www.chron.com/opinion/outlook/article/Comparing-our- Blacks-to-their- Blacks-2252651.php.
2 Alexander, Michelle. *The New Jim Crow: Mass Incarceration in the Age of Colorblindness*. New York: New Press, 2010.

3 Ibid., 49.
4 Ibid., 50.
5 Williams. *Race and Economics.* 31.
6 Ibid.
7 Ibid., 32.
8 Ibid., 34.
9 Ibid.
10 Ibid., 34–35.
11 Ibid., 42–43.
12 Ibid., 40–41.
13 Ibid., 45.
14 Thernstrom. *America in Black and White.* 19.
15 Ibid.
16 Ibid., 594.
17 Ibid.
18 Ibid., 252.
19 Ibid.
20 Ibid., 594.
21 Sowell. *Ethnic America.* 219.
22 Ibid.
23 Perazzo. *The Myths That Divide Us.* 307.
24 Alexander. *The New Jim Crow.* 206–207.
25 Murray, Charles. *Losing Ground.* New York: Basic Books, 1984. 275, 274.
26 Ibid.
27 Alexander. *The New Jim Crow.* 49.
28 Ibid., 206.
29 Murray. *Losing Ground.* 31.
30 Ibid.
31 Thernstrom. *America in Black and White.* 161.
32 Ibid.
33 Ibid., 165.
34 Ibid., 167.
35 Ibid.
36 Murray. *Losing Ground.* 181.
37 Ibid.
38 Ibid.
39 Ibid., 162-163.
40 Ibid., 151.
41 Ibid.
42 Ibid., 152.
43 Ibid., 152–153.
44 Alexander. *The New Jim Crow.* 206–207.
45 Murray. *Losing Ground.* 5.
46 Ibid., 266, tables.
47 Ibid.
48 Ibid.

Notes

[49] Tanner, Michael D. "More Proof We Can't Stop Poverty By Making It More Comfortable." *Investors.com*. September 17, 2010.

[50] Ibid.

[51] Thernstrom. *America in Black and White*. 236.

[52] Sowell, Thomas. "On the Right." *Investors.com*. August 3, 2011.

[53] Page, Benjamin I., and James Roy Simmons. *What Government Can Do: Dealing with Poverty and Inequality*. Chicago: University of Chicago Press, 2000. 24.

[54] Sowell. "On the Right." *Investors.com*. August 3, 2011.

[55] Page, and Simmons. *What Government Can Do*. 258.

[56] Ibid.

[57] Sowell. "On the Right." *Investors.com*. August 3, 2011.

[58] Ibid.

[59] Williams. *Race and Economics*. 2.

[60] Ibid.

[61] Ibid., 2–3.

[62] Ibid., 15.

[63] Ibid.

[64] Ibid., 16.

[65] Ibid.

[66] Ibid., 17.

[67] Ibid.

[68] Ibid., 22.

[69] Ibid.

[70] Ibid.

[71] Ibid., 23.

[72] Ibid.

[73] Ibid.

[74] Thernstrom. *America in Black and White*.

[75] Williams, Walter. *Race and Economics*. 29.

[76] Ibid., 36–37.

[77] Ibid.

[78] Ibid.

[79] Ibid. 59.

[80] Ibid.

[81] Ibid.

[82] Ibid., 60.

[83] Ibid.

[84] Ibid.

[85] Ibid., 62.

[86] Ibid.

[87] Ibid., 60.

[88] Ibid., 77.

[89] Ibid., 79.

[90] Ibid., 103.

[91] Ibid.

[92] Ibid., 105.

[93] Ibid., 106.

94 Ibid., 106–107.

95 Ibid., 109.

96 Ibid., 108.

97 Ibid., 109.

98 Perazzo. *The Myths That Divide Us.* 183–184.

99 Ibid.

100 Hester, Jere. "Rev. Al's Caught On Protest Tape Called Mart Owner A 'White Interloper'" *NY Daily News.* December 13, 1995. Accessed January 5, 2015. http://www.nydailynews.com/archives/news/rev-al-caught-protest-tape-called-mart-owner-white-interloper-article-1.693222.

CHAPTER 4

1 Obama, Barack. *Dreams From My Father: A Story of Race and Inheritance.* New York: Three Rivers Press, 2004. 257.

2 204 Ibid.

3 205 Murray. *Losing Ground.* 97.

4 206 Samuelson, Robert J. "Why One School Reform After Another Fails." Investor's Business Daily. September 3, 2010. Accessed January 19, 2015. http://news.*Investors.com*/ibd-editorials-perspective/090310-546134-why-one-school-reform-after-another-fails.htm.

5 207 Page and Simmons. What Government Can Do.

6 208 Schlafly, Phyllis. "Why Not Cut Education Spending." Investor's Business Daily. March 23, 2011. Accessed January 19, 2015. http://news.*Investors.com*/ibd-editorials-viewpoint/032311-566952-why-not-cut-education-spending-.htm.

7 209 Samuelson. "Why One School Reform After Another Fails."

8 210 Schlafly. "Why Not Cut Education Spending."

9 211 Ibid.

10 212 Thernstrom. *America in Black and White.* 351.

11 213 Ibid.

12 214 Obama. Dreams From My Father.

13 215 Ibid., 257.

14 216 Ibid.

15 217 Thernstrom. *America in Black and White.* 369.

16 218 Shermer, Michael. Why People Believe Weird Things: Pseudoscience, Superstition, and Other Confusions of Our Time. New York: Holt Paperbacks, 2002. 34.

17 219 Thernstrom. *America in Black and White.* 369.

18 220 Ibid., 370.

19 221 Ibid., 372.

20 222 Perazzo. *The Myths That Divide Us.* 238.

21 223 Horowitz and Laksin. *One-party Classroom.* 34.

22 224 Williams, Walter. "Teacher Union Holding Back Black Students." Investor's Business Daily. December 22, 2009. Accessed January 19, 2015. http://news.*Investors.com*/ibd-editorials-on-the-right/122209-516029-teacher-union-holding-back-black-students.htm.

Notes

23 Williams, Walter. "Black Education." *Creators.com*. December 23, 2009. Accessed January 19, 2015. http://econfaculty.gmu.edu/wew/articles/09/BlackEducation. htm

24 Williams, Walter. "Teacher Union Holding Back Black Students."

25 Thernstrom. *America in Black and White*.

26 Ibid., 376.

27 Ibid., 363.

28 Ibid., 364.

29 Williams, Walter. "Teacher Union Holding Back Black Students."

30 Sowell. *Black Rednecks and White Liberals*.

31 Ibid.

32 Ibid.

33 Ibid.

34 Ibid.

35 Ibid., 208.

36 Ibid.

37 Ibid.

38 Ibid.

39 Ibid.

40 Ibid.

41 Ibid.

42 Shermer. The Believing Brain.

43 Sowell. *Black Rednecks and White Liberals*.

44 Shermer. Why People Believe Weird Things. 24.

45 Study Duke Howard University

46 Sowell. *Intellectuals and Society*. 423.

47 Sowell. *Race and Culture*.

48 Sowell. *Intellectuals and Society*. 423.

49 Sowell. *Race and Culture*. 105.

50 Ibid., 296.

51 Ibid.

52 Sowell. *Ethnic America*. 5.

53 Thernstrom. *America in Black and White*. 264.

54 Henserling. *Principles of Sociology*.

55 Sporting News Magazine. May 29, 2009.

56 Henserling. *Principles of Sociology*.

57 Sowell. *Intellectuals and Society*. 121.

58 Perazzo. *The Myths That Divide Us*. 411.

59 Ibid., 90.

60 "Concealing Black Hate Crimes." *Investor's Business Daily*, August 15, 2011.

61 Sowell. *Race and Culture*. 22.

62 Sowell. *Ethnic America*. 38.

63 Ibid., 37.

64 Ibid., 73.

65 Ibid., 86.

66 Samuelson. "Why One School Reform After Another Fails."

67 Ibid.

[68] Friedman, Thomas L. "How About Better Parents." *Sunday Review*, November 19, 2011. Accessed January 19, 2015.

[69] Ibid.

CHAPTER 5
PART I

[1] Alexandre, Michelle. "Special Report: Mixed Race America." *Ebony Magazine*, May 1, 2011.

[2] MacDonald, Heather. "Is the Criminal-Justice System Racist?" *City Journal.* March 1, 2008.

[3] Alexander. *The New Jim Crow.* 13.

[4] MacDonald. "Is the Criminal-Justice System Racist?"

[5] Wilson, James Q., and Richard J. Herrnstein. *Crime and Human Nature.* New York: Simon and Schuster, 1985. 32 - 33.

[6] Thernstrom. *America in Black and White.* 271.

[7] Ibid., 272.

[8] Wilson and Herrnstein. *Crime and Human Nature.* 463.

[9] Ibid.

[10] Thernstrom. *America in Black and White.* 264.

[11] Ibid.

[12] MacDonald. "Is the Criminal-Justice System Racist?"

[13] Perazzo. *The Myths That Divide Us.* 99.

[14] Ibid.

[15] MacDonald. "Is the Criminal-Justice System Racist?"

[16] Ibid.

[17] Thernstrom. *America in Black and White.* 273.

[18] McClain, John. "Texans LB Loiseau Relishes Second Chance." Ultimate Texans. May 29, 2012. Accessed January 20, 2015.

[19] Pitts, Leonard. "Blame society's stereotypes in slaying of Trayvon Martin." *Houston Chronicle.* May 6, 2012. Accessed January 19, 2015. http://www.chron.com/opinion/outlook/article/Pitts-Blame-society-s-stereotypes-in-slaying-of-3535953.php

[20] Pitts, Leonard. "Pitts: White Denotes Not Race, but the Privilege of Basic Rights." *Houston Chronicle.* March 23, 2012. Accessed January 19, 2015. http://www.chron.com/opinion/outlook/article/Pitts-White-denotes-not-race-but-the-privilege-3430895.php.

[21] Ibid.

[22] Ibid.

[23] Bello, Marisol. "Stand-your-ground Law Looms Large in Phoenix Shooting." usatoday.com. May 31, 2012. Accessed January 20, 2015. http://usatoday30.usatoday.com/news/nation/story/2012-05-27/stand-your-ground-law-trayvon-martin/55208980/1.

[24] Perazzo. *The Myths That Divide Us.* 104.

[25] Ibid., 95.

Notes

[26] Ibid.

[27] Pitts, Leonard. "Helping to Spread Word about 'The New Jim Crow'" *Houston Chronicle*. January 13, 2012. Accessed January 19, 2015. http://www.chron.com/opinion/outlook/article/Pitts-Helping-to-spread-word-about-The-New-Jim-2518033.php.

[28] Ibid.

[29] Ibid.

[30] Alexander. *The New Jim Crow*. 16–18.

[31] Ibid., 24–25.

[32] Sowell. *Black Rednecks and White Liberals*.

[33] Ibid.

[34] Alexander. *The New Jim Crow*. 26.

[35] Ibid., 28.

[36] Perazzo. *The Myths That Divide Us*.

[37] Thernstrom. *America in Black and White*. 260.

[38] Perazzo. *The Myths That Divide Us*.

[39] Sowell. *Black Rednecks and White Liberals*.

[40] Alexander. *The New Jim Crow*. 16.

[41] Ibid., 22.

[42] Ibid., 40.

[43] Ibid., 44.

[44] Ibid., 42–43.

[45] Murray. *Losing Ground*. 115.

[46] Alexander. *The New Jim Crow*. 42.

[47] Murray. *Losing Ground*. 117.

[48] Ibid., 118.

[49] Thernstrom. *America in Black and White*. 376.

[50] *Webster's Dictionary*. Random House.

[51] Webb, James H. *Born Fighting: How the Scots-Irish Shaped America*. New York: Broadway Books, 2004.

[52] 325 Alexander. *The New Jim Crow*. 182.

[53] Murray. *Losing Ground*. 168.

[54] Ibid., 283.

[55] Ibid., 261.

[56] Ibid.

[57] MacDonald. *Is the Criminal-Justice System Racist?*

[58] Alexander. "The Lockdown." In *The New Jim Crow*.

[59] Ibid., 58.

[60] Ibid., 59.

[61] MacDonald. *Is the Criminal-Justice System Racist?*

[62] Thernstrom. *America in Black and White*. 279.

[63] Ibid.

[64] Ibid.

[65] Alexander. *The New Jim Crow*. 88.

[66] Alexander. *The New Jim Crow*. 88.

[67] Ibid., 201.

[68] Ibid., 202.

[69] MacDonald. *Is the Criminal-Justice System Racist?*

[70] Ibid.

[71] Ibid.

[72] Ibid.

[73] Dalrymple, Theodore. *Our Culture, What's Left of It: The Mandarins and the Masses.* Chicago: Ivan R. Dee, 2005. 231.

[74] Ibid., 226.

[75] Ibid., 230.

[76] Ibid., 232.

[77] Ibid.

[78] Alexander. *The New Jim Crow.*

[79] Ibid.

[80] Thernstrom. *America in Black and White.* 176.

[81] Ibid., 177.

[82] Alexander. *The New Jim Crow.*

[83] Thernstrom. *America in Black and White.*

[84] Alexander. *The New Jim Crow.* 48–49.

[85] Wilson and Herrnstein. *Crime and Human Nature.* 462.

[86] Thernstrom. *America in Black and White.* 264.

[87] Wilson and Herrnstein. *Crime and Human Nature.* 367–369.

[88] Alexander. *The New Jim Crow.* 97.

[89] Ibid.

[90] Ibid.

[91] National Survey on Drug Use and Health. 2010.

[92] Wilson and Herrnstein. *Crime and Human Nature.* 37.

[93] Thernstrom. *America in Black and White.* 182.

[94] Wilson and Herrnstein. *Crime and Human Nature.* 371.

[95] Ibid., 462–463.

[96] Ibid., 37.

[97] Ibid., 37–38.

[98] Alexander. *The New Jim Crow.* 97.

[99] Wilson and Herrnstein. *Crime and Human Nature.* 311.

[100] Alexander. *The New Jim Crow.* 99.

[101] Thernstrom. *America in Black and White.* 262.

[102] Alexander. *The New Jim Crow.* 124–125.

[103] Ibid.

[104] Sowell. *The Quest for Cosmic Justice.*

[105] Alexander. *The New Jim Crow.* 17.

[106] Sowell. *Black Rednecks and White Liberals.* 277–278.

[107] Alexander. *The New Jim Crow.* 138.

[108] Ibid.

[109] Webb. *Born Fighting.*

[110] Williams, Walter. "The Epidemic of Black-on-Black Violence." *Creators.com.*

[111] Perazzo. *The Myths That Divide Us.* 147.

[112] *Webster's Dictionary.* Random House.

[113] Sowell. *Race and Culture.* 113–118.

[114] Sowell. *Intellectuals and Society.* 288.

Notes

115 Alexander. *The New Jim Crow*. 141.

116 Ibid., 145.

117 MacDonald. *Is the Criminal-Justice System Racist?*

118 *Houston Chronicle*. August 20, 2011.

119 Ibid.

120 Alexander. *The New Jim Crow*. 139.

121 Dalrymple. *Our Culture, What's Left of It*. 40–90.

122 MacDonald. *Is the Criminal-Justice System Racist?*

123 Ibid.

124 Alexander. *The New Jim Crow*. 163.

125 Ibid., 159.

126 Ibid., 163.

127 Ibid., 159.

128 Wilson and Herrnstein. *Crime and Human Nature*. 485.

129 Alexander. *The New Jim Crow*. 173–174.

130 Thernstrom. *America in Black and White*. 238.

131 Alexander. *The New Jim Crow*. 175.

132 Ibid., 182–183.

133 Thernstrom. *America in Black and White*. 282.

134 Ibid.

135 Alexander. *The New Jim Crow*. 193.

136 Wilson and Herrnstein. *Crime and Human Nature*. 483.

137 Ibid.

138 Ibid.

139 Prager, Dennis. "On the Right: Mainstream Media Cover Up Left's Immaturity and Nihilism." *Investors.com*.

140 Uniform Crime Report. 2007.

141 Alexander. *The New Jim Crow*. 204.

142 Ibid., 227.

143 Thernstrom. *America in Black and White*. 280.

144 Ibid.

145 Cohen, Richard. "On The Left: Liberal Theories Can't Explain Crime Rate Fall." *Investors.com*. May 31, 2011.

146 Alexander. *The New Jim Crow*. 248.

147 Ibid., 224.

148 Ibid., 225.

149 Ibid., 228.

150 Ibid., 230.

151 Ibid., 231.

152 Bruckner, Pascal. *The Tyranny of Guilt: An Essay on Western Masochism*. Princeton: Princeton University Press, 2010. 143.

153 Ibid., 148.

154 Ibid., 147.

155 Ibid., 142–143.

156 Sowell. *Intellectuals and Society*. 119.

157 Sowell. *The Quest for Cosmic Justice*. 36–37.

158 Sowell. *Intellectuals and Society*. 121.

[159] Ibid.

[160] Sowell. *The Quest for Cosmic Justice*. 37.

[161] Sowell. *Black Rednecks and White Liberals*.

[162] Sowell. *The Quest for Cosmic Justice*. 62.

[163] Alexander. *The New Jim Crow*. 225.

[164] Sowell. *Intellectuals and Society*. 121.

[165] Ibid., 288–294.

[166] Ibid.

[167] Wilson and Herrnstein. *Crime and Human Nature*. 390.

[168] Ibid.

[169] Ibid., 393.

[170] Ibid., 294.

[171] Alexander. *The New Jim Crow*. 224.

[172] MacDonald. *Is the Criminal-Justice System Racist?*

[173] Thernstrom. *America in Black and White*.

[174] Sowell. *Intellectuals and Society*. 288–289.

[175] Ibid., 291.

[176] Alexander. *The New Jim Crow*. 226.

[177] Ibid., 225.

[178] Ibid., 247.

[179] Thernstrom. *America in Black and White*. 272.

[180] McWhorter, John H. *Authentically Black: Essays for the Black Silent Majority*. New York: Gotham Books, 2003. 215.

[181] Litwack, Leon F. *Been in the Storm so Long: The Aftermath of Slavery*. New York: Knopf: 1979. 65, 95, 147.

[182] Alexander. *The New Jim Crow*. 226.

[183] Sowell. *The Quest for Cosmic Justice*. 31–32.

[184] Sowell. *Black Rednecks and White Liberals*. 282–284.

[185] *Higher Learning*. Columbia TriStar Home Entertainment, 2001. Film.

[186] Ibid., 284.

[187] Alexander. *The New Jim Crow*. 242.

[188] Sowell. *Black Rednecks and White Liberals*. 284.

[189] Ibid., 285.

[190] Obama. *Dreams From My Father*. 182.

[191] Ibid., 285.

[192] Associated Press, *Houston Chronicle*. August 2008.

[193] Pitts, Leonard. Various Miami Herald Editorials.

[194] MacDonald. *Is the Criminal-Justice System Racist?*

[195] Wilson and Herrnstein. *Crime and Human Nature*. 37–38.

[196] Ibid., 473.

PART II

[1] Thernstrom. *America in Black and White*. 9.

[2] Perazzo. *The Myths That Divide Us*. 87.

[3] Ibid., 81.

⁴ Ibid., 56.

⁵ Census Bureau.

⁶ Perazzo. *The Myths That Divide Us*. 87–88.

⁷ Ibid., 68.

⁸ Ibid., 85.

⁹ Ibid., 88.

¹⁰ Uniform Crime Reports. FBI.

¹¹ Perazzo. *The Myths That Divide Us*. 89.

¹² Ibid.

¹³ Ibid., 90.

¹⁴ Ibid.

¹⁵ Ibid.

¹⁶ Webb. *Born Fighting*.

¹⁷ Williams. "The Epidemic of Black-on-Black Violence."

¹⁸ Perazzo. *The Myths That Divide Us*. 169.

¹⁹ Ibid.

²⁰ Ibid., 170.

²¹ Ibid., 175.

²² Horowitz and Laksin. *One-party Classroom*. 13.

²³ Ibid., 14.

²⁴ Ibid., 15.

²⁵ *Avatar*. 20th Century Fox Home Entertainment, 2010. Film.

²⁶ *American Beauty*. DreamWorks Home Entertainment, 2000. Film.

²⁷ *Gangs of New York*. Miramax Home Entertainment, 2003. Film.

²⁸ *A Time to Kill*. Warner Home Video, 1997. Film.

²⁹ "Cold Case." CBS Broadcasting Inc.

³⁰ Perazzo. *The Myths That Divide Us*. 174.

³¹ *Tyler Perry's Daddy's Little Girls*. Lions Gate Home Entertainment, 2007. Film.

³² Martin, Crystal G. "Gabrielle Union's Aha! Moment: Surrounding Myself with the Right People." Oprah.com. http://www.oprah.com/spirit/Gabrielle-Union-Interview-Victims-of-Rape#ixzz3S9lxHZCx.

³³ Thernstrom. *America in Black and White*. 515.

³⁴ Ibid., 517.

³⁵ Ibid.

³⁶ Sowell, Thomas. "James Q. Wilson (1931-2012)." *Creators.com*. January 1, 2012. Accessed December 27, 2014. http://www.*Creators.com*/conservative/thomas-sowell/james-q-wilson-1931-2012.html.

CHAPTER 6

¹ Sowell. *Intellectuals and Society*. 76.

² Bon Jovi, Jon. "Sante Fe." *Blaze of Glory: Songs inspired by the movie 'Young Guns.'* 1990.

³ Wilson and Herrnstein. *Crime and Human Nature*. 463.

⁴ Ibid.

⁵ Ibid., 81.

[6] Ibid., 85–86.

[7] Ibid., 87.

[8] Ibid., 88.

[9] Ibid., 89.

[10] Wilson and Herrnstein. *Crime and Human Nature*. 469.

[11] Ibid., 96.

[12] Ibid., 97.

[13] Peper, Jiska, S.P. Cedric, M.P. Koolschijn, and Eveline A. Crone. "Development of Risk Taking: Contributions from Adolescent Testosterone and the Orbitofrontal Cortex." *Journal of Cognitive Neuroscience*, July 16, 2013.

[14] Wilson and Herrnstein. *Crime and Human Nature*.

[15] Ibid., 154.

[16] Ibid., 156.

[17] Ibid., 160–161.

[18] Ibid., 169.

[19] Ibid., 205.

[20] Ibid., 165.

[21] Ibid., 166.

[22] Ibid., 168.

[23] Ibid., 205.

[24] Ibid., 209.

[25] Ibid., 509.

[26] Ibid., 461.

[27] Ibid., 469.

[28] Ibid.

[29] Ibid., 186.

[30] Ibid., 469.

[31] Ibid., 469–470.

[32] Ibid., 186.

[33] Ibid., 188.

[34] Brockman, John. *What Is Your Dangerous Idea?: Today's Leading Thinkers on the Unthinkable*. New York: Harper Perennial, 2007.

[35] Wilson and Herrnstein. *Crime and Human Nature*. 470.

[36] Sowell. *Race and Culture*. 170.

[37] Ibid., 171.

[38] Wilson and Herrnstein. *Crime and Human Nature*. 472.

[39] Sowell. *Black Rednecks and White Liberals*. 33.

[40] Webb. *Born Fighting*. 25.

[41] Ibid., 8.

[42] Ibid., 35.

[43] Ibid., 88.

[44] Ibid., 89.

[45] Sowell. *Black Rednecks and White Liberals*. 3.

[46] Ibid., 5.

[47] Webb. *Born Fighting*. 136.

[48] Sowell. *Black Rednecks and White Liberals*. 9.

[49] Ibid.

[50] Ibid., 27.

[51] Ibid., 28.

[52] Ibid., 24.

[53] Sowell. *Ethnic America.*

[54] Sowell. *Black Rednecks and White Liberals.*

[55] Wilson and Herrnstein. *Crime and Human Nature.* 473–474.

[56] Webb. *Born Fighting.* 8.

[57] Eagleman, David. *Incognito: The Secret Lives of the Brain.* New York: Pantheon Books, 2011. 182.

[58] Ibid.

[59] Ibid., 184.

[60] Ibid., 185.

[61] Ibid.

[62] MacDonald, Heather. "Undisciplined." *City Journal.* Summer 2012, 26.

[63] Ibid.

Chapter 7

[1] Flynn, Daniel J. *Intellectual Morons: How Ideology Makes Smart People Fall for Stupid Ideas.* New York: Crown Forum, 2004. 15.

[2] Ibid., 19.

[3] Ibid., 15–16.

[4] Ibid., 24.

[5] Ibid.

[6] Ibid., 21.

[7] Ibid., 22.

[8] Ibid., 21.

[9] Ibid., 23.

[10] Ibid., 19.

[11] Ibid., 29.

[12] Ibid., 15.

[13] "The Harvard Hug: What Else Are Media Hiding?" *Investor's Business Daily.* March 2012. Accessed January 2015. http://news.investors.com/ibd-editorials/030912-603914-obama-radicalism-at-harvard-hidden-from-voters.htm., 9–10

[14] Thernstrom. *America in Black and White.* 496.

[15] Perazzo. *The Myths That Divide Us.* 20.

[16] Sowell, Thomas. "Racial Quota Fallout." *Jewish World Review.* March 15, 2012. Accessed January 10, 2015. http://jewishworldreview.com/cols/sowell031512.php.

[17] Flynn. *Intellectual Morons.* 24.

[18] Ibid., 34.

[19] Smith, Starita. "Churches Need to Keep out of Politics Keep out of Politics." *Houston Chronicle.* October 4, 2008. Accessed January 10, 2015. http://www.chron.com/news/article/Churches-need-to-keep-out-of-politics-keep-out-82288.php.

[20] Kever, Jeannie. "Houston Region is now the most diverse in the U.S." *Houston Chronicle*. March 5, 2012. Accessed January 10, 2015. http://www.chron.com/news/houston-texas/article/Houston-region-is-now-the-most-diverse-in-the-U-S-3384174.php

[21] "VIDEO: Damon Wayans Stuns the Ladies on The View." PEOPLE.com. November 7, 2007. Accessed January 10, 2015. http://www.people.com/people/article/0,,20158913,00.html.

[22] Cube, Ice. "Cave Bitch." *Lethal Injection*. 1993.

[23] Robinson, Eugene. "A Sotomayor Sense of Justice." Washington Post. July 14, 2009. Accessed February 10, 2015. http://www.washingtonpost.com/wp-dyn/content/article/2009/07/13/AR2009071302605.html.

[24] Cohen, Richard. "Sonia Sotomayor: A Safe, Soporific Bet for the High Court." *Washington Post*. July 21, 2009. Accessed February 10, 2015. http://www.washingtonpost.com/wp-dyn/content/article/2009/07/20/AR2009072002179.html.

[25] Buchanan, Patrick J. *Suicide of a Superpower: Will America Survive to 2025?* New York: Thomas Dunne Books, 2011. 151.

[26] Krauthammer, Charles. "Foreign Trip a Triumph, Belying Spin from Media." *Houston Chronicle*. August 3, 2012. Accessed February 10, 2015. http://www.chron.com/opinion/outlook/article/Krauthammer-Foreign-trip-a-triumph-belying-spin-3761365.php.

[27] Perazzo. *The Myths That Divide Us*.

[28] Gardner, David. "Is Political Correctness to Blame for Lack of Coverage over Horrific Black-on-white Killings in America's Deep South?" *Mail Online*. October 16, 2009. Accessed February 10, 2015. http://www.dailymail.co.uk/news/article-1220695/Is-political-correctness-blame-lack-coverage-horrific-black-white-killings-Americas-Deep-South-Tennessee-Channon-Christian-Christopher-Newsom-carjack.html.

[29] Williams, Walter. "Killings Only Get Attention When They Fit Mold." *Creators Syndicate*.

[30] Ibid.

[31] Perazzo. *The Myths That Divide Us*.

[32] Ibid.

[33] Ibid.

[34] Ibid., 113.

[35] Ibid., 76.

[36] Ibid.

[37] Ibid., 59.

[38] Ibid.

[39] Ibid., 90.

[40] Ibid., 90.

[41] Ibid., 71.

[42] Sowell. *Race and Culture*. 174.

[43] Perazzo. *The Myths That Divide Us*. 71.

[44] McCall, Nathan. *Makes Me Wanna Holler: A Young Black Man in America*. New York: Random House, 1994. 3–4.

[45] Ibid., 58, 78–79.

[46] Ibid., 196.

47 Ibid., 236.
48 Ibid., 254.
49 Barron, David. "The Express Stretches the Truth." *Houston Chronicle*. October 10, 2008. Accessed February 10, 2015. http://www.chron.com/entertainment/movies/article/The-Express-stretches-the-truth-1783470.php.
50 "The Tuskegee Timeline." *Centers for Disease Control and Prevention*. September 24, 2013. Accessed February 10, 2015. http://www.cdc.gov/tuskegee/timeline.htm.
51 Sowell. *Black Rednecks and White Liberals*. 114.
52 McPhail, Beverly. "We Must Acknowledge the Existence of Racism in America." *Houston Chronicle*. March 30, 2012. Accessed February 10, 2015. http://www.chron.com/opinion/outlook/article/We-must-acknowledge-the-existence-of-racism-in-3448338.php.
53 Medved, Michael. *The 10 Big Lies about America: Combating Destructive Distortions about Our Nation*. New York: Crown Forum, 2008. 69.
54 Ibid.
55 Ibid., 60.
56 Sowell. *Black Rednecks and White Liberals*. 158.
57 Williams. *Race and Economics*. 214.
58 Medved. *The 10 Big Lies about America*. 60.
59 Ibid., 61.
60 Perazzo. *The Myths That Divide Us*. 351–352.
61 Ibid., 354.
62 Ibid.
63 Ibid., 355.
64 Ibid.
65 Feldman, George Franklin. *Cannibalism, Headhunting and Human Sacrifice in North America: A History Forgotten*. Chambersburg, Pa.: Alan C. Hood &, 2008. 50.
66 Ibid., 4.
67 Ibid., 38.
68 Ibid., 150.
69 Medved. *The 10 Big Lies about America*. 40.
70 Sowell. *Race and Culture*. 188–189.
71 Sowell. *Ethnic America*. 18.
72 Sowell. *Black Rednecks and White Liberals*. 116.
73 Sowell. *Race and Culture*. 210.
74 Ibid., 210–211.
75 Ibid.
76 Sowell. *Black Rednecks and White Liberals*. 117.
77 Ibid., 117–118.
78 Sowell. *Race and Culture*. 210.
79 Sowell. *Black Rednecks and White Liberals*. 123.
80 Ibid.
81 Ibid., 124.
82 Ibid.
83 Ibid., 124–125.

[84] Ibid.
[85] Ibid., 126.
[86] Ibid.
[87] Sowell. *Race and Culture*. 187.

CHAPTER 8

[1] Buchanan, Patrick J. *Suicide of a Superpower: Will America Survive to 2025?* New York: Thomas Dunne Books, 2011. 134.
[2] Bruckner, Pascal. *The Tyranny of Guilt: An Essay on Western Masochism.* Princeton: Princeton University Press, 2010. 2–3.
[3] "Leonard Pitts: Looking Back Can Help Us Navigate Road to the Future." *Houston Chronicle.* May 15, 2011. Accessed January 17, 2015. http://www. chron.com/opinion/outlook/article/Leonard-Pitts-Looking-back-can-help-us-navigate-1688250.php.
[4] Ibid.
[5] Ibid.
[6] Bruckner. The Tyranny of Guilt. 3–4.
[7] Buchanan. Suicide of a Superpower. 143.
[8] Ibid.
[9] Webb. *Born Fighting.*
[10] Williams. "The Epidemic of Black-on-Black Violence." *Creators.com*
[11] http://www.chesnuttarchive.org/classroom/lynchingstat.html
[12] Thernstrom. *America in Black and White*. 9.
[13] Franklin, John Hope. *Mirror to America: The Autobiography of John Hope Franklin*. New York: Farrar, Straus and Giroux, 2005. 362.
[14] Ibid., 43.
[15] Ibid., 62.
[16] Ibid., 118.
[17] Ibid., 317.
[18] Sowell. *Intellectuals and Society*. 254.
[19] Ibid., 255.
[20] Long v. State, 10 S.W.3d 389 (Tex. App. 2000)
[21] Franklin. *Mirror to America*. 248.
[22] Ibid., 217.
[23] Sowell. *Intellectuals and Society*. 451.
[24] Ibid., 454–455.
[25] Litwack. *Been in the Storm so Long*. 255.
[26] Bruckner. *The Tyranny of Guilt*. 161.
[27] Chua, Amy. *World on Fire: How Exporting Free Market Democracy Breeds Ethnic Hatred and Global Instability*. New York: Doubleday, 2003. 136.
[28] Ibid., 112.
[29] Ibid., 142.
[30] Chua. "A World on the Edge." In *World on Fire:*
[31] Sowell. *Intellectuals and Society*. 444.
[32] Bruckner. *The Tyranny of Guilt*. 999.

33 Ibid.
34 Sowell. *Intellectuals and Society*. 474.
35 Bruckner. *The Tyranny of Guilt*. 284.
36 Ibid.
37 Sowell. *Intellectuals and Society*. 445–446.
38 Buchanan. *Suicide of a Superpower*. 284.
39 Ibid., 279.
40 Ravat, Safiyat. "Witnesses Dispute HPD's Account of Fatal Shooting." *Houston Chronicle*, July 10, 2012. Accessed February 18, 2015. http://www.chron.com/news/houston-texas/article/Witnesses-dispute-HPD-s-account-of-fatal-shooting-3697666.php.
41 Checkoway, Laura. *My Infamous Life: The Autobiography of Mobb Deep's Prodigy*. New York: Simon & Schuster, 2011. 128.
42 Ibid., 129.
43 Sowell, Thomas. "Who's Responsible?" *Creators.com*. 2014. Accessed January 20, 2015. http://www.*Creators.com*/opinion/thomas-sowell/whos-responsible.html.

Epilogue

1 Sowell. Intellectuals and Society. 445–446.
2 Buchanan. Suicide of a Superpower. 284.
3 Ibid., 279.
4 Dougherty, Jude P. "Why I Am a Conservative." *First Principles Journal*. September 22, 2008. Accessed January 28, 2015. http://www.firstprinciplesjournal.com/articles.aspx?article=177.
5 Ravat, Safiyat. "Witnesses Dispute HPD's Account of Fatal Shooting." *Houston Chronicle*, July 10, 2012. Accessed February 18, 2015. http://www.chron.com/news/houston-texas/article/Witnesses-dispute-HPD-s-account-of-fatal-shooting-3697666.php.
6 Checkoway, Laura. *My Infamous Life: The Autobiography of Mobb Deep's Prodigy*. New York: Simon & Schuster, 2011. 128.
7 Ibid., 129
8 Sowell, Thomas. "Who's Responsible?" *Creators.com*. 2014. Accessed January 20, 2015. http://www.creators.com/opinion/thomas-sowell/whos-responsible.html

INDEX

A

C

INDEX

INDEX

America Apart